Behavioral Finance and Wealth Management

Founded in 1807, John Wiley & Sons is the oldest independent publishing company in the United States. With offices in North America, Europe, Australia and Asia, Wiley is globally committed to developing and marketing print and electronic products and services for our customers' professional and personal knowledge and understanding.

The Wiley Finance series contains books written specifically for finance and investment professionals as well as sophisticated individual investors and their financial advisors. Book topics range from portfolio management to e-commerce, risk management, financial engineering, valuation, and financial instrument analysis, as well as much more.

For a list of available titles, visit our Web site at www.WileyFinance.com.

Behavioral Finance and Wealth Management

How to Build Investment Strategies
That Account for Investor Biases

Second Edition

MICHAEL M. POMPIAN

WILEY

John Wiley & Sons, Inc.

Published by John Wiley & Sons, Inc., Hoboken, New Jersey.
Published simultaneously in Canada.

For general information on our other products and services or for technical support, please contact our Customer Care Department within the United States at (800) 762-2974, outside the United States at (317) 572-3993 or fax (317) 572-4002.

Wiley also publishes its books in a variety of electronic formats. Some content that appears in print may not be available in electronic books. For more information about Wiley products, visit our web site at www.wiley.com.

Library of Congress Cataloging-in-Publication Data

Pompian, Michael M., 1963–
  Behavioral finance and wealth management : how to build investment strategies that account for investor biases / Michael Pompian. — 2nd ed.
     p. cm. — (Wiley finance series)
  Includes index.
  ISBN 978-1-118-01432-5 (cloth); ISBN 978-1-118-18227-7 (ebk);
  ISBN 978-1-118-18228-4 (ebk); ISBN 978-1-118-18229-1 (ebk)
  1. Investments–Psychological aspects.   2. Investments–Decision making.   I. Title.
  HG4515.15.P66 2012
  332.601′9—dc23   2011039271

Printed in the United States of America.

10 9 8 7 6 5 4 3 2 1

*I would like to dedicate this book
to my brother Dave and his family.*

Contents

Preface

It is with great satisfaction that I write this preface. Fifteen years ago, I embarked upon a quest to introduce the benefits of applying behavioral finance in practice with my first published article. Six years ago the first edition of this book was published. In that edition, I noted that behavioral finance was an emerging topic and that, hopefully, it would become a well-recognized discipline in finance. At the time, the debate as to whether or not behavioral finance was to be taken seriously by, mainly, academics and some practitioners, was in full force. Six years on, this debate appears to essentially be over. Behavioral finance is now part of the financial lexicon in many circles, such as the advisor-client relationship, the financial press, the academic literature, financial journals, and so on. It's not whether behavioral finance exists, but rather how can we begin to learn from the research that has been done and help ourselves become better investors. This second edition continues to help both clients and their advisors benefit from the practical application of behavioral finance.

This book is intended to be a guide both to understanding irrational investor behavior and to creating individual investors' portfolios that account for these irrational behaviors. The investment business is dominated by "benchmarks" against which performance of an investment portfolio should be judged. Often, investor think they should "beat the market" just because that is what they think defines success. In my view, private clients should begin thinking about their benchmarks in terms of how well they help them progress toward their financial goals, not so much whether an investment manager beats their benchmark or their portfolio outperformed the policy benchmark. Knowledge of behavioral biases and their affect on the investment process can go a long way to changing the way we view investment success. Often times, when applying behavioral finance to real-world investment programs, an optimal portfolio is one with which an investor can comfortably live, so that he or she has the ability to adhere to his or her investment program, while at the same time reach long-term financial goals.

The last edition of the book was written in the wake of the run-up in stock prices in the late 1990s and the subsequent popping of the technology bubble. This time, the latest financial bombshell was the 2008–2009 bursting of the housing and credit bubbles. And given the response to this financial crisis by central banks around the world, by keeping interest rates ultra-low, similar to the years preceding the most recent crisis, my view is we may be in store for continued volatility. Therefore, understanding irrational investor behavior is as important as it has ever been, probably more so. This is true not only for the markets in general but most especially for individual investors. This book will be used primarily by financial advisors, but it can also be effectively used by sophisticated individual investors who wish to become more introspective about their own behaviors and to truly try to understand how to create a portfolio that works for them. The book is not intended to sit on the polished mahogany bookcases of successful advisors as a showpiece: It is a guidebook to be used and implemented in the pursuit of building better portfolios.

The reality of today's advisor-investor relationship demands a better understanding of individual investors' behavioral biases and an awareness of these biases when structuring investment portfolios. Advisors need to focus more acutely on why their clients make the decisions they do and whether behaviors need to be modified or adapted. If advisors can successfully accomplish this difficult task, the relationship will be strengthened considerably, and advisors can enjoy the loyalty of clients who end the search for a new advisor.

In the past 250 years, many schools of economic and social thought have been developed, some of which have come and gone, while others are still very relevant today. We will explore some of these ideas to give some perspective on where behavioral finance is today. In the past 30 years, the interest in behavioral finance as a discipline has not only emerged but rather exploded onto the scene, with many articles written by very prestigious authors in prestigious publications and now is consistently in the mainstream media. We will review some of the key people who have shaped the current body of behavioral finance thinking and the work done by them. The intent is to take the study of behavioral finance to another level: reviewing the most important behavioral biases in terms that advisors and investors can understand, and demonstrating how biases are to be used in practice through the use of case studies—a "how-to" of behavioral finance. We will also explore some of the new frontiers of behavioral finance, things not even discussed by today's advisors that may be commonly discussed in the next 30 years.

A CHALLENGING ENVIRONMENT

In the last edition, I noted that investment advisors have never had a more challenging environment to work in. I wrote: "Many advisors thought they had found nirvana in the late 1990s, only to find themselves in quicksand in 2001 and 2002." Now, we merely need to substitute the years 2005 through 2007 and 2008–2009 into the same sentence. As the old adage goes, the more things change the more they stay the same. And once again we find ourselves in a low-return environment. Like then, advisors are still being peppered with the vexing questions from their clients:

"Why is this fund not up as much as that fund?"

"The market has not done well the past quarter—what should we do?"

"Why is asset allocation so important?"

"Why are we investing in alternative investments?"

"Why aren't we investing in alternative investments?"

"Why don't we take the same approach to investing in college money and retirement money?"

"Why don't we buy fewer stocks so we can get better returns?"

Advisors need a handbook that can help them deal with the behavioral and emotional sides of investing, so that they can help their clients understand why they have trouble sticking to a long-term program of investing.

WHY THIS BOOK?

The first edition of the book was conceived only after many hours, weeks, and years of researching, studying, and applying behavioral finance concepts to real-world investment situations. When I began taking an interest in how portfolios might be adjusted for behavioral biases back in the late 1990s, when the technology bubble was in full force, I sought a book like this one but couldn't find one. I did not set a goal of writing a book at that time; I merely took an interest in the subject and began reading. It wasn't until my wife, who was going through a job transition, came home one night talking about the Myers-Briggs personality type test she took that I began to consider the idea of writing about behavioral finance. My thought process at the time was relatively simple: Doesn't it make sense that people of differing personality types would want to invest differently? I couldn't find any literature on this topic. So, with the help of a colleague on the private wealth committee at NYSSA (the New York Society of Securities Analysts—the local CFA chapter), John Longo, PhD, I began my quest to write on the practical application of behavioral finance. Our paper, entitled "A New Paradigm for Practical Application of Behavioral Finance: Correlating Personality Type and Gender with Established Behavioral Biases," was ultimately published in the *Journal of Wealth Management* in the fall of 2003 and, at the time, was one of the most popular articles in that issue.

Since that time, I have written several papers, a new Wiley book entitled *Advising Ultra Affluent Clients and Family Offices*, and a monthly column for MorningstarAdvisor.com that have expanded my work. In 2008, I published "Behavioral Investor Types," an article that ran in the *Journal of Financial Planning*. This work attempts to categorize investors into four "behavioral investor types," which will be reviewed in this book briefly and fully explained in my next Wiley book, entitled *Behavioral Finance and Investor Types*, coming out later in 2012 or 2013. As a wealth manager, I have found the value of understanding the behavioral finance and have discovered some useful ways to adjust investment programs for behavioral biases. You will learn about these methods. By writing this book, I hope to spread the knowledge that I have developed and accumulated so that other advisors and clients can benefit from these insights.

WHO SHOULD USE THIS BOOK?

The book was originally intended as a handbook for wealth management practitioners who help clients create and manage investment portfolios. As the book evolved, it became clear that individual investors could also greatly benefit from it. The following are the target audience for the book:

- *Traditional Wire-house Financial Advisors.* A substantial portion of the wealth in the United States and abroad is in the very capable hands of traditional wire-house financial advisors. From a historical perspective, these advisors have not traditionally been held to a fiduciary standard, as the client relationship was based primarily on financial planning being "incidental" to the brokerage of investments. In today's modern era, many believe that this will have to change, as "wealth management," "investment advice," and brokerage will merge to become one. And the change is indeed taking place within these hallowed organizations. Thus, it is crucial that financial advisors develop stronger relationships with their clients because advisors will be held to a higher standard of responsibility. Applying behavioral finance will be a critical step in this process as the financial services industry continues to evolve.
- *Private Bank Advisors and Portfolio Managers.* Private banks, such at U.S. Trust, Bessemer Trust, and the like, have always taken a very solemn, straightlaced approach to client portfolios. Stocks, bonds, and cash were really it for hundreds of years. Lately, many of these banks have added such nontraditional offerings as venture capital, hedge

funds, and others to their lineup of investment product offerings. However, many clients, including many extremely wealthy clients, still have the big three—stocks, bonds, and cash—for better or worse. Private banks would be well served to begin to adopt a more progressive approach to serving clients. Bank clients tend to be conservative, but they also tend to be trusting and hands-off clients. This client base represents a vast frontier to which behavioral finance could be applied because these clients either do not recognize that they do not have an appropriate portfolio or tend to recognize only too late that they should have been more or less aggressive with their portfolios. Private banks have developed a great trust with their clients and should leverage this trust to include behavioral finance in these relationships.

- *Independent Financial Advisors.* Independent registered representatives (wealth managers who are Series 7 registered but who are not affiliated with major stock brokerage firms) have a unique opportunity to apply behavioral finance to their clients. They are typically not part of a vast firm and may have fewer restrictions than their wire-house brethren. These advisors, although subject to regulatory scrutiny, can for the most part create their own ways of serving clients; and with many seeing that great success is growing their business, they can deepen and broaden these relationships by including behavioral finance.

- *Registered Investment Advisors.* Of all potential advisors that could include behavioral finance as a part of the process of delivering wealth management services, it is my belief that registered investment advisors (RIAs) are well positioned to do so. Why? Because RIAs are typically smaller firms, which have fewer regulations than other advisors. I envision RIAs asking clients, "How do you feel about this portfolio?" "If we changed your allocation to more aggressive, how might your behavior change?" Many other types of advisors cannot and will not ask these types of questions for fear of regulatory or other matters, such as pricing, investment choices, or others.

- *Consultants and Other Financial Advisors.* Consultants to individual investors, family offices, or other entities that invest for individuals can also greatly benefit from this book. Understanding how and why their clients make investment decisions can greatly impact the investment choices consultants can recommend. When the investor is happy with his or her allocation and feels good about the selection of managers from a psychological perspective, the consultant has done his or her job and will likely keep that client for the long term.

- *Individual Investors.* For those individual investors who have the ability to look introspectively and assess their behavioral biases, this book is ideal. Many individual investors who choose either to do it themselves or to rely on a financial advisor only for peripheral advice often find themselves unable to separate their emotions from the investment decision-making process. This does not have to be a permanent condition. By reading this book and delving deep into their behaviors, individual investors can indeed learn to modify behaviors and to create portfolios that help them stick to their long-term investment programs and, thus, reach their long-term financial goals.

WHEN TO USE THIS BOOK?

First and foremost, this book is generally intended for those who want to apply behavioral finance to the asset allocation process to create better portfolios for their clients or themselves. This book can be used:

- *When there is an opportunity to create or re-create an asset allocation from scratch.* Advisors know well the pleasure of having only cash to invest for a client. The lack of such baggage as emotional ties to certain investments, tax implications, and a host of other issues that accompany an existing allocation is ideal. The time to apply the principles learned in this book is at the moment that one has the opportunity to invest only cash or to clean house on an existing portfolio.
- *When a life trauma has taken place.* Advisors often encounter a very emotional client who is faced with a critical investment decision during a traumatic time, such as a divorce, a death in the family, or job loss. These are the times that the advisor can add a significant amount of value to the client situation by using the concepts learned in this book.
- *When a concentrated stock position is held.* When a client holds a single stock or other concentrated stock position, emotions typically run high. In my practice, I find it incredibly difficult to get people off the dime and to diversify their single-stock holdings. The reasons are well known: "I know the company, so I feel comfortable holding the stock," "I feel disloyal selling the stock," "My peers will look down on me if I sell any stock," "My grandfather owned this stock, so I will not sell it." The list goes on and on. This is the exact time to employ behavioral finance. Advisors must isolate the biases that are being employed by the client and then work together with the client to relieve the stress caused by these biases. This book is essential in these cases.
- *When retirement age is reached.* When a client enters the retirement phase, behavioral finance becomes critically important. This is so because the portfolio structure can mean the difference between living a comfortable retirement and outliving one's assets. Retirement is

typically a time of reassessment and reevaluation and is a great opportunity for the advisor to strengthen and deepen the relationship to include behavioral finance.

- *When wealth transfer and legacy are being considered.* Many wealthy clients want to leave a legacy. Is there any more emotional an issue than this one? Having a frank discussion about what is possible and what is not possible is difficult and is often fraught with emotional crosscurrents that the advisor would be well advised to stand clear of. However, by including behavioral finance into the discussion and taking an objective, outside-councilor's viewpoint, the client may well be able to draw his or her own conclusion about what direction to take when leaving a legacy.
- *When a trust is being created.* Creating a trust is also a time of emotion that may bring psychological biases to the surface. Mental accounting comes to mind. If a client says to himself or herself, "Okay, I will have this pot of trust money over here to invest, and that pot of spending money over there to invest," the client may well miss the big picture of overall portfolio management. The practical application of behavioral finance can be of great assistance at these times.

Naturally, there are many more situations not listed here that can arise where this book will be helpful.

PLAN OF THE BOOK

This edition of the book has an updated structure. In the last edition, Part One of the book not only provided an introduction to the practical application of behavioral finance but also an introduction to incorporating investor behavior into the asset allocation process for private clients. In this edition, Part One includes a definition of behavioral finance, a review of its history, and a new chapter that introduces behavioral biases. Asset allocation topics are covered in Part Five, Case Studies. Parts Two, Three, and Four are a comprehensive review of some of the most commonly found biases, complete with a general description, technical description, practical application, research review, implications for investors, diagnostic, and advice. This time, biases are broken out into three categories: Belief Perseverance Biases, Information Processing Biases, Emotional Biases to correspond to Part's Two, Three, and Four. Part Five includes completely updated case studies as well as the previously referenced "Application of Behavioral Finance to Asset Allocation" section. Lastly, Part Six includes my latest research into defining four "Behavioral Investor Types."

MICHAEL M. POMPIAN

Acknowledgments

I would like to acknowledge all my colleagues, both present and past, who have contributed to broadening my knowledge not only in the topic of this book but also in wealth management in general. You know who you are. I would also like to acknowledge all of the behavioral finance academics and professionals who have granted permission for me to use their brilliant work. I also would like to acknowledge Cristina Hensel and all Wiley staff for their help in editing the book. Finally, I would like to thank my parents and extended family for giving me the support to write this book.

M. M. P.

Behavioral Finance and Wealth Management

One

Introduction to Behavioral Finance

In Part One, we present three chapters: Chapter 1 poses the question "What is Behavioral Finance?" This chapter also includes a review of some of the most important figures in the field of behavioral finance. In Chapter 2, we review the history of behavioral finance placing particular emphasis on understanding the differences between rational and irrational behavioral economic theories that have been developed over the year. Chapter 3 provides an introduction to behavioral biases, 20 of which will be reviewed in the book.

Throughout this part of the book, the goal is to have readers understand the basics of as well as the effects of behavioral biases on the investment process. By doing so investors and their advisors may be able to improve economic outcomes and attain stated financial objectives.

CHAPTER 1

What Is Behavioral Finance?

People in standard finance are rational. People in behavioral finance are normal.

—Meir Statman, PhD, Santa Clara University

At its core, behavioral finance attempts to understand and explain actual investor and market behaviors versus theories of investor behavior. This idea differs from traditional (or standard) finance, which is based on assumptions of how investors and markets should behave. Wealth managers from around the world who want to better serve their clients have begun to realize that they cannot rely solely on theories or mathematical models to explain individual investor and market behavior. As Meir Statman's quote puts it, standard finance people are modeled as "rational," whereas behavioral finance people are modeled as "normal." This can be interpreted to mean that "normal" people may behave irrationally—but the reality is that almost no one (actually, I will go so far as to say absolutely no one) behaves perfectly rationally, and dealing with normal people is what this book is all about. We will delve into the topic of the irrational behaviors of markets at times; however, the focus of the book is on individual investor behavior.

Fundamentally, behavioral finance is about understanding how people make financial decisions, both individually and collectively. By understanding how investors and markets behave, it may be possible to modify or adapt to these behaviors in order to improve financial outcomes. In many instances, knowledge of and integration of behavioral finance may lead to better than expected results for both advisors and their clients. But advisors cannot view behavioral finance as a panacea or "the answer" to problems with clients. Working with clients is as much an art as it is a science. Behavioral finance can add many arrows to the art quiver.

We will begin this chapter with a review of the prominent researchers in the field of behavioral finance, all of whom promote a deeper understanding of the benefits of the behavioral finance discipline. We will then review the key differences debate between standard finance and behavioral finance. By doing so, we can establish a common understanding of what we mean when we say *behavioral finance*, which will in turn permit us to understand the use of this term as it applies directly to the practice of wealth management. This chapter will finish with a summary of the role of behavioral finance in dealing with private clients and how the practical application of behavioral finance can enhance an advisory relationship.

BEHAVIORAL FINANCE: THE BIG PICTURE

Behavioral finance, commonly defined as the application of psychology to finance, has become a very hot topic, generating credence with the rupture of the tech-stock bubble in March of 2000, and has been pushed to the forefront of both investors' and advisors' minds with the financial market meltdown of 2008–2009. While the term *behavioral finance* is bandied about in books, magazine articles, and investment papers, many people lack a firm understanding of the concepts behind behavioral finance. Additional confusion may arise from a proliferation of topics resembling behavioral finance, at least in name, including: behavioral science, investor psychology, cognitive psychology, behavioral economics, experimental economics, and cognitive science, to name a few. Furthermore, many investor psychology books that have entered the market recently refer to various aspects of behavioral finance but fail to fully define it. This section will try to communicate a more detailed understanding of the term *behavioral finance*. First, we will discuss some of the popular authors in the field and review the outstanding work they have done (not an exhaustive list), which will provide a broad overview of the subject. We will then examine the two primary subtopics in behavioral finance: behavioral finance micro and behavioral finance macro. Finally, we will observe the ways in which behavioral finance applies specifically to wealth management, the focus of this book.

Key Figures in the Field

In Chapter 2 we will review a history of behavioral finance. In this section, we will review some key figures in the field who have more recently contributed exceptionally brilliant work to the field of behavioral finance. Most of the people we will review here are active academics, but many of them have also

FIGURE 1.1 Robert Shiller, former president of the Eastern Economic Association and best-selling author.

been applying their work to the "real world," which makes them especially worthy of our attention. While this is clearly not an exhaustive list, the names of the people we will review are: Professor Robert Shiller, Professor Richard Thaler, Professor Meir Statman, Professor Daniel Kahnemann, and Professor Vernon Smith.

The first prominent figure we will discuss is Professor Robert Shiller (Figure 1.1). Some readers may be familiar with the work *Irrational Exuberance,* by Yale University professor Robert Shiller, PhD. Certainly, the title resonates; it's a reference to a now-famous admonition by Federal Reserve Chairman Alan Greenspan during his remarks at the Annual Dinner and Francis Boyer Lecture of the American Enterprise Institute for Public Policy Research in Washington, D.C., on December 5, 1996. In his speech, Greenspan acknowledged that the ongoing economic growth spurt had been accompanied by low inflation, generally an indicator of stability. "But," he posed, "how do we know when irrational exuberance has unduly escalated asset values, which then become subject to unexpected and prolonged contractions as they have in Japan over the past decade?"[1] In Shiller's *Irrational Exuberance,* which hit bookstores only days before the 1990s' market peaked, Professor Shiller warns investors that stock prices, by various historical measures, have climbed too high. He cautions that the "public may be very disappointed with the performance of the stock market in coming years."[2] It was reported that Shiller's editor at Princeton University Press rushed the book to print, perhaps fearing a market crash and wanting to

FIGURE 1.2   Richard Thaler, PhD, renowned behavioral finance theorist.

warn investors. Sadly, few heeded the alarm. Mr. Greenspan's prediction came true, and the bubble burst. Though the correction came earlier than the Fed Chairman had foreseen, the damage did not match the aftermath of the collapse of the Japanese asset price bubble (the specter Greenspan raised in his speech).

More recently, Professor Shiller has been active in indentifying the next bubble—in the U.S. housing market. Together with researcher Karl E. Case, Shiller has been collecting data on housing, which is now known as the S&P/Case-Shiller U.S. National Home Price Index. This is a composite of single-family home price indices for the nine U.S. Census divisions. As early as 2004, Shiller and Case asked, "Is there a bubble in the housing market?" They were early, but they were also quite correct. Mr. Shiller is an active commentator on news programs and is someone to whom, in my opinion, we should listen closely.

Another high-profile behavioral finance researcher, Professor Richard Thaler, PhD (Figure 1.2), of the University of Chicago Graduate School of Business, penned a classic commentary with Owen Lamont entitled "Can the Market Add and Subtract? Mispricing in Tech Stock Carve-Outs,"[3] also on the general topic of irrational investor behavior set amid the tech bubble. The work relates to 3Com Corporation's 1999 spin-off of Palm, Inc., and argues that if investor behavior was indeed rational, then 3Com would have sustained a positive market value for a few months after the Palm Pilot spin-off. In actuality, after 3Com distributed shares of Palm

Pilot to shareholders in March 2000, Palm Pilot traded at levels exceeding the inherent value of the shares of the original company. "This would not happen in a rational world," Thaler notes. Professor Thaler is also the author of the book *Advances in Behavioral Finance,* which was published in 1993.

More recently, Professor Thaler, in conjunction with Professor Cass Sunstein, wrote *Nudge: Improving Decisions About Health, Wealth, and Happiness.* In this work, Thaler and Sunstein support the idea that by "tilting" people's decision making in a positive direction, everyone can make society a better place. The following is an interesting and insightful excerpt from an interview Amazon.com did with Thaler and Sunstein.[4] I particularly like the reference to choice architecture.

Amazon.com: What do you mean by "nudge" and why do people sometimes need to be nudged?

Thaler and Sunstein: By a nudge we mean anything that influences our choices. A school cafeteria might try to nudge kids toward good diets by putting the healthiest foods at front. We think that it's time for institutions, including government, to become much more user-friendly by enlisting the science of choice to make life easier for people and by gentling nudging them in directions that will make their lives better.

Amazon.com: Can you describe a nudge that is now being used successfully?

Thaler and Sunstein: One example is the *Save More Tomorrow* program. Firms offer employees who are not saving very much the option of joining a program in which their saving rates are automatically increased whenever the employee gets a raise. This plan has more than tripled saving rates in some firms, and is now offered by thousands of employers.

Amazon.com: What is "choice architecture" and how does it affect the average person's daily life?

Thaler and Sunstein: Choice architecture is the context in which you make your choice. Suppose you go into a cafeteria. What do you see first, the salad bar or the burger and fries stand? Where's the chocolate cake? Where's the fruit? These features influence what you will choose to eat, so the person who decides how to display the food is the choice architect of the cafeteria. All of our choices are similarly influenced by choice architects. The architecture includes rules deciding what happens if you do nothing; what's said and what isn't said; what you see and what you don't. Doctors, employers, credit card companies, banks, and even parents are choice architects.

We show that by carefully designing the choice architecture, we can make dramatic improvements in the decisions people make, without forcing anyone to do anything. For example, we can help people save more and invest better in their retirement plans, make better choices when picking a mortgage, save on their utility bills, and improve the environment simultaneously. Good choice architecture can even improve the process of getting a divorce—or (a happier thought) getting married in the first place!

Amazon.com: You point out that most people spend more time picking out a new TV or audio device than they do choosing their health plan or retirement investment strategy? Why do most people go into what you describe as "auto-pilot mode" even when it comes to making important long-term decisions?

Thaler and Sunstein: There are three factors at work. First, people procrastinate, especially when a decision is hard. And having too many choices can create an information overload. Research shows that in many situations people will just delay making a choice altogether if they can (say by not joining their 401(k) plan), or will just take the easy way out by selecting the default option, or the one that is being suggested by a pushy salesman.

Second, our world has gotten a lot more complicated. Thirty years ago, most mortgages were of the 30-year fixed-rate variety, making them easy to compare. Now mortgages come in dozens of varieties, and even finance professors can have trouble figuring out which one is best. Since the cost of figuring out which one is best is so hard, an unscrupulous mortgage broker can easily push unsophisticated borrowers into taking a bad deal.

Third, although one might think that high stakes would make people pay more attention, instead it can just make people tense. In such situations some people react by curling into a ball and thinking, well, err, I'll do something else instead, like stare at the television or think about baseball. So, much of our lives is lived on auto-pilot, just because weighing complicated decisions is not so easy, and sometimes not so fun. Nudges can help ensure that even when we're on auto-pilot, or unwilling to make a hard choice, the deck is stacked in our favor.

Another prolific contributor to behavioral finance is Meir Statman, PhD, of the Leavey School of Business, Santa Clara University (Figure 1.3).

Statman has authored many significant works in the field of behavioral finance, including an early paper entitled "Behavioral Finance: Past Battles and Future Engagements,"[5] which is regarded as another classic in behavioral finance research. His research posed decisive questions: What are the cognitive errors and emotions that influence investors? What are investor aspirations? How can financial advisors and plan sponsors help investors?

FIGURE 1.3   Meir Statman, PhD, Glenn Klimek Professor of Finance at the Leavey School of Business, Santa Clara University.

What is the nature of risk and regret? How do investors form portfolios? How important are tactical asset allocation and strategic asset allocation? What determines stock returns? What are the effects of sentiment? Statman produces insightful answers to all of these points. Professor Statman has won the William F. Sharpe Best Paper Award, a Bernstein Fabozzi/Jacobs Levy Outstanding Article Award, and two Graham and Dodd Awards of Excellence.

More recently, Professor Statman has written a book entitled *What Investors Really Want.*[6] According to Statman, what investors really want is three kinds of benefits from their investments: utilitarian, expressive, and emotional. Utilitarian benefits are those investment benefits that drop to the bottom line: what money can buy. Expressive benefits convey to us and to others an investor's values, tastes, and status. For example, Statman contends that hedge funds express status, and socially responsible funds express virtue. Emotional benefits of investments express how people feel. His examples are: insurance policies make people feel safe, lottery tickets and speculative stocks give hope, and stock trading gives people excitement.

Perhaps the greatest realization of behavioral finance as a unique academic and professional discipline is found in the work of Daniel Kahneman and Vernon Smith, who shared the Bank of Sweden Prize in Economic Sciences in Memory of Alfred Nobel in 2002. The Nobel Prize organization honored Kahneman for "having integrated insights from

FIGURE 1.4   Daniel Kahneman, Prize winner in Economic Sciences 2002.
Source: Jon Roemer. © The Nobel Foundation.

psychological research into economic science, especially concerning human judgment and decision-making under uncertainty." Smith similarly "established laboratory experiments as a tool in empirical economic analysis, especially in the study of alternative market mechanisms," garnering the recognition of the committee.[7]

Professor Kahneman (Figure 1.4) found that under conditions of uncertainty, human decisions systematically depart from those predicted by standard economic theory. Kahneman, together with Amos Tversky (deceased in 1996), formulated prospect theory. An alternative to standard models, prospect theory provides a better account for observed behavior and is discussed at length in later chapters. Kahneman also discovered that human judgment may take heuristic shortcuts that systematically diverge from basic principles of probability. His work has inspired a new generation of research, employing insights from cognitive psychology to enrich financial and economic models.

Vernon Smith (Figure 1.5) is known for developing standards for laboratory methodology that constitute the foundation for experimental economics. In his own experimental work, he demonstrated the importance of alternative market institutions, for example, the rationale by which a seller's expected revenue depends on the auction technique in use. Smith also performed "wind-tunnel tests" to estimate the implications of alternative market configurations before such conditions are implemented in practice. The deregulation of electricity markets, for example, was one scenario

FIGURE 1.5   Vernon L. Smith, Prize winner in Economic Sciences 2002.
© The Nobel Foundation.

that Smith was able to model in advance. Smith's work has been instrumental in establishing experiments as an essential tool in empirical economic analysis.

Behavioral Finance Micro versus Behavioral Finance Macro

As we have observed, behavioral finance models and interprets phenomena ranging from individual investor conduct to market-level outcomes. Therefore, it is a difficult subject to define. For practitioners and investors reading this book, this is a major problem, because our goal is to develop a common vocabulary so that we can apply to our benefit the very valuable body of behavioral finance knowledge. For purposes of this book, we adopt an approach favored by traditional economics textbooks; we break our topic down into two subtopics: behavioral finance micro and behavioral finance macro.

1. Behavioral finance micro (BFMI) examines *behaviors or biases of individual investors* that distinguish them from the rational actors envisioned in classical economic theory.
2. Behavioral finance macro (BFMA) detects and describe *anomalies* in the efficient market hypothesis that behavioral models may explain.

As wealth management practitioners and investors, our primary focus will be BFMI, the study of individual investor behavior. Specifically, we want to identify relevant psychological biases and investigate their influence on asset allocation decisions so that we can manage the effects of those biases on the investment process.

Each of the two subtopics of behavioral finance corresponds to a distinct set of issues within the standard finance versus behavioral finance discussion. With regard to BFMA, the debate asks: Are markets "efficient," or are they subject to behavioral effects? With regard to BFMI, the debate asks: Are individual investors perfectly rational, or can cognitive and emotional errors impact their financial decisions? These questions are examined in the next section of this chapter; but to set the stage for the discussion, it is critical to understand that much of economic and financial theory is based on the notion that individuals act rationally and consider all available information in the decision-making process. In academic studies, researchers have documented abundant evidence of irrational behavior and repeated errors in judgment by adult human subjects.

Finally, one last thought before moving on. It should be noted that there is an entire body of information available on what the popular press has termed the *psychology of money*. This subject involves individuals' relationship with money—how they spend it, how they feel about it, and how they use it. There are many useful books in this area; however, this book will not focus on these topics.

STANDARD FINANCE VERSUS BEHAVIORAL FINANCE

This section reviews two basic concepts in standard finance that behavioral finance disputes: rational markets and the rational economic man. It also covers the basis on which behavioral finance proponents challenge each tenet and discusses some evidence that has emerged in favor of the behavioral approach.

Overview

On Monday, October 18, 2004, a significant but mostly unnoticed article appeared in the *Wall Street Journal*. Eugene Fama, one of the pillars of the efficient market school of financial thought, was cited admitting that stock prices could become "somewhat irrational."[8] Imagine a renowned and rabid Boston Red Sox fan proposing that Fenway Park be renamed Yogi Berra Stadium (after the colorful New York Yankees catcher), and you may begin to grasp the gravity of Fama's concession. The development raised eyebrows and pleased many behavioralists. (Fama's paper, "Market Efficiency, Long-Term Returns, and Behavioral Finance," noting this concession at the Social Science Research Network, is one of the most popular investment downloads on the web site.) The *Journal* article also featured remarks by Roger Ibbotson, founder of Ibboston Associates: "There is a shift taking place," Ibbotson observed. "People are recognizing that markets are less efficient than we thought."[9]

As Meir Statman eloquently put it, "Standard finance is the body of knowledge built on the pillars of the arbitrage principles of Miller and Modigliani, the portfolio principles of Markowitz, the capital asset pricing theory of Sharpe, Lintner, and Black, and the option-pricing theory of Black, Scholes, and Merton."[10] Standard finance theory is designed to provide mathematically elegant explanations for financial questions that, when posed in real life, are often complicated by imprecise, inelegant conditions. The standard finance approach relies on a set of assumptions that oversimplify reality. For example, embedded within standard finance is the notion of *Homo economicus,* or rational economic man. It prescribes that humans make perfectly rational economic decisions at all times. Standard finance, basically, is built on rules about how investors "should" behave, rather than on principles describing how they actually behave. Behavioral finance attempts to identify and learn from the human psychological phenomena at work in financial markets and within individual investors. Behavioral finance, like standard finance, is ultimately governed by basic precepts and assumptions. However, standard finance grounds its assumptions in idealized financial behavior; behavioral finance grounds its assumptions in observed financial behavior.

Efficient Markets versus Irrational Markets

During the 1970s, the standard finance theory of market efficiency became the model of market behavior accepted by the majority of academics and a good number of professionals. The efficient market hypothesis had matured in the previous decade, stemming from the doctoral dissertation of Eugene Fama. Fama persuasively demonstrated that in a securities market populated by many well-informed investors, investments will be appropriately priced and will reflect all available information. There are three forms of the efficient market hypothesis:

1. The "Weak" form contends that all past market prices and data are fully reflected in securities prices; that is, technical analysis is of little or no value.

2. The "Semistrong" form contends that all publicly available information is fully reflected in securities prices; that is, fundamental analysis is of no value.
3. The "Strong" form contends that all information is fully reflected in securities prices; that is, insider information is of no value.

If a market is efficient, then no amount of information or rigorous analysis can be expected to result in outperformance of a selected benchmark. An efficient market can basically be defined as a market wherein large numbers of rational investors act to maximize profits in the direction of individual securities. A key assumption is that relevant information is freely available to all participants. This competition among market participants results in a market wherein, at any given time, prices of individual investments reflect the total effects of all information, including information about events that have already happened, and events that the market expects to take place in the future. In sum, at any given time in an efficient market, the price of a security will match that security's intrinsic value.

At the center of this market efficiency debate are the actual portfolio managers who manage investments. Some of these managers are fervently passive, believing that the market is too efficient to "beat"; some are active managers, believing that the right strategies can consistently generate alpha (alpha is performance above a selected benchmark). In reality, active managers beat their benchmarks only roughly one-third of the time on average. This may explain why the popularity of exchange-traded funds (ETFs) has exploded in the past five years and why venture capitalists are now supporting new ETF companies, many of which are offering variations on the basic ETF theme.

The implications of the efficient market hypothesis are far-reaching. Most individuals who trade stocks and bonds do so under the assumption that the securities they are buying (selling) are worth more (less) than the prices that they are paying. If markets are truly efficient and current prices fully reflect all pertinent information, then trading securities in an attempt to surpass a benchmark is a game of luck, not skill.

The market efficiency debate has inspired literally thousands of studies attempting to determine whether specific markets are in fact "efficient." Many studies do indeed point to evidence that supports the efficient market hypothesis. Researchers have documented numerous, persistent anomalies, however, that contradict the efficient market hypothesis. There are three main types of market anomalies: Fundamental Anomalies, Technical Anomalies, and Calendar Anomalies.

Fundamental Anomalies

Irregularities that emerge when a stock's performance is considered in light of a fundamental assessment of the stock's value are known as fundamental anomalies. Many people, for example, are unaware that value investing—one of the most popular and effective investment methods—is based on fundamental anomalies in the efficient market hypothesis. There is a large body of evidence documenting that investors consistently overestimate the prospects of growth companies and underestimate the value of out-of-favor companies.

One example concerns stocks with low price-to-book-value (P/B) ratios. Eugene Fama and Kenneth French performed a study of low price-to-book-value ratios that covered the period between 1963 and 1990.[11] The study considered all equities listed on the New York Stock Exchange (NYSE), the American Stock Exchange (AMEX), and the Nasdaq. The stocks were divided into 10 groups by book/market and were reranked annually. The lowest book/market stocks outperformed the highest book/market stocks 21.4 percent to 8 percent, with each decile performing more poorly than the previously ranked, higher-ratio decile. Fama and French also ranked the deciles by beta and found that the value stocks posed lower risk and that the growth stocks had the highest risk. Another famous value investor, David Dreman, found that for the 25-year period ending in 1994, the lowest 20 percent P/B stocks (quarterly adjustments) significantly outperformed the market; the market, in turn, outperformed the 20 percent highest P/B of the largest 1,500 stocks on Compustat.[12]

Securities with low price-to-sales ratios also often exhibit performance that is fundamentally anomalous. Numerous studies have shown that low P/B is a consistent predictor of future value. In *What Works on Wall Street,* however, James P. O'Shaughnessy demonstrated that stocks with low price-to-sales ratios outperform markets in general and also outperform stocks with high price-to-sales ratios. He believes that the price/sales ratio is the strongest single determinant of excess return.[13]

Low price-to-earnings ratio (P/E) is another attribute that tends to anomalously correlate with outperformance. Numerous studies, including David Dreman's work, have shown that low P/E stocks tend to outperform both high P/E stocks and the market in general.[14]

Ample evidence also indicates that stocks with high dividend yields tend to outperform others. The Dow Dividend Strategy, which has received a great deal of attention recently, counsels purchasing the 10 highest-yielding Dow stocks.

Technical Anomalies

Another major debate in the investing world revolves around whether past securities prices can be used to predict future securities prices. "Technical analysis" encompasses a number of techniques that attempt to forecast securities prices by studying past prices. Sometimes, technical analysis reveals inconsistencies with respect to the efficient market hypothesis; these are technical anomalies. Common technical analysis strategies are based on relative strength and moving averages, as well as on support and resistance. While a full discussion of these strategies would prove too intricate for our purposes, there are many excellent books on the subject of technical analysis. In general, the majority of research-focused technical analysis trading methods (and, therefore, by extension, the weak-form efficient market hypothesis) finds that prices adjust rapidly in response to new stock market information and that technical analysis techniques are not likely to provide any advantage to investors who use them. However, proponents continue to argue the validity of certain technical strategies.

Calendar Anomalies

One calendar anomaly is known as "The January Effect." Historically, stocks in general and small stocks in particular have delivered abnormally high returns during the month of January. Robert Haugen and Philippe Jorion, two researchers on the subject, note that "the January Effect is, perhaps, the best-known example of anomalous behavior in security markets throughout the world."[15] The January Effect is particularly illuminating because it hasn't disappeared, despite being well known for 25 years (according to arbitrage theory, anomalies should disappear as traders attempt to exploit them in advance).

The January Effect is attributed to stocks rebounding following year-end tax selling. Individual stocks depressed near year-end are more likely to be sold for tax-loss harvesting. Some researchers have also begun to identify a "December Effect," which stems both from the requirement that many mutual funds report holdings as well as from investors buying in advance of potential January increases.

Additionally, there is a Turn-of-the-Month Effect. Studies have shown that stocks show higher returns on the last and on the first four days of each month relative to the other days. Frank Russell Company examined returns of the Standard & Poor's (S&P) 500 over a 65-year period and found that U.S. large-cap stocks consistently generate higher returns at the turn of the month.[16] Some believe that this effect is due to end-of-month cash flows (salaries, mortgages, credit cards, etc.). Chris Hensel and William Ziemba found that returns for the turn of the month consistently and significantly exceeded averages during the interval from 1928 through 1993 and "that the total return from the S&P 500 over this sixty-five-year period was received mostly during the turn of the month."[17] The study implies that investors making regular purchases may benefit by scheduling those purchases prior to the turn of the month.

Finally, as of this writing, during the course of its existence, the Dow Jones Industrial Average (DJIA) has never posted a net decline over any year ending in a "5." Of course, this may be purely coincidental.

Validity exists in both the efficient market and the anomalous market theories. In reality, markets are neither perfectly efficient nor completely anomalous. Market efficiency is not black or white but rather, varies by degrees of gray, depending on the market in question. In markets exhibiting substantial inefficiency, savvy investors can strive to outperform less savvy investors. Many believe that large-capitalization stocks, such as GE and Microsoft, tend to be very informative and efficient stocks but that small-capitalization stocks and international stocks are less efficient, creating opportunities for outperformance. Real estate, while traditionally an inefficient market, has become more transparent and, during the time of this writing, could be entering a bubble phase. Finally, the venture capital market, lacking fluid and continuous prices, is considered to be less efficient due to information asymmetries between players.

Rational Economic Man versus Behaviorally Biased Man

Stemming from neoclassical economics, Homo economicus is a simple model of human economic behavior, which assumes that principles of perfect self-interest, perfect rationality, and perfect information govern economic decisions by individuals. Like the efficient market hypothesis, Homo economicus is a tenet that economists uphold with varying degrees of stringency. Some have adopted it in a semistrong form; this version does not see rational economic behavior as perfectly predominant but still assumes an abnormally high occurrence of rational economic traits. Other economists support a weak form of Homo economicus, in which the corresponding traits exist but are not strong. All of these versions share the core assumption that humans are "rational maximizers" who are purely self-interested and make perfectly rational economic decisions. Economists like to use the concept of rational economic man for two primary reasons:

1. Homo economicus makes economic analysis relatively simple. Naturally, one might question how useful such a simple model can be.

2. Homo economicus allows economists to quantify their findings, making their work more elegant and easier to digest. If humans are perfectly rational, possessing perfect information and perfect self-interest, then perhaps their behavior can be quantified.

Most criticisms of Homo economicus proceed by challenging the bases for these three underlying assumptions—perfect rationality, perfect self-interest, and perfect information.

1. *Perfect rationality.* When humans are rational, they have the ability to reason and to make beneficial judgments. However, rationality is not the sole driver of human behavior. In fact, it may not even be the primary driver, as many psychologists believe that the human intellect is actually subservient to human emotion. They contend, therefore, that human behavior is less the product of logic than of subjective impulses, such as fear, love, hate, pleasure, and pain. Humans use their intellect only to achieve or to avoid these emotional outcomes.

2. *Perfect self-interest.* Many studies have shown that people are not perfectly self-interested. If they were, philanthropy would not exist. Religions prizing selflessness, sacrifice, and kindness to strangers would also be unlikely to prevail as they have over centuries. Perfect self-interest would preclude people from performing such unselfish deeds as volunteering, helping the needy, or serving in the military. It would also rule out self-destructive behavior, such as suicide, alcoholism, and substance abuse.

3. *Perfect information.* Some people may possess perfect or near-perfect information on certain subjects; a doctor or a dentist, one would hope, is impeccably versed in his or her field. It is impossible, however, for every person to enjoy perfect knowledge of every subject. In the world of investing, there is nearly an infinite amount to know and learn; and even the most successful investors don't master all disciplines.

Many economic decisions are made in the absence of perfect information. For instance, some economic theories assume that people adjust their buying habits based on the Federal Reserve's monetary policy. Naturally, some people know exactly where to find the Fed data, how to interpret it, and how to apply it; but many people don't know or care who or what the Federal Reserve is. Considering that this inefficiency affects millions of people, the idea that all financial actors possess perfect information becomes implausible.

Again, as with market efficiency, human rationality rarely manifests in black or white absolutes. It is better modeled across a spectrum of gray.

People are neither perfectly rational nor perfectly irrational; they possess diverse combinations of rational and irrational characteristics, and benefit from different degrees of enlightenment with respect to different issues.

THE ROLE OF BEHAVIORAL FINANCE WITH PRIVATE CLIENTS

Private clients can greatly benefit from the application of behavioral finance to their unique situations. Because behavioral finance is a relatively new concept in application to individual investors, investment advisors may feel reluctant to accept its validity. Moreover, advisors may not feel comfortable asking their clients psychological or behavioral questions to ascertain biases, especially at the beginning of the advisory relationship.

One of the objectives of this book is to position behavioral finance as a more mainstream aspect of the wealth management relationship, for both advisors and clients.

As behavioral finance is increasingly adopted by practitioners, clients will begin to see the benefits. There is no doubt that an understanding of how investor psychology impacts investment outcomes will generate insights that benefit the advisory relationship. The key result of a behavioral finance–enhanced relationship will be a portfolio to which the advisor can comfortably adhere while fulfilling the client's long-term goals. This result has obvious advantages—advantages that suggest that behavioral finance will continue to play an increasing role in portfolio structure.

HOW PRACTICAL APPLICATION OF BEHAVIORAL FINANCE CAN CREATE A SUCCESSFUL ADVISORY RELATIONSHIP

Wealth management practitioners have different ways of measuring the success of an advisory relationship. Few could argue that every successful relationship shares some fundamental characteristics:

- The advisor understands the client's financial goals.
- The advisor maintains a systematic (consistent) approach to advising the client.
- The advisor delivers what the client expects.
- The relationship benefits both client and advisor.

So, how can behavioral finance help?

Formulating Financial Goals

Experienced financial advisors know that defining financial goals is critical to creating an investment program appropriate for the client. To best define financial goals, it is helpful to understand the psychology and the emotions underlying the decisions behind creating the goals. Upcoming chapters in this book will suggest ways in which advisors can use behavioral finance to discern why investors are setting the goals that they are. Such insights equip the advisor in deepening the bond with the client, producing a better investment outcome and achieving a better advisory relationship.

Maintaining a Consistent Approach

Most successful advisors exercise a consistent approach to delivering wealth management services. Incorporating the benefits of behavioral finance can become part of that discipline and would not mandate large-scale changes in the advisor's methods. Behavioral finance can also add more professionalism and structure to the relationship because advisors can use it in the process for getting to know the client, which precedes the delivery of any actual investment advice. This step will be appreciated by clients, and it will make the relationship more successful.

Delivering What the Client Expects

Perhaps there is no other aspect of the advisory relationship that could benefit more from behavioral finance. Addressing client expectations is essential to a successful relationship; in many unfortunate instances, the advisor doesn't deliver the client's expectations because the advisor doesn't understand the needs of the client. Behavioral finance provides a context in which the advisor can take a step back and attempt to really understand the motivations of the client. Having gotten to the root of the client's expectations, the advisor is then more equipped to help realize them.

Ensuring Mutual Benefits

There is no question that measures taken that result in happier, more satisfied clients will also improve the advisor's practice and work life. Incorporating insights from behavioral finance into the advisory relationship will enhance that relationship, and it will lead to more fruitful results.

It is well known by those in the individual investor advisory business that investment results are not the primary reason that a client seeks a new advisor. The number-one reason that practitioners lose clients is that clients do not feel as though their advisors understand, or attempt to understand, the clients' financial objectives—resulting in poor relationships. The primary benefit that behavioral finance offers is the ability to develop a strong bond between client and advisor. By getting inside the head of the client and developing a comprehensive grasp of his or her motives and fears, the advisor can help the client to better understand why a portfolio is designed the way it is and why it is the "right" portfolio for him or her—regardless of what happens from day to day in the markets.

NOTES

1. The Federal Reserve Board, www.federalreserve.gov/boarddocs/speeches/ 1996/19961205.htm.
2. Robert Shiller, *Irrational Exuberance* (New Haven, CT: Yale University Press, 2000).
3. Owen A. Lamont and Richard H. Thaler, "Can the Market Add and Subtract? Mispricing in Tech Stock Carve-Outs," *Journal of Political Economy* 111(2) (2003): 227–268.
4. www.amazon.com/Nudge-Improving-Decisions-Health-Happiness/dp/ 014311526X/ref=sr_1_1?ie=UTF8&qid=1315651564&sr=8-1
5. This paper can be found on Meir Statman's home page at http://lsb. scu.edu/finance/faculty/Statman/Default.htm.
6. Meir Statman, *What Investors Really Want: Discover What Drives Investor Behavior and Make Smarter Financial Decisions* (New York: McGraw Hill, 2011).
7. Nobel Prize web site: http://nobelprize.org/economics/laureates/2002/.
8. Jon E. Hilsenrath, "Belief in Efficient Valuation Yields Ground to Role of Irrational Investors: Mr. Thaler Takes on Mr. Fama," *Wall Street Journal,* October 18, 2004.
9. Ibid.
10. Meir Statman, "Behavioral Finance: Past Battles and Future Engagements," *Financial Analysts Journal* 55 (6) (November/December 1999): 18–27.
11. Eugene Fama and Kenneth French, "The Cross-Section of Expected Stock Returns," *Journal of Finance* 47(2) (1992): 427–465.
12. Dream Value Management web site: www.dreman.com/.
13. James O'Shaughnessy, *What Works on Wall Street* (New York: McGraw-Hill Professional, 2005).
14. See note 12.
15. Robert Haugen and Philippe Jorion, "The January Effect: Still There after All These Years," *Financial Analysts Journal* 52(1) (January–February 1996): 27–31.
16. Russell Investment Group web site: www.russell.com/us/education_center/.
17. Chris R. Hensel and William T. Ziemba, "Investment Results from Exploiting Turn-of-the-Month Effects," *Journal of Portfolio Management* 22 (3) (Spring 1996): 17–23.

CHAPTER 2

The History of Behavioral Finance Micro

If you go into what I call a "bubble boom," every bubble bursts.
—Margaret Thatcher, British Prime Minister

T his chapter traces the development of behavioral finance micro (BFMI). There are far too many authors, papers, and disciplines that touch on various aspects of behavioral finance (behavioral science, investor psychology, cognitive psychology, behavioral economics, experimental economics, and cognitive science) to examine every formative influence in one chapter. Instead, the emphasis will be on major milestones of the past 250 years. The focus is, in particular, on recent developments that have shaped applications of behavioral finance in private-client situations.

HISTORICAL PERSPECTIVE ON THE LINK BETWEEN PSYCHOLOGY AND ECONOMICS

Historical Roots

Investor irrationality has existed as long as the markets themselves have. Perhaps the best-known historical example of irrational investor behavior dates back to the *early modern* or *mercantilist* period during the sixteenth century. A man named Conrad Guestner transported tulip bulbs from Constantinople, introducing them to Holland. Beautiful and difficult to obtain, tulips were a consumer sensation and an instant status symbol for the Dutch elite. Although most early buyers sought the flowers simply because they adored them, speculators soon joined the fray to make a profit. Trading activity escalated and, eventually, tulip bulbs were placed onto the local market exchanges.

The obsession with owning tulips trickled down to the Dutch middle class. People were selling everything they owned—including homes, livestock, and other essentials—so they could acquire tulips, based on the expectation that the bulbs' value would continue to grow. At the peak of the tulip frenzy, a single bulb would have sold for about the equivalent of several tons of grain, a major item of furniture, a team of oxen, or a breeding stock of pigs. Basically, consumers valued tulips about as highly as they valued pricey, indispensable, durable goods. By 1636, tulip bulbs had been established on the Amsterdam stock exchange, as well as exchanges in Rotterdam, Harlem, and other locations in Europe. They became such a prominent commodity that tulip notaries were hired to record transactions, and public laws and regulations developed to oversee the tulip trade. Can you imagine? Later that year, however, the first speculators began to liquidate their tulip holdings. Tulip prices weakened slowly at first and then plunged; within a month, the bulbs lost 90 percent of their value. Many investors, forced to default on their tulip contracts, incurred huge losses. Do we notice any parallels to the economic events of 1929 or 2000, or similar bubbles?

It wasn't until the mid-eighteenth-century onset of the classical period in economics, however, that people began to study the human side of economic decision making, which subsequently laid the groundwork for BFMI. At this time, the concept of utility was introduced to measure the satisfaction associated with consuming a good or a service. Scholars linked economic utility with human psychology and even morality, giving it a much broader meaning than it would take on later, during neoclassicism, when it survived chiefly as a principle underlying laws of supply and demand.

Many people think that the legendary *Wealth of Nations* (1776) was what made Adam Smith (Figure 2.1) famous; in fact, Smith's crowning composition focused far more on individual psychology than on production of wealth in markets. Published in 1759, *The Theory of Moral Sentiments* described the mental and emotional underpinnings of human interaction, including economic interaction. In Smith's time, some believed that people's behavior could be modeled in completely rational, almost mathematical terms. Others, like Smith, felt that each human was born possessing an intrinsic moral compass, a source of influence superseding externalities like logic or law. Smith argued that this "invisible hand" guided both social and economic conduct. The prospect of "perfectly rational" economic decision making never entered into Smith's analysis. Instead, even when addressing financial matters, *The Theory of Moral Sentiments* focused on elements like pride, shame, insecurity, and egotism:

FIGURE 2.1　Adam Smith

It is the vanity, not the ease, or the pleasure, which interests us. But vanity is always founded upon the belief of our being the object of attention and approbation. The rich man glories in his riches, because he feels that they naturally draw upon him the attention of the world, and that mankind are disposed to go along with him in all those agreeable emotions with which the advantages of his situation so readily inspire him. At the thought of this, his heart seems to swell and dilate itself within him, and he is fonder of his wealth, upon this account, than for all the other advantages it procures him. The poor man, on the contrary, is ashamed of his poverty. He feels that it either places him out of the sight of mankind, or, that if they take any notice of him, they have, however, scarce any fellow-feeling with the misery and distress which he suffers. He is mortified upon both accounts. For though to be overlooked, and to be disapproved of, are things entirely different, yet as obscurity covers us from the daylight of honour and approbation, to feel that we are taken no notice of, necessarily damps the most agreeable hope, and disappoints the most ardent desire, of human nature.[1]

The topic of this passage is money; yet humanity and emotion play huge roles, reflecting the classical-era view on economic reasoning by individuals. Another famous thinker of the time, Jeremy Bentham, wrote extensively on the psychological aspects of economic utility. Bentham asserted that "the principle of utility is that principle which approves or disapproves of every action whatsoever, according to the tendency which it appears to have to augment or diminish the happiness of the party whose interest is in question: or, what is the same thing in other words, to promote or to oppose that happiness."[2] For Bentham, "every action whatsoever" seeks to maximize utility. Happiness, a subjective experience, is the ultimate human concern—rendering impossible any moral or economic calculation entirely devoid of emotion.

Smith, Bentham, and others recognized the role of psychological idiosyncrasies in economic behavior, but their consensus lost ground over the course of the next century. By the 1870s, three famous economists began to introduce the revolutionary neoclassical framework. William Stanley Jevons's *Theory of Political Economy* (1871), Carl Menger's *Principles of Economics* (1871), and Leon Walras's *Elements of Pure Economics* (1874 to 1877) defined economics as the study of the allocation of scarce resources among competing forces. Neoclassical theory sought equilibrium solutions whereby individuals maximized marginal utility, subject to situational constraints. Regularities in economies derived from the uniform, simultaneous behavior of individuals optimizing their marginal gains; and large-scale economic phenomena could be explained by simply aggregating the behavior of these individuals. Neoclassical economists distanced themselves from psychology, reframing their discipline as a quantitative science that deduced explanations of economic behavior from assumptions regarding the nature of economic agents.

Pursuing a simple model suited to the neoclassical focus on profit maximization, economists of this period conceived *Homo economicus,* or rational economic man, to serve as a mathematical representation of an individual economic actor. Based on the assumption that individuals make perfectly rational economic decisions, Homo economicus ignores important aspects of human reasoning.

Rational Economic Man

Rational economic man (REM) describes a simple model of human behavior. REM strives to maximize his economic well-being, selecting strategies that are contingent on predetermined, utility-optimizing goals, on the information that REM possesses, and on any other postulated constraints. The amount of utility that REM associates with any given outcome is represented by the output of his algebraic utility function. Basically, REM is an individual who tries to achieve discretely specified goals to the most comprehensive, consistent extent possible while minimizing economic costs. REM's choices are dictated by his utility function. Often, predicting how REM will negotiate complex trade-offs, such as the pursuit of wages versus leisure, simply entails computing a derivative. REM ignores social values, unless adhering to them gives him pleasure (i.e., registers as a term expressed in his utility function).

The validity of Homo economicus has been the subject of much debate since the model's introduction. As was shown in the previous chapter, those who challenge Homo economicus do so by attacking the basic assumptions of perfect information, perfect rationality, and perfect self-interest. Economists Thorstein Veblen, John Maynard Keynes, and many others criticize Homo economicus, contending that no human can be fully informed of "all circumstances and maximize his expected utility by determining his complete, reflexive, transitive, and continuous preferences over alternative bundles of consumption goods at all times."[3] They posit, instead, "bounded rationality," which relaxes the assumptions of standard expected utility theory in order to more realistically represent human economic decision making. Bounded rationality assumes that individuals' choices are rational but subject to limitations of knowledge and cognitive capacity. Bounded rationality is concerned with ways in which final decisions are shaped by the decision-making process itself.

Some psychological researchers argue that Homo economicus disregards inner conflicts that real people face. For instance, Homo economicus does not account for the fact that people have difficulty prioritizing short-term versus long-term goals (e.g., spending versus saving) or reconciling inconsistencies between individual goals and societal values. Such conflicts, these researchers argue, can lead to "irrational" behavior.

MODERN BEHAVIORAL FINANCE

By the early twentieth century, neoclassical economics had largely displaced psychology as an influence in economic discourse. In the 1930s and 1950s, however, a number of important events laid the groundwork for the renaissance of behavioral economics. First, the growing field of *experimental economics* examined theories of individual choice, questioning the theoretical underpinnings of Homo economicus. Some very useful early experiments generated insights that would later inspire key elements of contemporary behavioral finance.

Twentieth-Century Experimental Economics: Modeling Individual Choice

In order to understand why economists began experimenting with actual people to assess the validity of rational economic theories, it is necessary to understand *indifference curves*. The aim of indifference curve analysis is to demonstrate, mathematically, the basis on which a rational consumer substitutes certain quantities of one good for another. One classic example

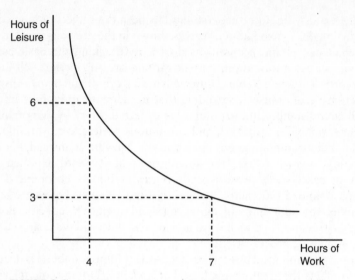

FIGURE 2.2   Indifference Curves Model Consumer Trade-Offs

models the effects of a wage adjustment on a worker's allocation of hours to work versus leisure. Indifference curve analysis also incorporates budget lines (constraints), which signify restrictions on consumption that stem from resource scarcity. In the work-versus-leisure model, for example, workers may not allocate any sum exceeding 24 hours per day.

An indifference curve is a line that depicts all of the possible combinations of two goods between which a person is indifferent; that is, consuming any bundle on the indifference curve yields the same level of utility.

Figure 2.2 maps an exemplary indifference curve. This consumer could consume four hours of work and six hours of leisure—or seven hours of work and three hours of leisure—and achieve equal satisfaction.

With this concept in mind, consider an experiment performed by Louis Leon Thurstone in 1931 on individuals' actual indifference curves.[4] Thurstone reported an experiment in which each subject was asked to make a large number of hypothetical choices between commodity bundles consisting of hats and coats, hats and shoes, or shoes and coats. For example, would an individual prefer a bundle consisting of eight hats and eight pairs of shoes or one consisting of six hats and nine pairs of shoes? Thurstone found that it was possible to estimate a curve that fit fairly closely to the data collected for choices involving shoes and coats and other subsets of the experiment. Thurstone concluded that choice data could be adequately represented by indifference curves, and that it was practical to estimate them this way.

Although some researchers felt that Thurston's experiment was too hypothetical, it was still considered important. In the 1940s, two researchers named Stephen W. Rousseas and Albert G. Hart performed some experiments on indifference curves designed to follow up on Thurstone's experiment and to respond to some of the experiment's critics. They constructed what they viewed as a more concrete and realistic choice situation by having subjects select among possible breakfast menus, with each potential breakfast consisting of a specified number of eggs and a specified quantity of bacon strips. They required that "each individual was obliged to eat all of what he chose; i.e., he could not save any part of the offerings for a future time."[5]

In this experiment, individual subjects made only a single choice (repeated subsequently a month later); and, in addition to selecting among available combinations, each was asked to state an ideal combination of bacon and eggs. While this experiment did not ask its subjects to make too many choices of the same type (i.e., different combinations of two goods), thereby averting a common criticism of Thurstone, it left Rousseas and Hart with the problem of trying to aggregate individual choice data collected from multiple individuals. They attempted to ascertain whether choices made by separate individuals stating similar "ideal" breakfast combinations could be pieced together to form consistent indifference curves. This last step presented complications, but overall the project was considered a success and led to further experiments in the same vein.

Also inspired by Thurstone, Frederick Mosteller and Phillip Nogee sought in 1951 to test expected utility theory by experimentally constructing utility curves.[6] Mosteller and Nogee tested subjects' willingness to accept lotteries with given stakes at varying payoff probabilities. They concluded, in general, that it was possible to construct subjects' utility functions experimentally and that the predictions derived from these utility functions were "not so good as might be hoped, but their general direction [was] correct." This is a conclusion that many experimental economists would still affirm, with differing degrees of emphasis.

As these types of experiments continued, various violations of expected utility were beginning to be observed. Perhaps the most famous of violations of expected utility was exposed by another Nobel Prize winner in Economic Sciences in 1988.

Maurice Allais (Figure 2.3), Memorial Prize in Economic Sciences winner (1988), made distinguished, pioneering, and highly original contributions in many areas of economic research. Outside of a rather small circle of economists, he is perhaps best known for his studies of risk theory and the so-called Allais paradox. He showed that the theory of maximization of expected utility, which had been accepted for many decades, did not apply

FIGURE 2.3   Maurice Allais,
Prize winner in Economic
Sciences (1988).
© The Nobel Foundation.

to certain empirically realistic decisions under risk and uncertainty. In the
Allais paradox, Allais asked subjects to make two hypothetical choices. The
first choice was between alternatives "A" and "B," defined as:

A — Certainty of receiving 100 million (francs).

B — Probability 0.1 of receiving 500 million.

Probability 0.89 of receiving 100 million.

Probability 0.01 of receiving zero.

The second choice was between alternatives "C" and "D," defined as:

C — Probability 0.11 of earning 100 million.

Probability 0.89 of earning zero.

D — Probability 0.1 of earning 500 million.

Probability 0.9 of earning zero.[7]

It is not difficult to show that an expected utility maximizer who
prefers A to B must also prefer C to D. However, Allais reported that A
was commonly preferred over B, with D preferred over C. Note that although Allais's choices were hypothetical, the phenomenon he reported has
subsequently been reproduced in experiments offering real—albeit much
smaller—quantities of money.

As the 1950s concluded and the 1960s progressed, the field of experimental economics expanded, with numerous researchers publishing volumes of data. Their important experiments brought to light new aspects of human economic decision making and drew intellectual attention to the field. Concurrently, two more intellectual disciplines were emerging that would contribute to the genesis of behavioral finance: cognitive psychology and decision theory. Researchers in these subjects would build on concepts learned in experimental economics to further refine the concepts of modern behavioral finance.

Cognitive Psychology

Many scholars of contemporary behavioral finance feel that the field's most direct roots are in cognitive psychology. *Cognitive psychology* is the scientific study of cognition, or the mental processes that are believed to drive human behavior. Research in cognitive psychology investigates a variety of topics, including memory, attention, perception, knowledge representation, reasoning, creativity, and problem solving.

Cognitive psychology is a relatively recent development in the history of psychological research, emerging only in the late 1950s and early 1960s. The term *cognitive psychology* was coined by Ulrich Neisser in 1967, when he published a book with that title. The cognitive approach was actually brought to prominence, however, by Donald Broadbent, who published *Perception and Communication* in 1958.[8] Broadbent promulgated the information processing archetype of cognition that, to this day, serves as the dominant cognitive psychological model. Broadbent's approach treats mental processes like software running on a computer (the brain). Cognitive psychology commonly describes human thought in terms of input, representation, computation or processing, and output.

As will be discussed later in this chapter, psychologists Amos Tversky and Daniel Kahneman would eventually create a theory—prospect theory—that is viewed as the intellectual foundation of BFMI. Tversky and Kahneman examined mental processes as they directly relate to decision making under conditions of uncertainty. We will look at this topic now, and then review the groundbreaking work behind prospect theory.

Decision Making under Uncertainty

Each day, people have little difficulty making hundreds of decisions. This is because the best course of action is often obvious and because many decisions do not determine outcomes significant enough to merit a great deal of attention. On occasion, however, many potential decision paths emanate, and the correct course is unclear. Sometimes, our decisions have significant consequences. These situations demand substantial time and effort to try to devise a systematic approach to analyzing various courses of action.

Even in a perfect world, when a decision maker must choose one among a number of possible actions, the ultimate consequences of most, if not every, available action will depend on uncertainties to be resolved in the future. When deciding under uncertainty, there are generally accepted guidelines that a decision maker should follow:

1. Take an inventory of all viable options available for obtaining information, for experimentation, and for action.
2. List the events that may occur.
3. Arrange pertinent information and choices/assumptions.
4. Rank the consequences resulting from the various courses of action.
5. Determine the probability of an uncertain event occurring.

Unfortunately, facing uncertainty, most people cannot and do not systematically describe problems, record all the necessary data, or synthesize information to create rules for making decisions. Instead, most people venture down somewhat more subjective, less ideal paths of reasoning in an attempt to determine the course of action consistent with their basic judgments and preferences. How, then, can decision making be faithfully modeled?

Raiffa In 1968, in *Decision Analysis: Introductory Lectures on Choices under Uncertainty*,[9] decision theorist Howard Raiffa introduced to the analysis of decisions three approaches that provide a more accurate view of a "real" person's thought process:

1. *Normative* analysis is concerned with the rational solution to the problem at hand. It defines an ideal that actual decisions should strive to approximate.
2. *Descriptive* analysis is concerned with the manner in which real people actually make decisions.
3. *Prescriptive* analysis is concerned with practical advice and tools that might help people achieve results more closely approximating those of normative analysis.

Raiffa's contribution laid the foundation for a significant work in the field of BFMI, an article by Daniel Kahneman and Mark Riepe entitled "Aspects of Investor Psychology: Beliefs, Preferences, and Biases Investment Advisors Should Know About." This work was the first to tie together decision theory and financial advising. According to Kahneman and Riepe, "to advise effectively, advisors must be guided by an accurate picture of the cognitive and emotional weaknesses of investors that relate to making investment decisions: their occasionally faulty assessment of their own interests and true wishes, the relevant facts that they tend to ignore, and the limits of their ability to accept advice and to live with the decisions they make."[10]

Kahnemann and Tversky At approximately the same time that Howard Raiffa published his work on decision theory, two relatively unknown cognitive psychologists, Amos Tversky and Daniel Kahneman, began research on decision making under uncertainty. This work ultimately produced a very important book published in 1982 entitled *Judgment under Uncertainty: Heuristics and Biases.*[11]

In an interview conducted by a publication called Current Contents of ISI in April 1983, Tversky and Kahneman discussed their findings with respect to mainstream investors' thinking:

> *The research was sparked by the realization that intuitive predictions and judgments under uncertainty do not follow the laws of probability or the principles of statistics. These hypotheses were formulated very early in conversations between us, but it took many years of research and thousands of subject hours to study the role of representativeness, availability, and anchoring, and to explore the biases to which they are prone. The approach to the study of judgment that is reflected in the paper is characterized by (1) a comparison of intuitive judgment to normative principles of probability and statistics, (2) a search for heuristics of judgment and the biases to which they are prone, and (3) an attempt to explore the theoretical and practical implications of the discrepancy between the psychology of judgment and the theory of rational belief.*[12]

Essentially, Tversky and Kahneman brought to light the incidence, causes, and effects of human error in economic reasoning. Building on the success of their 1974 paper, the two researchers published in 1979 what is now considered the seminal work in behavioral finance: "Prospect Theory: An Analysis of Decision under Risk." The following is the abstract of the paper.

> *This paper presents a critique of expected utility theory as a descriptive model of decision making under risk, and develops an alternative model, called prospect theory. Choices among risky prospects exhibit several pervasive effects that are inconsistent with the basic*

tenets of utility theory. In particular, people underweight outcomes that are merely probable in comparison with outcomes that are obtained with certainty. This tendency, called the certainty effect, contributes to risk aversion in choices involving sure gains and to risk seeking in choices involving sure losses. In addition, people generally discard components that are shared by all prospects under consideration. This tendency, called the isolation effect, leads to inconsistent preferences when the same choice is presented in different forms. An alternative theory of choice is developed, in which value is assigned to gains and losses rather than to final assets and in which probabilities are replaced by decision weights. The value function is normally concave for gains, commonly convex for losses, and is generally steeper for losses than for gains. Decision weights are generally lower than the corresponding probabilities, except in the range of low probabilities. Overweighting of low probabilities may contribute to the attractiveness of both insurance and gambling.[13]

Prospect theory, in essence, describes how individuals evaluate gains and losses. The theory names two specific thought processes: editing and evaluation. During the editing state, alternatives are ranked according to a basic "rule of thumb" (heuristic), which contrasts with the elaborate algorithm in the previous section. Then, during the evaluation phase, some reference point that provides a relative basis for appraising gains and losses is designated. A value function, passing through this reference point and assigning a "value" to each positive or negative outcome, is S shaped and asymmetrical in order to reflect loss aversion (i.e., the tendency to feel the impact of losses more than gains). This can also be thought of as risk seeking in domain losses (the reflection effect). Figure 2.4 depicts a value function, as typically diagrammed in prospect theory.

It is important to note that prospect theory also observes how people mentally "frame" predicted outcomes, often in very subjective terms; this accordingly affects expected utility. An exemplary instance of framing is given by the experimental data cited in the 1979 article by Kahneman and Tversky, where they reported that they presented groups of subjects with a number of problems.[14] One group was presented with this problem:

1. In addition to whatever you own, you have been given $1,000. You are now asked to choose between:
   A. A sure gain of $500.
   B. A 50 percent chance to gain $1,000 and a 50 percent chance to gain nothing.

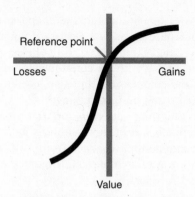

Reference point

Losses   Gains

Value

FIGURE 2.4 The Value Function—
a Key Tenet of Prospect Theory
Source: The Econometric Society.

Another group of subjects was presented with a different problem:

1. In addition to whatever you own, you have been given $2,000. You are
   now asked to choose between:
   A. A sure loss of $500.
   B. A 50 percent chance to lose $1,000 and a 50 percent chance to lose
   nothing.

In the first group, 84 percent of participants chose A. In the second
group, the majority, 69 percent, opted for B. The net expected value of
the two prospective prizes was, in each instance, identical. However, the
phrasing of the question caused the problems to be interpreted differently.

Kahnemann and Riepe   One of the next significant steps in the evolution
of BFMI also involves Daniel Kahneman. Along with Mark Riepe, Kahneman wrote a paper entitled "Aspects of Investor Psychology: Beliefs,
Preferences, and Biases Investment Advisors Should Know About."[15] This
work leveraged the decision theory work of Howard Raiffa, categorizing
behavioral biases on three grounds: (1) *biases of judgment,* (2) *errors of
preference,* and (3) *biases associated with living with the consequences of
decisions.* Kahneman and Riepe also provide examples of each type of bias
in practice.

Biases of judgment include overconfidence, optimism, hindsight, and
overreaction to chance events. Errors of preference include nonlinear weight-
ing of probabilities; the tendency of people to value changes, not states; the

value of gains and losses as a function; the shape and attractiveness of gambles; the use of purchase price as a reference point; narrow framing; tendencies related to repeated gambles and risk policies; and the adoption of short versus long views. Living with the consequences of decisions gives rise to regrets of omission and commission, and also has implications regarding the relationship between regret and risk taking.[16]

One of the reasons that this paper is so important from the practical application perspective is that it was the first scholarly work to really challenge financial advisors to examine their practice from a behavioral standpoint. Moreover, the authors encapsulate their challenge in the form of a detailed "Checklist for Financial Advisors."

PSYCHOGRAPHIC MODELS USED IN BEHAVIORAL FINANCE

Psychographic models are designed to classify individuals according to certain characteristics, tendencies, or behaviors. Psychographic classifications are particularly relevant with regard to individual strategy and risk tolerance. An investor's background and past experiences can play a significant role in decisions made during the asset allocation process. If investors fitting specific psychographic profiles are more likely to exhibit specific investor biases, then practitioners can attempt to recognize the relevant telltale behavioral tendencies before investment decisions are made. Hopefully, resulting considerations would yield better investment outcomes.

Two studies—Barnewall (1987) and Bailard, Biehl, and Kaiser (1986)—apply useful models of investor psychographics.

Barnewall Two-Way Model

One of the oldest and most prevalent psychographic investor models, based on the work of Marilyn MacGruder Barnewall, was intended to help investment advisors interface with clients. Barnewall distinguished between two relatively simple investor types: passive investors and active investors. Barnewall noted:

> *"Passive investors" are defined as those investors who have become wealthy passively—for example, by inheritance or by risking the capital of others rather than risking their own capital. Passive investors have a greater need for security than they have tolerance for risk. Occupational groups that tend to have passive investors*

include corporate executives, lawyers with large regional firms, certified public accountants with large CPA firms, medical and dental non-surgeons, individuals with inherited wealth, small business owners who inherited the business, politicians, bankers, and journalists. The smaller the economic resources an investor has, the more likely the person is to be a passive investor. The lack of resources gives individuals a higher security need and a lower tolerance for risk. Thus, a large percentage of the middle and lower socioeconomic classes are passive investors as well.

"Active investors" are defined as those individuals who have earned their own wealth in their lifetimes. They have been actively involved in the wealth creation, and they have risked their own capital in achieving their wealth objectives. Active investors have a higher tolerance for risk than they have need for security. Related to their high risk tolerance is the fact that active investors prefer to maintain control of their own investments. If they become involved in an aggressive investment of which they are not in control, their risk tolerance drops quickly. Their tolerance for risk is high because they believe in themselves. They get very involved in their own investments to the point that they gather tremendous amounts of information about the investments and tend to drive their investment managers crazy. By their involvement and control, they feel that they reduce risk to an acceptable level.[17]

Barnewall's work suggests that a simple, noninvasive overview of an investor's personal history and career record could signal potential pitfalls to guard against in establishing an advisory relationship. Her analysis also indicates that a quick, biographic glance at a client could provide an important context for portfolio design.

Bailard, Biehl, and Kaiser Five-Way Model

The Bailard, Biehl, and Kaiser (BB&K) model features some principles of the Barnewall model; but by classifying investor personalities along two axes—level of confidence and method of action—it introduces an additional dimension of analysis. Thomas Bailard, David Biehl, and Ronald Kaiser provided a graphic representation of their model (Figure 2.5) and explain:

The first aspect of personality deals with how confidently the investor approaches life, regardless of whether it is his approach to his career, his health, his money. These are important emotional

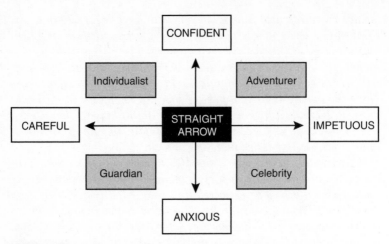

FIGURE 2.5   BB&K Five-Way Model: Graphic Representation
Source: Thomas Bailard, David Biehl, and Ronald Kaiser. *Personal Money Management,* 5th ed. (Chicago: Science Research Associates, 1986).

choices, and they are dictated by how confident the investor is about some things or how much he tends to worry about them. The second element deals with whether the investor is methodical, careful, and analytical in his approach to life or whether he is emotional, intuitive, and impetuous. These two elements can be thought of as two "axes" of individual psychology; one axis is called "confident-anxious" and the other is called the "careful-impetuous" axis.[18]

The following inset includes BB&K's descriptions of each of the five investor personality types that the model generates. The authors also suggest approaches to advising each type of client.[19]

In the past five to ten years, there have been some new and exciting developments in the practical application of BFMI. Specifically, there is some very thoughtful work being done in the field of brain research that is attempting to demonstrate how the brain works when making financial decisions. Additionally, research is also conducted on how various personality types behave when it comes to making financial decisions. Later in this book, a chapter is devoted to each of several of these new, exciting topics. For now, however, basic strategies for incorporating behavioral finance into the asset allocation decision are introduced in Chapter 3.

BB&K FIVE INVESTOR PERSONALITY TYPES

The Adventurer. People who are willing to put it all on one bet and go for it because they have confidence. They are difficult to advise because they have their own ideas about investing. They are willing to take risks, and they are volatile clients from an investment counsel point of view.

The Celebrity. These people like to be where the action is. They are afraid of being left out. They really do not have their own ideas about investments. They may have their own ideas about other things in life, but not investing. As a result they are the best prey for maximum broker turnover.

The Individualist. These people tend to go their own way and are typified by the small businessperson or an independent professional, such as a lawyer, certified public accountant (CPA), or engineer. These are people who are trying to make their own decisions in life, carefully going about things, having a certain degree of confidence about them, but also being careful, methodical, and analytical. These are clients whom everyone is looking for—rational investors with whom the portfolio manager can talk sense.

The Guardian. Typically, as people get older and begin considering retirement, they approach this personality profile. They are careful and a little bit worried about their money. They recognize that they face a limited earning time span and have to preserve their assets. They are definitely not interested in volatility or excitement. Guardians lack confidence in their ability to forecast the future or to understand where to put money, so they look for guidance.

The Straight Arrow. These people are so well balanced, they cannot be placed in any specific quadrant, so they fall near the center. On average, this group of clients is the average investor, a relatively balanced composite of each of the other four investor types, and by implication a group willing to be exposed to medium amounts of risk.

Source: Thomas Bailard, David Biehl, and Ronald Kaiser, *Personal Money Management,* 5th ed. (Chicago: Science Research Associates, 1986).

Behavioral Investor Types

Building on the idea of classifying investors by their psychographic characteristics, as did the works of BB&K and Barnewall, I have identified four behavioral investor types (BITs) which I will review in detail in Chapter 26using a process called behavioral alpha (BA). The objective of the BIT categorization scheme, similar to that of BB&K and Barnewall's work, is to assist advisors and investors in better understanding their behaviors in an effort to make better investment decisions.

This section will review the basics of this process, building on key concepts in previous articles published in the *Journal of Financial Planning* and the first edition of this book. These early works outlined a method of applying behavioral finance to private clients in a way that I now refer to as "bottom-up." This means that for advisors or investors to diagnose and treat behavioral biases, they must first test for all behavioral biases in the client (listed in this book), and then determine which ones apply before creating a behaviorally modified investment plan such as those presented in the first reading. Using the BA method, advisors and investors can simplify this process by testing for the behavioral biases they are likely to encounter, based on the psychological profile of clients, and then considering how to correct for or adapt to the biases.

The reason that I created the BA method is that it is easier to implement. In one of my early papers,[20] I explain how to plot the bias type and wealth level information on a chart to create a "best practical allocation" or "best behaviorally modified allocation" for the client. However, some advisors may find this bottom-up approach too time consuming or complex. BA is a simpler, more efficient approach to bias identification that is "top-down," a shortcut if you will, that makes bias identification more efficient for the purpose of determining which type of bias a client might have. Efficiency is essential for advisors and investors to be able to apply behavioral finance in practice.

This introduction will hopefully whet your appetite for learning more about behavioral investor types. We will now move on to incorporating investor behavior into the asset allocation process in Chapter 3. For a more complete review of BITs, please turn to Chapter 26

NOTES

1. Adam Smith, *The Theory of Moral Sentiments* (1759).
2. Jeremy Bentham, *An Introduction to the Principles of Morals and Legislation* (1789).

3. John Maynard Keynes, *The General Theory of Employment* (New York: Harcourt, Brace, 1936).
4. A. E. Roth, "On the Early History of Experimental Economics," *Journal of the History of Economic Thought* 15 (Fall 1993): 184–209.
5. Ibid.
6. Ibid.
7. Ibid.
8. Donald Broadbent, *Perception and Communication* (New York: Pergamon Press, 1958).
9. H. Raiffa, *Decision Analysis: Introductory Lectures on Choices under Uncertainty* (Reading, MA: Addison-Wesley, 1968).
10. Daniel Kahneman and Mark Riepe, "Aspects of Investor Psychology: Beliefs, Preferences, and Biases Investment Advisors Should Know About," *Journal of Portfolio Management* 24 (1998): 52–65.
11. Daniel Kahneman, Paul Slovic, and Amos Tversky, eds., *Judgment under Uncertainty: Heuristics and Biases* (New York: Cambridge University Press, 1982).
12. This paper can be found at www.garfield.library.upenn.edu/classics 1983/ A1983QG78800001.pdf.
13. Daniel Kahneman and Amos Tversky, "Prospect Theory: An Analysis of Decisions under Risk," *Econometrica* 47 (1979): 313–327.
14. Ibid.
15. See note 10.
16. Ibid.
17. M. Barnewall, "Psychological Characteristics of the Individual Investor," in William Droms, ed., *Asset Allocation for the Individual Investor* (Charlottesville, VA: Institute of Chartered Financial Analysts, 1987).
18. Thomas Bailard, David Biehl, and Ronald Kaiser, *Personal Money Management*, 5th ed. (Chicago: Science Research Associates, 1986).
19. Ibid.
20. Michael Pompian and John Longo, "Incorporating Behavioral Finance into Your Practice," *Journal of Financial Planning* (March 2005): 58–63.

CHAPTER 3

Introduction to Behavioral Biases

*What we believe to be the motives of our conduct are usually but
the pretexts for it.*
                    —Miguel de Unamuno, Spanish Philosopher,
                                            1864 to 1936

INTRODUCTION

Numerous research studies have shown that when people are faced with
complex decision-making problems that demand substantial time and cognitive decision-making requirements, they have difficulty devising a rational
approach to developing and analyzing a proper course of action. This problem is exacerbated by the fact that many consumers need to contend with
a potential overload of information to process. Have you walked down the
toothpaste aisle lately? Way too many choices—how do you pick? And this
is one of the easier decisions we face! For more meaningful decisions, people
don't systematically describe problems, record necessary data, and/or synthesize information to create rules for making decisions, which is really the
best way make complex decisions. Instead, people usually follow a more
subjective path of reasoning to determine a course of action consistent with
their desired outcome or general preferences.

Individuals make decisions, although typically suboptimal ones, by sim-
plifying the choices presented to them, typically using a subset of the information available, and discarding some (usually complicated but potentially
good) alternatives to get down to a more manageable number. They are
content to find a solution that is "good enough" rather than arriving at the
optimal decision. In doing so, they may (unintentionally) bias the decision-
making process. These biases may lead to irrational behaviors and flawed
decisions. In the investment realm, this happens a lot; many researchers have
documented numerous biases that investors have. This chapter will introduce

these biases, which we will review in the next 20 chapters and highlight the importance of understanding them and dealing with them before they have a chance to negatively impact the investment decision-making process.

BEHAVIORAL BIASES DEFINED

The dictionary defines a "bias" in several different ways, including: (a) a statistical sampling or testing error caused by systematically favoring some outcomes over others; (b) a preference or an inclination, especially one that inhibits impartial judgment; (c) an inclination or prejudice in favor of a particular viewpoint; and (d) an inclination of temperament or outlook, especially, a personal and sometimes unreasoned judgment. In this book, we are naturally concerned with biases that cause irrational financial decisions due to either (1) faulty cognitive reasoning or (2) reasoning influenced by emotions which can also be considered feelings, or, unfortunately, due to both. The first dictionary definition (a) of bias is consistent with faulty *cognitive* reasoning or thinking while (b), (c), and (d) are more consistent with impaired reasoning influenced by feelings or *emotion*.

Behavioral biases are defined, essentially, the same way as systematic errors in judgment. Researchers distinguish a long list of specific biases, and have applied over 50 of these to individual investor behaviors in recent studies. When one considers the derivative and the undiscovered biases awaiting application in personal finance, the list of systematic investor errors seems very long indeed. More brilliant research seeks to categorize these biases according to a meaningful framework. Some authors refer to biases as heuristics (rules of thumb), while others call them beliefs, judgments, or preferences. Psychologists' factors include cognitive information processing shortcuts or heuristics, memory errors, emotional and/or motivational factors, and social influences such as family upbringing or societal culture. Some biases identified by psychologists are understood in relation to human needs such as those identified by Maslow—physiological, safety, social, esteem, and self-actualizing. In satisfying these needs, people will generally attempt to avoid pain and seek pleasure. The avoidance of pain can be as subtle as refusing to acknowledge mistakes in order to maintain a positive self-image. The biases that help to avoid pain and instead produce pleasure may be classified as emotional. Other biases are attributed by psychologists to the particular way the brain perceives, forms memories, and makes judgments; the inability to do complex mathematical calculations, such as updating probabilities; and the processing and filtering of information.

This sort of bias taxonomy is helpful as an underlying theory about why and how people operate under bias, but no universal theory has been developed. Instead of a universal theory of investment behavior, behavioral finance research relies on a broad collection of evidence pointing to the ineffectiveness of human decision making in various economic decision-making circumstances.

WHY UNDERSTANDING AND IDENTIFYING BEHAVIORAL BIASES IS IMPORTANT

By understanding the effects of behavioral biases on the investment process, investors and their advisors may be able to improve economic outcomes and attain stated financial objectives. In my experience, simply identifying a behavioral bias at the right time can save clients from potential financial disaster. During my 20-plus-year career, spanning numerous market meltdowns, including but not limited to 1987, 1998, 2001, and 2008–2009, I've talked many of my clients "down from the ledge" and out of selling their risky assets at the wrong time. This behavior-modifying advice has built copious amounts of goodwill for me and also helped clients continue on the path to reaching their financial goals. In other cases, I identified a behavioral bias or a group of biases and decided to adapt to the biased behavior in the investment process so that overall financial decisions improved. For example, some investors have a gambling instinct and want to take a risk with some of their capital. My advice in many of these cases is to carve out a small percentage of the portfolio for risky bets, leaving the vast majority of wealth in a prudent, well-organized portfolio. In short, knowledge of the biases reviewed in this book and the modification of or adaption to irrational behavior may lead to superior results.

How to Identify Behavioral Biases

Biases can be diagnosed by means of a specific series of questions. In this book, Chapters 4 through 23 contain a list of diagnostic questions to determine susceptibility to each bias. In addition, a case-study approach is used to illustrate susceptibility to biases. In either case, as advisors begin to incorporate behavioral analysis into their wealth management practices, they will need to administer diagnostic "tests" with utmost discretion, especially at the outset of a relationship. When one becomes very good at diagnosing irrational behavior, it can be done without fanfare or much notice. As they get to know their clients better, advisors reading this book should try to apply what they've learned in order to gain a tentative sense of a client's biases prior to administering any tests. This will improve the quality of advice when taking into account behavioral factors.

CATEGORIZATION OF BEHAVIORAL BIASES

In the first edition of this book, I noted that the classification or categorization of biases was not as important as identifying and acting upon biased behavior in actual private-client situations. I made no attempt to distinguish elaborately among types of biases, except to note whether a bias was cognitive or emotional. In this edition of the book, however, we will delve more deeply into cognitive and emotional differences. The cognitive/emotional distinction becomes quite relevant in the investor case studies, namely in Chapter 25, in which it helps to determine if an asset allocation should undergo behavioral modification. As with the last edition, the focus will be on gauging the presence or the absence—not the magnitude—of each bias examined; that is, the degree to which someone is overconfident will not be decided, but rather if he or she is overconfident or not. Furthermore, the discussion is not concerned with how certain biases relate to one another, unless to make a practical application point. Finally, it is important to note that the study of behavioral finance is still nascent, and therefore an overarching theory of investor behavior should not be a realistic expectation.

In its simplest form, cognitive biases are those biases based on faulty cognitive reasoning (cognitive errors), while emotional biases are those based on reasoning influenced by feelings or emotions. Cognitive errors stem from basic statistical, information processing, or memory errors; cognitive errors may be considered to be the result of faulty reasoning. Emotional biases stem from impulse or intuition; emotional biases may be considered to result from reasoning influenced by feelings. Behavioral biases, regardless of source, may cause decisions to deviate from the assumed rational decisions of traditional finance. A more elaborate distinction between cognitive and emotional biases is made in the next section.

DIFFERENCES BETWEEN COGNITIVE AND EMOTIONAL BIASES

In this book, behavioral biases are classified as either cognitive or emotional biases, not only because the distinction is straightforward but also because the cognitive-emotional breakdown provides a useful framework for understanding how to effectively deal with them in practice. I recommend thinking about investment decision making as occurring along a (somewhat unrealistic) spectrum, from the completely rational decision making of traditional finance to purely emotional decision making. In that context, cognitive biases are basic statistical, information processing, or memory errors that cause the decision to deviate from rationality. Emotional biases are those that arise spontaneously as a result of attitudes and feelings and that cause the decision to deviate from the rational decisions of traditional finance.

Cognitive errors, which stem from basic statistical, information processing, or memory errors, are more easily corrected for than are emotional biases. Why? Investors are better able to adapt their behaviors or modify their processes if the source of the bias is illogical reasoning, even if the investor does not fully understand the investment issues under consideration. For example, an individual may not understand the complex mathematical process used to create a correlation table of asset classes, but he can understand that the process he is using to create a portfolio of uncorrelated investments is best. In other situations, cognitive biases can be thought of as "blind spots" or distortions in the human mind. Cognitive biases do not result from emotional or intellectual predispositions toward certain judgments, but rather from subconscious mental procedures for processing information. In general, because cognitive errors stem from faulty reasoning, better information, education, and advice can often correct for them.

DIFFERENCE AMONG COGNITIVE BIASES

In this book, we review 13 cognitive biases, their implications for financial decision making, and suggestions for correcting for the biases. As previously mentioned, cognitive errors are statistical, information processing, or memory errors—a somewhat broad description. An individual may be attempting to follow a rational decision-making process but fails to do so because of cognitive errors. For example, they may fail to update probabilities correctly, to properly weigh and consider information, or to gather information. If corrected by supplemental or educational information, an individual attempting to follow a rational decision-making process may be receptive to correcting the errors.

To make things simpler, I have identified and classified cognitive biases into two categories. The first category contains "belief perseverance" biases. In general, belief perseverance may be thought of as the tendency to cling to one's previously held beliefs irrationally or illogically. The belief continues to be held and justified by committing statistical, information processing, or memory errors.

Belief Perseverance Biases

Belief perseverance biases are closely related to the psychological concept of cognitive dissonance, a bias I will review in the next chapter. Cognitive dissonance is the mental discomfort that one feels when new information conflicts with previously held beliefs or cognitions. To resolve this discomfort, people tend to notice only information of interest to them (called selective exposure), ignore or modify information that conflicts with existing beliefs (called selective perception), and/or remember and consider only information that confirms existing beliefs (called selective retention). Aspects of these behaviors are contained in the biases categorized as belief perseverance. The six belief perseverance biases covered in this book are cognitive dissonance, conservatism, confirmation, representativeness, illusion of control, and hindsight.

Information Processing Biases

The second category of cognitive biases has to do with "processing errors," and describes how information may be processed and used illogically or irrationally in financial decision making. As opposed to belief perseverance biases, these are less related to errors of memory or in assigning and updating probabilities and instead have more to do with how information is processed. The seven processing errors discussed are anchoring and adjustment, mental accounting, framing, availability, self-attribution bias, outcome bias, and recency bias.

Individuals are less likely to make cognitive errors if they remain vigilant to the possibility that they may occur. A systematic process to describe problems and objectives; to gather, record, and synthesize information; to document decisions and the reasoning behind them; and to compare the actual outcomes with expected results will help reduce cognitive errors.

EMOTIONAL BIASES

Although *emotion* has no single universally accepted definition, it is generally agreed upon that an emotion is a mental state that arises spontaneously rather than through conscious effort. Emotions are related to feelings, perceptions, or beliefs about elements, objects, or relations between them; these can be a function of reality or the imagination. Emotions may result in physical manifestations, often involuntary. Emotions can cause investors to make suboptimal decisions. Emotions may be undesired to the individuals feeling them, and while they may wish to control the emotion and their response to it, they often cannot.

Emotional biases are harder to correct for than cognitive errors because they originate from impulse or intuition rather than conscious calculations. In other words, a bias that is an inclination of temperament or outlook, especially a personal and sometimes unreasonable judgment, is harder to correct. When clients adapt to a bias, they accept it and make decisions that recognize and adjust for it rather than making an attempt to reduce it. To moderate the impact of a bias is to recognize it and to attempt to reduce or even eliminate it within the individual rather than to accept the bias. In the case of emotional biases, it may be possible to only recognize the bias and adapt to it rather than correct for it.

Emotional biases stem from impulse, intuition, and feelings and may result in personal and unreasoned decisions. When possible, focusing on cognitive aspects of the biases may be more effective than trying to alter an emotional response. Also, educating the client about the investment decision-making process and portfolio theory can be helpful in moving the decision making from an emotional basis to a cognitive basis. When biases are emotional in nature, drawing them to the attention of the individual making the decision is unlikely to lead to positive outcomes. The individual is likely to become defensive rather than receptive to considering alternatives. Thinking of the appropriate questions to ask and to focus on as well as potentially altering the decision-making process are likely to be the most effective options.

Emotional biases can cause investors to make suboptimal decisions. The emotional biases are rarely identified and recorded in the decision-making process because they have to do with how people feel rather than what and how they think. The six emotional biases discussed are loss aversion, overconfidence, self-control, status quo, endowment, and regret aversion. In the discussion of each of these biases, some related biases may be discussed.

A FINAL WORD ON BIASES

The cognitive-emotional distinction will help us determine when and how to adjust for behavioral biases in financial decision making. However, it should be noted that specific biases may have some common aspects and that a specific bias may seem to have both cognitive and emotional aspects. Researchers in financial decision making have identified numerous and specific behavioral biases. This book will not attempt to discuss all identified biases but rather will discuss what I consider to be the most important biases within the cognitive-emotional framework for considering potential biases. This framework will be useful in developing an awareness of biases, their implications, and ways of moderating their impact or adapting to them. The intent is to help investors and their advisors to have a heightened awareness of biases so that financial decisions and resulting economic outcomes are potentially improved.

SUMMARY OF PART ONE

Congratulations! We have now completed Part One of this book. We introduced the basics of behavioral finance, focusing on the aspects most relevant to individual wealth management. In Chapter 1, we reviewed some of the most important academic scholarship in modern behavioral finance. We also distinguished between micro- and macro-level applications, reviewed the differences characterizing standard versus behavioralist camps, and discussed how incorporating insights from behavioral finance can enhance the private-client advisory relationship.

In Chapter 2, we traced the emergence of the modern behavioral finance discipline, beginning with its roots in the premodern era. We started with a review of the work by Adam Smith and continued our way forward in time to cover Homo economicus and the dawn of the twentieth century. More influences on behavioral finance, which we also examined, included studies in cognitive psychology and decision making under uncertainty. Here, we focused often on the contributions of Kahneman and Tversky, and of Kahneman and Riepe, as well as on psychographic modeling. We also looked at new developments in the practical application of behavioral finance micro.

This chapter dealt with incorporating investor behavior into the asset allocation process. We discussed some of the limitations of risk tolerance questionnaires, introduced the concept of best practical allocation, and looked at methodology for diagnosing behavioral biases in clients. Of critical importance was our discussion of how detecting certain types of biases in particular types of clients might impact asset allocation decisions. The quantitative guidelines laid out for adjusting portfolio structure comprised another key element of this chapter. We are now ready to move on to Part Two, which investigates specific investor biases as well as their implications in practice.

Two

Belief Perseverance Biases Defined and Illustrated

In Chapters 4 through 23, 20 behavioral biases, both cognitive and emotional, will be discussed. Two types of cognitive biases will be reviewed in Chapters 4 through 16. Belief perseverance cognitive biases will be covered in Chapters 4 through 9, and information processing cognitive biases covered in Chapters 10 through 16. Emotional biases are covered in Chapters 17 through 23.

In each of the 20 bias chapters, I use the same basic format in discussing the bias in order to promote greater accessibility. First, each bias is named, categorized as emotional or cognitive, including subtype (belief perseverance or information processing), and then generally described and technically described. This is followed by the all-important concrete practical application, where it is demonstrated how each bias has been used or can be used in a practical situation. The practical application portion varies in content, consisting of either an intensive review of applied research or a case study. Implications for investors are then delineated. At the end of the practical application section is a research review of work directly applicable to each chapter's topic. A diagnostic test and test results analysis follow, providing a tool to indicate the potential bias of susceptibility. Finally, advice on managing the effects of each bias in order to minimize the effects of biases is offered.

CHAPTER 4

Cognitive Dissonance Bias

This above all: to thine own self be true,
And it must follow, as the day the night.
                    —Polonius to Laertes, in Shakespeare's *Hamlet*

BIAS DESCRIPTION

Bias Name: Cognitive dissonance
Bias Type: Cognitive
Subtype: Belief perseverance

General Description

When newly acquired information conflicts with preexisting understandings, people often experience mental discomfort—a psychological phenomenon known as cognitive dissonance. *Cognitions,* in psychology, represent attitudes, emotions, beliefs, or values; *cognitive dissonance* is a state of imbalance that occurs when contradictory cognitions intersect.

The term *cognitive dissonance* encompasses the response that arises as people struggle to harmonize cognitions and thereby relieve their mental discomfort. For example, a consumer might purchase a certain brand of mobile phone, initially believing that it is the best mobile phone available. However, when a new cognition that favors a substitute mobile phone is introduced, representing an imbalance, cognitive dissonance occurs in an attempt to relieve the discomfort that comes with the notion that perhaps the buyer did not purchase the right mobile phone. People will go to great

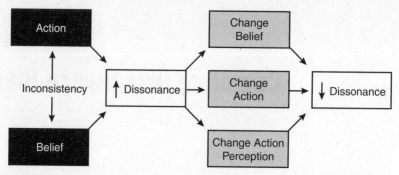

FIGURE 4.1   Cognitive Dissonance Theory
Reprinted from R. H. Rolla, "Cognitive Dissonance Theory," with
permission by *Psychology World*. Department of Psychology, University of
Missouri—www. umr.edu/~psyworld.

lengths to convince themselves that the mobile phone they actually bought
is better than the one they just learned about, to avoid mental discomfort
associated with their initial purchase. In essence, they persist in their belief
that they are correct. In that sense, cognitive dissonance bias is the basis for
all of the belief perseverance biases in this section, with different variations
on the same theme.

Technical Description

Psychologists conclude that people often perform far-reaching rationaliza-
tions in order to synchronize their cognitions and maintain psychological
stability. When people modify their behaviors or cognitions to achieve cognitive harmony, however, the modifications that they make are not always
rational or in their self-interest. Figure 4.1 illustrates this point.

Any time someone feels compelled to choose between alternatives, some
sense of conflict is sure to follow the decision. This is because the selected
alternative often poses downsides, while the rejected alternative has redeem-
ing characteristics. These factors challenge the decision maker's confidence
in the trade-off he or she has just negotiated. Commitment, which indicates
an emotional attachment by an individual to the final decision, always precedes the surfacing of cognitive dissonance. If facts challenge the course to
which a subject is emotionally attached, then those facts pose emotional
threats. Most people try to avoid dissonant situations and will even ignore
potentially relevant information to avoid psychological conflict. Theorists

have identified two different aspects of cognitive dissonance that pertain to decision making.

1. *Selective perception.* Subjects suffering from selective perception register only information that appears to affirm a chosen course, thus producing a view of reality that is incomplete and, hence, inaccurate. Unable to objectively understand available evidence, people become increasingly prone to subsequent miscalculations.
2. *Selective decision making.* Selective decision making usually occurs when commitment to an original decision course is high. Selective decision making rationalizes actions that enable a person to adhere to that course, even if at an exorbitant economic cost. Selective decision makers might, for example, continue to invest in a project whose prospects have soured in order to avoid "wasting" the balance of previously sunk funds. Many studies show that people will subjectively reinforce decisions or commitments they have already made.

PRACTICAL APPLICATION

Example of Cognitive Dissonance

Smoking is a classic example of cognitive dissonance. Although it is widely accepted by the general public that cigarettes cause lung cancer and heart disease, virtually everyone who smokes wants to live a long and healthy life. In terms of cognitive dissonance theory, the desire to live a long life is dissonant with the activity of doing something that will most likely shorten one's life. The tension produced by these contradictory ideas can be reduced by denying the evidence of lung cancer and heart disease or justifying one's smoking because it reduces stress or provides a similar benefit. A smoker might rationalize his or her behavior by believing that only a few smokers become ill (it won't be me), that it only happens to two-pack-a-day smokers, or that if smoking does not kill them, something else will. While chemical addiction may operate in addition to cognitive dissonance for existing smokers, new smokers may exhibit a simpler case of the latter.

This case of dissonance could also be interpreted in terms of a threat to the self-concept.[1] The thought, "I am increasing my risk of lung cancer," is dissonant with the self-related belief, "I am a smart, reasonable person who makes good decisions." Because it is often easier to make excuses than it is

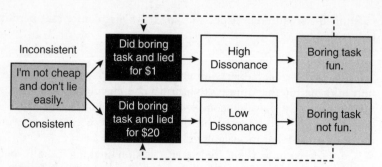

FIGURE 4.2 Modeling Cognitive Dissonance in Festinger's
Peg Experiment
Reprinted from R. H. Rolla, "Cognitive Dissonance Theory," with
permission by *Psychology World*. Department of Psychology, University
of Missouri—www. umr.edu/~psyworld.

to change behavior, dissonance theory leads to the conclusion that humans
are sometimes rationalizing, and not always rational beings.

Investors, like everyone else, sometimes have trouble living with their
decisions. Many wealth management practitioners note that clients often
go to great lengths to rationalize decisions on prior investments, especially
failed investments. Moreover, people displaying this tendency might also irrationally delay unloading assets that are not generating adequate returns. In
both cases, the effects of cognitive dissonance are preventing investors from
acting rationally and, in certain cases, preventing them from realizing losses
for tax purposes and reallocating at the earliest opportunity. Furthermore,
and perhaps even more important, the need to maintain self-esteem may
prevent investors from learning from their mistakes. To ameliorate dissonance arising from the pursuit of what they perceive to be two incompatible
goals—self-validation and acknowledgment of past mistakes—investors will
often attribute their failures to chance rather than to poor decision making.
Of course, people who miss opportunities to learn from past miscalculations
are likely to miscalculate again, renewing a cycle of anxiety, discomfort, dissonance, and denial (see Figure 4.2).

Both selective perception (information distortion to meet a need, which
gives rise to subsequent decision-making errors) and selective decision making (an irrational drive to achieve some specified result for the purpose of
vindicating a previous decision) can have significant effects on investors.
The following inset illustrates four behaviors that result from cognitive dissonance and that cause investment losses.

RESEARCH REVIEW

COGNITIVE DISSONANCE BIAS: BEHAVIORS THAT CAN CAUSE INVESTMENT MISTAKES

1. Cognitive dissonance can cause investors to hold losing securities positions that they otherwise would sell because they want to avoid the mental pain associated with admitting that they made a bad decision.
2. Cognitive dissonance can cause investors to continue to invest in a security that they already own after it has gone down (average down) to confirm an earlier decision to invest in that security without judging the new investment with objectivity and rationality. A common phrase for this concept is "throwing good money after bad."
3. Cognitive dissonance can cause investors to get caught up in herds of behavior; that is, people avoid information that counters an earlier decision (cognitive dissonance) until so much counter information is released that investors herd together and cause a deluge of behavior that is counter to that decision.
4. Cognitive dissonance can cause investors to believe "it's different this time." People who purchased high-flying, hugely overvalued growth stocks in the late 1990s ignored evidence that there were no excess returns from purchasing the most expensive stocks available. In fact, many of the most high-flying companies are now far below their peaks in price.

In their superb work entitled "Cognitive Dissonance and Mutual Fund Investors," Professor William N. Goetzmann of the Yale School of Management, and Nadav Peles of J. P. Morgan, examined the tendency of investors to "stick," irrationally, with struggling mutual funds. Their theory was that cognitive dissonance played a significant role in compelling investors to hold losing fund positions. The researchers theorized that people do not permit themselves to accept new evidence that suggests that it might be time to evacuate a fund because they feel committed to whatever rationale initially inspired the purchase. In 1998, Goetzmann told CNN that investors "are selective about the information they collect about their mutual funds. People like to think that they made a good choice in the past and don't like to look at evidence that their fund did poorly."[2]

The study by Goetzmann and Peles[3] showed that investors, when deciding whether to sell or to retain an investment, are affected by the disparity in value between the security's purchase price and its current price. The researchers observed an imbalance between cash inflows and outflows for most mutual funds and discovered that investors rapidly poured money into funds that performed well but tended to vacate the poorest-performing funds. This behavior suggests susceptibility to availability bias but also indicates that investors in a losing fund may suffer from selective perception, ignoring evidence that discredits the earlier decision to buy into the fund. In some instances, people also feel compelled to "double down," or to continue an investment in a risky situation in an attempt to break even, just to avoid the embarrassment of reporting a losing investment.

Goetzmann and Peles noted:

> We present evidence from questionnaire studies of mutual fund investors about recollections of past fund performance. We find that investor memories exhibit a positive bias, consistent with current psychological models. We find that the degree of bias is conditional upon previous investor choice, a phenomenon related to the well-known theory of cognitive dissonance.
>
> The magnitude of psychological and economic frictions in the mutual fund industry is examined via a cross-sectional study of equity mutual funds. We find an unusually high frequency of poorly performing funds, consistent with investor "inertia." Analysis of aggregate dollar investments, however, shows the net effect of this inertia is small. Thus the regulatory implications with respect to additional disclosure requirements are limited. We examine one widely documented empirical implication of mutual fund investor inertia: the differential response of investment dollars to past performance. We perform tests that control for the crucial problem of survivorship. These confirm the presence of differential response, but find the effect is confined to the top quartile. There is little evidence that the response to poor performance is unusual.[4]

The researchers' final comment here—that the response documented in their study appears widespread—suggests that this chapter might have especially broad implications. Understanding, detecting, and countering the behavioral biases associated with cognitive dissonance are objectives that, when undertaken successfully, could help numerous individual investors.

DIAGNOSTIC TESTING

This test begins with a scenario that illustrates some criteria that can determine susceptibility to cognitive dissonance.

Cognitive Dissonance Bias Test

Scenario: Suppose that you recently bought a new car, Brand A, Model B. You are very pleased with your purchase. One day, your neighbor finds you in your driveway washing your new car and comments on your new purchase: "Wow, love the new car. I know this model. Did you know that Brand Y, Model Z (Model Z is nearly identical to Model B), was giving away a free navigation system when you bought the car?"

You are initially confused. You were unaware, until now, that Model Z was including a navigation system with purchase of the car. You would have liked to have it. Perhaps, you wonder, was getting Model B a bad decision? You begin to second-guess yourself. After your neighbor leaves, you return to your house.

Question: Your next action is, most likely, which of the following?
  a. You immediately head to your home office and page through the various consumer magazines to determine whether you should have purchased Model B.
  b. You proceed with washing the car and think, "If I had it to do all over again, I may have purchased Model Z. Even though mine doesn't have a navigation system, I'm still pleased with Model B."
  c. You contemplate doing some additional research on Model Z. However, you decide not to follow through on the idea. The car was a big, important purchase, and you've been so happy with it—the prospect of discovering an error in your purchase leaves you feeling uneasy. Better to just put this thought to rest and continue to enjoy the car.

Test Results Analysis

Answering "c" may indicate a propensity for cognitive dissonance. The next section gives advice on coping with this bias.

ADVICE

Cognitive dissonance does not in and of itself preordain biased decision making. The driving force behind most of the irrational behavior discussed is the tendency of individuals to adopt certain detrimental *responses* to cognitive dissonance in an effort to alleviate their mental discomfort. Therefore, the first step in overcoming the negative effects of cognitive dissonance is to recognize and to attempt to abandon such counterproductive coping techniques. People who can recognize this behavior become much better investors. Specifically, there are three common responses to cognitive dissonance that have potentially negative implications for personal finance and, consequently, should be avoided: (1) modifying beliefs, (2) modifying actions, and (3) modifying perceptions of relevant action(s). Each will be addressed in detail, following a brief overview. Advisors should take note of how these types of resolutions can affect investors.

Cognitive Dissonance: Common Coping Responses

People can and do recognize inconsistencies between actions and beliefs. When they act in ways that contradict their own beliefs, attitudes, or opinions, some natural "alarm" tends to alert them. For example, you believe that it is wrong to hit your dog; yet, somehow, if you find yourself engaged in the act of hitting your dog, you will register the inconsistency. This moment of recognition will generate cognitive dissonance, and the unease that you experience will motivate you to resolve the contradiction. You will be expected, usually, to try to reconcile your conflicting cognitions in one of three ways:

1. *Modifying beliefs.* Perhaps the easiest way to resolve dissonance between actions and beliefs is simply to alter the relevant beliefs. In the aforementioned incident, for example, you could just recategorize "hitting one's dog" as a perfectly acceptable behavior. This would take care of any dissonance. When the principle in question is important to you, however, such a course of action becomes unlikely. People's most basic beliefs tend to remain stable; they don't just go around modifying their fundamental moral matrices on a day-to-day basis.

Investors, however, do sometimes opt for this path of least resistance when attempting to eliminate dissonance (although the belief-modification mechanism is the least common, in finance, of the three coping tactics discussed here). For example, if the behavior in question was not "hitting your dog" but rather "selling a losing investment," you might concoct some rationale along the lines of "it is okay not to sell a losing investment" in order to resolve cognitive dissonance and permit yourself to hold onto a stock. This behavior, obviously, can pose serious hazards to your wealth.

2. *Modifying actions.* On realizing that you have engaged in behavior contradictory to some preexisting belief, you might attempt to instill fear and anxiety into your decision in order to averse-condition yourself against committing the same act in the future. Appalled at what you have done, you may emphasize to yourself that you will never hit your dog again, and this may aid in resolving cognitive dissonance. However, averse conditioning is often a poor mechanism for learning, especially if you can train yourself, over time, to simply tolerate the distressful consequences associated with a "forbidden" behavior.

Investors may successfully leverage averse conditioning. For example, in the instance wherein a losing investment must be sold, an individual could summon such anxiety at the prospect of ever again retaining an unprofitable stock that actually doing so seems inconceivable. Thus, the dissonance associated with having violated a basic precept of investment strategy dissipates. However, some investors might undergo repeated iterations of this process and eventually become numb to their anxieties, nullifying the effects of averse conditioning on behavior.

3. *Modifying perceptions of relevant action(s).* A more difficult approach to reconciling cognitive dissonance is to rationalize whatever action has brought you into conflict with your beliefs. For example, you may decide that while hitting a dog is generally a bad idea, the dog whom you hit was not behaving well; therefore, you haven't done anything wrong. People relying on this technique try to recontextualize whatever action has generated the current state of mental discomfort so that the action no longer appears to be inconsistent with any particular belief.

An investor might rationalize retaining a losing investment: "I don't really need the money right now, so I won't sell" is a justification that might resolve cognitive dissonance. It is also a very dangerous attitude and must be avoided.

CONCLUSION

The bottom line in overcoming the negative behavioral effects of cognitive dissonance is that investors need to immediately admit that a faulty cognition has occurred. Rather than adapting beliefs or actions in order to circumnavigate cognitive dissonance, investors must address feelings of unease at their source and take an appropriate *rational* action. If you think you may have made a bad investment decision, analyze the decision; if your fears prove correct, confront the problem head-on and rectify the situation. In the long run, you'll become a better investor.

NOTES

1. E. Aronson, "The Theory of Cognitive Dissonance: A Current Perspective," in L. Berkowitz, ed., *Advances in Experimental Social Psychology*, Vol. 4 (New York: Academic Press, 1969), 1–34.
2. L. Festinger, *A Theory of Cognitive Dissonance* (Stanford, CA: Stanford University Press, 1957).
3. See www.money.cnn.com/1998/06/12/mutualfunds/q_worstfunds.
4. W. N. Goetzmann and N. Peles, "Cognitive Dissonance and Mutual Fund Investors," *Journal of Financial Research* 10 (Summer 1997): 145–158.

CHAPTER 5

Conservatism Bias

*To invest successfully over a lifetime does not require a
stratospheric IQ, unusual business insight, or inside information.
What's needed is a sound intellectual framework for decisions and
the ability to keep emotions from corroding that framework.*
                                                      —Warren Buffett

BIAS DESCRIPTION

Bias Name: Conservatism

Bias Type: Cognitive

Subtype: Belief perseverance

General Description

Conservatism bias is a mental process in which people cling to their prior
views or forecasts at the expense of acknowledging new information. For
example, suppose that an investor receives some bad news regarding a company's earnings and that this news negatively contradicts another earnings estimate issued the previous month. Conservatism bias may cause the
investor to *underreact* to the new information, maintaining impressions
derived from the previous estimate rather than acting on the updated information. Investors persevere in a previously held belief rather than acknowledging new information; this is again a variation on the cognitive dissonance
theme described in Chapter 4.

Technical Description

Conservatism causes individuals to overweight base rates and to underreact
to sample evidence. As a result, they fail to react as a rational person would

in the face of new evidence. A classic experiment by Ward Edwards[1] in 1968 eloquently illustrated the technical side of conservatism bias. Edwards presented subjects with two urns—one containing three blue balls and seven red balls, the other containing seven blue balls and three red ones. Subjects were given this information and then told that someone had drawn randomly 12 times from one of the urns, with the ball after each draw restored to the urn in order to maintain the same probability ratio. Subjects were told that this draw yielded eight reds and four blues. They were then asked, "What is the probability that the draw was made from the first urn?" While the correct answer is 0.97, most people estimate a number around 0.7. They apparently overweight the base rate of 0.5—the random likelihood of drawing from one of two urns as opposed to the other—relative to the "new" information regarding the produced ratio of reds to blues.

Professor David Hirshleifer of Ohio State University[2] noted that one explanation for conservatism is that processing new information and updating beliefs is cognitively costly. He noted that information that is presented in a cognitively costly form, such as information that is abstract and statistical, is weighted less. Furthermore, people may overreact to information that is easily processed, such as scenarios and concrete examples. The argument for costly processing can be extended to explain base rate underweighting. If an individual underweights new information received about population frequencies (base rates), then base rate underweighting is really a form of conservatism. Indeed, base rates are underweighted less when they are presented in more salient form or in a fashion that emphasizes their causal relation to the decision problem. This argument for costly processing of new information does not suggest that an individual will underweight his or her preexisting internalized prior belief. If base rate underweighting is a consequence of the use of the representativeness heuristic, there should be underweighting of priors.

Portions of this analysis resonate interestingly with Edwards's experiment. For example, perhaps people overweight the base rate probability of drawing randomly from one of two urns, relative to the sample data probability of drawing a specific combination of items, because the former quantity is simply easier to compute.

PRACTICAL APPLICATION

James Montier is author of the 2002 book *Behavioural Finance: Insights into Irrational Minds and Markets*[3] and analyst for DKW in London. Montier has done some exceptional work in the behavioral finance field. Although Montier primarily studied the stock market in general, concentrating on the behavior of securities analysts in particular, the concepts presented here can and will be applied to individual investors later on.

Commenting on conservatism as it relates to the securities markets in general, Montier noted: "The stock market has a tendency to underreact to fundamental information—be it dividend omissions, initiations, or an earnings report. For instance, in the United States, in the 60 days following an earnings announcement, stocks with the biggest positive earnings surprise tend to outperform the market by 2 percent, even after a 4 to 5 percent outperformance in the 60 days prior to the announcement."

In relating conservatism to securities analysts, Montier wrote:

> *People tend to cling tenaciously to a view or a forecast. Once a position has been stated, most people find it very hard to move away from that view. When movement does occur, it does so only very slowly. Psychologists call this conservatism bias. The chart below [Figure 5.1] shows conservatism in analysts' forecasts. We have taken a linear time trend out of both the operating earnings numbers and the analysts' forecasts. A cursory glance at the chart reveals that analysts are exceptionally good at telling you what has just happened. They have invested too heavily in their view and hence will only change it when presented with indisputable evidence of its falsehood.*[4]

This is clear evidence of conservatism bias in action. Montier's research documents the behavior of securities analysts, but the trends observed can easily be applied to individual investors, who also forecast securities prices, and will cling to these forecasts even when presented with new information.

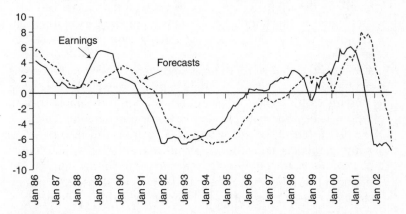

FIGURE 5.1 Montier Observes that Analysts Cling to Their Forecasts
Source: Dresdner Kleinwort Wasserstein, 2002.

Implications for Investors

Investors too often give more attention to forecast outcomes than to new data that actually describes emerging outcomes. Many wealth management practitioners have observed clients who are unable to rationally act on updated information regarding their investments because the clients are "stuck" on prior beliefs. The inset following lists three behaviors stemming from conservatism bias that can cause investment mistakes.

CONSERVATISM BIAS: BEHAVIORS THAT CAN CAUSE INVESTMENT MISTAKES

1. Conservatism bias can cause investors to cling to a view or a forecast, behaving too inflexibly when presented with new information. For example, assume an investor purchases a security based on the knowledge that the company is planning a forthcoming announcement regarding a new product. The company then announces that it has experienced problems bringing the product to market. The investor may cling to the initial, optimistic impression of some imminent, positive development by the company and may fail to take action on the negative announcement.

2. When conservatism-biased investors do react to new information, they often do so too slowly. For example, if an earnings announcement depresses a stock that an investor holds, the conservative investor may be too slow to sell. The preexisting view that, for example, the company has good prospects, may linger too long and exert too much influence, causing an investor exhibiting conservatism to unload the stock only after losing more money than necessary.

3. Conservatism can relate to an underlying difficulty in processing new information. Because people experience mental stress when presented with complex data, an easy option is to simply stick to a prior belief. For example, if an investor purchases a security on the belief that the company is poised to grow and then the company announces that a series of difficult-to-interpret accounting changes may affect its growth, the investor might discount the announcement rather than attempt to decipher it. More clear-cut and, therefore, easier to maintain is the prior belief that the company is poised to grow.

RESEARCH REVIEW

What happens when important news hits the financial markets? Suppose a company reports earnings much higher than expected or announces a big acquisition. Traders and investors rush to digest the information and push stock prices to a level they think is consistent with what they have heard. But do they get it right? Do they react properly to the news they receive? Recent evidence suggests investors make systematic errors in processing new information that may be profitably exploited by others. In a 1997 paper, "A Model of Investor Sentiment," University of Chicago Graduate School of Business assistant professor of finance Nicholas Barberis and finance professor Robert Vishny, along with former Chicago faculty member Andrei Shleifer of Harvard University, argued that there is evidence that in some cases investors react too little to news and that in other cases they react too much.[5]

Investor Overreaction

In an important paper published in 1985, Werner De Bondt of the University of Wisconsin and Richard Thaler of the University of Chicago Graduate School of Business discovered what they claimed was evidence that investors overreact to news. Analyzing data dating back to 1933, De Bondt and Thaler found that stocks with extremely poor returns over the previous five years subsequently dramatically outperformed stocks with extremely high previous returns, even after making the standard risk adjustments.[6] Barberis, Vishy, and Shleifer's work corroborated these findings. Barberis observed:

> *In other words, if an investor ranks thousands of stocks based on how well they did over the past three to five years, he or she can then make a category for the biggest losers, the stocks that performed badly, and another for the biggest winners. What you will find is that the group of the biggest losers will actually do very well on average over the next few years. So it is a good strategy to buy these previous losers or undervalued stocks.[7]*

How might investor overreaction explain these findings? Suppose that a company announces good news over a period of three to five years, such as earnings reports that are consistently above expectations. It is possible that investors overreact to such news and become excessively optimistic about the company's prospects, pushing its stock price to unnaturally high levels. In the subsequent years, however, investors realize that they were unduly optimistic about the business and that the stock price will correct itself downward. In a similar way, loser stocks may simply be stocks that investors have become excessively pessimistic about. As the misperception is corrected, these stocks earn high returns.

Investor Underreaction

Barberis, Vishny, and Shleifer believe that investors sometimes also make the mistake of underreacting to certain types of financial news. Suppose a company announces quarterly earnings that are substantially higher than expected. The evidence suggests that investors see this as good news and send the stock price higher but, for some reason, not high enough. Over the next six months, this mistake is gradually corrected as the stock price slowly drifts upward toward the level it should have attained at the time of the announcement. Investors who buy the stock immediately after the announcement will benefit from this upward drift and enjoy higher returns.

The same underreaction principle applies to bad news. If bad news is announced—like if a company announces it is cutting its dividend—then the stock price will fall. However, it does not fall enough at the time of the announcement and instead continues to drift downward for several months. In both cases, when investors are faced with either good or bad announcements, they initially underreact to this news and only gradually incorporate its full import into the stock price. This signals an inefficient market. So what strategy should smart investors adopt? In the long run, it is better to invest in value stocks, stocks with low valuations (overreaction theory); but in the short run, the best predictor of returns in the next six months is returns over the preceding six months (underreaction theory). "In the short run, you want to buy relative strength," explained Vishny. "This might seem contradictory, but we can explain how both of those facts might be true using some basic psychology and building that into a model for how people form their expectations for future earnings."[8]

Psychological Evidence

In the new field of behavioral finance, researchers seek to understand whether aspects of human behavior and psychology might influence the way prices are set in financial markets. "Our idea is that these market anomalies—underreaction and overreaction—are the results of investors' mistakes," said Vishny. "In this paper, we present a model of investor sentiment—that is, of how investors form beliefs—that is consistent with the empirical findings."[9] In explaining investor behavior, Barberis, Vishny, and Shleifer's model is consistent with two important psychological theories:

convervatism and the *representative heuristic,* the latter referring to the fact that people tend to see patterns in random sequences. Certainly, it would be to an investor's advantage to see patterns in financial data, if they were really there.

Unfortunately, investors are often too quick to see patterns that aren't genuine features of the data. In reality, long-run changes in company earnings follow a fairly random pattern. However, when people see a company's earnings go up several years in a row, they believe they have spotted a trend and think that it is going to continue. Such excessive optimism pushes prices too high and produces effects that support Barberis and Vishny's theory of overreaction. There are also well-known biases in human information processing that would predict underreaction to new pieces of information. One such bias, conservatism, states that once individuals have formed an impression, they are slow to change that impression in the face of new evidence. This corresponds directly to underreaction to news. Investors remain skeptical about new information and only gradually update their views.

DIAGNOSTIC TESTING

The following diagnostic quiz can help to detect elements of conservatism bias.

Conservatism Bias Test

Question 1: Suppose that you live in Baltimore, Maryland, and you make a forecast such as, "I think it will be a snowy winter this year." Furthermore, suppose that, by mid-February, you realize that no snow has fallen. What is your natural reaction to this information?
   a. There's still time to get a lot of snow, so my forecast is probably correct.
   b. There still may be time for some snow, but I may have erred in my forecast.
   c. My experience tells me that my forecast was probably incorrect. Most of the winter has elapsed; therefore, the cumulative amount of snow is not likely to be significant.

Question 2: When you recently hear news that has potentially negative implications for the price of an investment you own, what is your natural reaction to this information?
   a. I tend to ignore the information. Because I have already made the investment, I've already determined that the company will be successful.

b. I will reevaluate my reasons for buying the stock, but I will probably stick with it because I usually stick with my original determination that a company will be successful.

c. I will reevaluate my reasoning for buying the stock and will decide, based on an objective consideration of all the facts, what to do next.

Question 3: When news comes out that has potentially negative implications for the price of a security that you own, how quickly do you react to this information?

a. I usually wait for the market to communicate the significance of the information and then I decide what to do.

b. Sometimes, I wait for the market to communicate the significance of the information, but other times, I respond without delay.

c. I respond without delay.

Test Results Analysis

People answering "a" or "b" to any of the preceding questions may indicate susceptibility to conservatism bias.

ADVICE

Because conservatism is a cognitive bias, advice and information can often correct or lessen its effect. Specifically, investors must first avoid clinging to forecasts; they must also be sure to react, decisively, to new information. This does not mean that investors should respond to events without careful analysis. However, when the wisest course of action becomes clear, it should be implemented resolutely and without hesitation. Additionally, investors should seek professional advice when trying to interpret information that they have difficulty understanding. Otherwise, investors may not take action when they should.

When new information is presented, ask yourself: How does this impact my forecast? Does it actually jeopardize my forecast? If investors can answer these questions honestly, then they have achieved a very good handle on conservatism bias. Conservatism can prevent good decisions from being made, and investors need to remain mindful of any propensities they might exhibit that make them cling to old views and react slowly toward promising, emerging developments. Offering high-quality, professional advice is probably the best way to help a client avoid the pitfalls of this common bias.

NOTES

1. Ward Edwards, "Conservatism in Human Information Processing," in B. Kleinmutz, ed., *Formal Representation of Human Judgment* (New York: John Wiley & Sons, 1968).
2. David Hirshleifer, "Investor Psychology and Asset Pricing" (working paper, Fisher College of Business, Ohio State University, 2001).
3. James Montier, *Behavioural Finance: Insights into Irrational Minds and Markets* (West Sussex, England: John Wiley & Sons, 2002).
4. James Montier, "Equity Research" (research report, Dresdner Kleinwort Wasserstein, 2002).
5. Nicholas Barberis, Robert W. Vishny, and Andrei Shleifer, "A Model of Investor Sentiment," *Capital Ideas* [University of Chicago] 1(2) (Winter 1998).
6. Werner F. M. De Bondt and Richard Thaler, "Does the Stock Market Overreact?" *Journal of Finance* 40 (3) (July 1985): 793–805.
7. See note 5.
8. Ibid.
9. Ibid.

CHAPTER 6

Confirmation Bias

It is the peculiar and perpetual error of the human understanding
to be more moved and excited by affirmatives than by negatives.
— Francis Bacon

BIAS DESCRIPTION

Bias Name: Confirmation bias
Bias Type: Cognitive
Subtype: Belief perseverance

General Description

Confirmation bias refers to a type of selective perception that emphasizes ideas that confirm our beliefs, while devaluing whatever contradicts our beliefs. For example, it is quite typical for someone to decide, after having bought a much desired item such as a television, to look for the same television at a store that is known to have higher prices in order to confirm that he or she made a good purchase decision. This behavior, going back to cognitive dissonance in the last chapter, is caused by our attempt to resolve the post-decisional dissonance between the decision made and the possibility of being wrong.

To describe this phenomenon another way, we might say that confirmation bias refers to our all-too-natural ability to convince ourselves of whatever it is that we want to believe. We attach undue emphasis to events that corroborate the outcomes we desire and downplay whatever contrary evidence arises.

A	2
9	X

FIGURE 6.1 Classic
Confirmation Bias
Experiment

Technical Description

Confirmation bias can be thought of as a form of selection bias in collecting evidence for supporting certain beliefs, whereby decision makers observe, overvalue, or actively seek out information that confirms their claims, while simultaneously ignoring or devaluing evidence that might discount their claims. A classic demonstration of confirmation bias, of which there are many versions, is one in which subjects are shown four cards, each with a number on one side and a letter on the other. They are then told the following rule: "If the card has a vowel on one side, then it *must* have an even number on the other side." The cards are then laid out as depicted in Figure 6.1. Subjects are then asked, "Which two cards would you turn over to test the rule?"

When this experiment is run, most participants do not choose the correct cards (the card reading "A" and the card reading "9"). Instead, the most frequent responses are "A" and "2." This pairing demonstrates a common logical fallacy: People choose "2" because the discovery of an accompanying vowel could indeed uphold the hypothesis. However, exposing the opposite side of the "2" card can't possibly invalidate the hypothesized condition, so this can't be the correct response. People more readily identify "2" rather than "9" because confirmation bias makes them *want* to validate the hypothesis—not refute it as directed.

Another lesson here is that beliefs don't need to be logically entrenched in order to kindle confirmation bias. The hypothesis as stated becomes an immediate if subtle aspect of the participant's choice of cards. Even though subjects have no reason to accept the hypothesis, they become loyal enough to its validity that they are unable to recognize the correct answer choice. In fact, when beliefs *are* firmly established in evidence, the effects of confirmation bias become less overt. This is due to a tendency to give more attention and weight to data that fit with beliefs with stronger foundations.

Numerous studies have demonstrated that people excessively value confirmatory information, that is, positive or supportive data. The "most likely reason for the excessive influence of confirmatory information is that it is easier to deal with cognitively"[1] than contradictory information is; that is, most people find it easier to discern how a piece of data might support rather than challenge a given position. Researchers are sometimes guilty of confirmation bias, as they occasionally design experiments or frame data in ways likely to confirm their hypotheses. To compound the problem, some scholars also avoid dealing with data that would contradict their hypotheses.

PRACTICAL APPLICATION

To demonstrate confirmation bias, we discuss employees' penchant for over-concentrating in company stock. Most practitioners have encountered clients who rationalize their disproportionate holdings by citing the promising "big things" that are developing at their companies. Numerous shareholders in Enron and WorldCom (during the technology bubble of the 1990s), and Lehman Brothers and Bear Stearns (during the most recent crisis) probably speculated that great growth was going to be sustained forever—if only these investors had had some clue as to the nature of the "big things" that would soon befall their employers! When employees load up on company stock en masse and bullish commentary on employer stock prices dominates water cooler conversation, inauspicious details can be easily overlooked. For a more elaborate example, we are going "retro" back to the early 1990s. A strong cautionary tale emerged during that time at a well-established tech firm: IBM.

In the early 1990s, many IBM employees were convinced that their company's OS/2 operating system would achieve industry standard status. They frequently ignored unfavorable signs, including evidence of competition from Microsoft Windows. These employees loaded up on IBM stock, anticipating that OS/2's performance would drive the company forward. In 1991, IBM stock reached a split-adjusted peak of $35 per share. Over the course of the next two years, however, IBM slid to a low of $10. It would not reach $35 again until the end of 1996. During this five-year slump, IBM employees rallied around seemingly positive developments that "confirmed" that IBM was making a comeback. Some even delayed retirement. Unfortunately, in an effort to engineer a turnaround, IBM laid off a number of its employees. In the end, OS/2 caused many people to become less wealthy. For some, the failed operating system even led to unemployment. This is a classic case of confirmation bias in action.

Experienced practitioners have seen similar scenarios play out repeatedly. Clients ignore downside risks of, for example, employer stock and focus only on the upside potential. Why? In this case, confirmation bias played a significant role in the behavior of the IBM employees. It led them to accept information that supported their rosy predictions regarding IBM while discounting evidence of increased competition from Microsoft. Consequently, these employees lost money as IBM's stock price fell. Only those few who were able to hang on, over the course of five years of uncertainty—history, remember, shows us that most investors "panic" in such a situation—had the opportunity to profit in the end.

Implications for Investors

Anyone who has played a hand or two of poker knows well the downside of confirmation bias. Suppose you are entrenched in a game, and you get three kings on the flop. Your opponent raises the pot, and you are only happy to raise him back. You aren't really paying attention as the turn card comes out. Your cards are telling you "I can't lose." You are oblivious to the fact that a series of hearts are showing up. A two comes up on the river and you are pretty much guaranteed to win. You bet big. You get called. Oops, someone had a flush, and you lose.

In the context of the poker analogy, what's important to note is that, by "listening" only to information that confirms your belief that you have the best hand, you ignore the other players' cards. Focusing on the payoff of the present hand might eventually earn a profit; however, you don't analyze the implications of a loss—even if some indication has cropped up during the game that another player might be collecting hearts. While the poker metaphor isn't flawless, it gets the point across: people believe what they want to believe and ignore evidence to the contrary. This is the essence of confirmation bias.

In finance, the effects of confirmation bias can be observed almost daily. Investors often fail to acknowledge anything negative about investments they've just made, even when substantial evidence begins to argue against these investments. A classic example took place on the Internet message boards during the technology stock boom of the late 1990s. Many of these chat roomers would harass anyone who voiced a negative opinion of the company they invested in. Rather than try to glean some useful insight into their company through other investors, they sought only confirmations of their own beliefs.

The following is a summary investment mistakes that can be caused by confirmation bias.

CONFIRMATION BIAS: BEHAVIORS THAT CAN CAUSE INVESTMENT MISTAKES

1. Confirmation bias can cause investors to seek out only information that confirms their beliefs about an investment that they have made and to not seek out information that may contradict their beliefs. This behavior can leave investors in the dark regarding, for example, the imminent decline of a stock.
2. When investors believe strongly in predetermined "screens," such as stocks breaking through a 52-week price high, confirmation bias is usually at work. These investors only use information that confirms their beliefs. They may blind themselves to information that demonstrates that a stock breaking through its 52-week high may not make a good investment.
3. Confirmation bias can cause employees to overconcentrate in company stock. As IBM and other examples demonstrate, intraoffice buzz about a company's prospects does not justify indiscriminate reliance by employees on company stock. People naturally tend to unduly emphasize evidence suggesting that the companies they work for will do well.
4. Confirmation bias can cause investors to continue to hold under-diversified portfolios. Many practitioners have seen clients become infatuated with certain stocks—not always the stocks of employer corporations. Over the course of years, such a client might accrue a large position that ultimately produces a lopsided portfolio. These clients do not want to hear anything negative about favored investments but rather seek, single-mindedly, confirmation that the position will pay off.

RESEARCH REVIEW

Professor Meir Statman and investment professional Ken Fisher provided an excellent example of confirmation bias in action in their paper "Cognitive Biases in Market Forecasts."[2] Here, Statman and Fisher test the commonly held belief that price/earnings ratios (P/Es) can forecast stock returns. It seems logical to most investors that when P/Es surpass historical averages, shareholders should sell. Likewise, conventional wisdom dictates that stocks whose P/Es fall below historical averages make good buys. Statman and Fisher examined the validity of these principles.

We can overcome the confirmation bias by examining all data, confirming as well as disconfirming. Consider, in particular, an examination of the hypothesis that low dividend yields forecast low returns while high dividend yields forecast high returns. Define dividend yields as high if they exceed their median over the 128 years from 1872 through 1999 and as low if they fall below it. The median dividend yield for the period was 4.43 percent. Define one-year returns as high and low in a similar fashion. The median return was 10.50 percent. [Table 6.1] presents a schematic view of the frequency of observations in the four cells of a matrix. The first cell includes observations where dividend yields were low and subsequent returns were low. These are positive hits. The fourth cell has observations where dividend yields were high and subsequent returns were also high. These are negative hits. Positive hits and negative hits are confirming evidence, observations consistent with the hypothesis that low dividend yields forecast low returns and high dividend yields forecast high returns. The other two cells have disconfirming evidence. That is, the second cell includes false positive observations where dividend yields were low but subsequent returns were high, and the third cell is the false negatives, observations where dividend yields were high but subsequent returns were low. False positives and false negatives are discomfirming evidence. Correct analysis of the hypothesis requires examination of all four cells. Those who examine only the positive and negative hits fall prey to the confirmation bias. The confirmation bias is common. Consider, for example, Prechter's discussion of low dividend yield as a forecaster of low returns, "August 1987 saw a historically high valuation of dividends, beating out even that of 1929. The result was a 1,000 point crash." Prechter's observation is a positive hit, an observation consistent with the hypothesis that low dividend yields (i.e., "high valuation of dividends") forecast low returns. But we need an account of false positives and false negatives as well. Consider dividend yields as forecasters of one-year returns. It turns out, as presented in [Table 6.2], that there are 33 positive hits in the first cell and 33 negative hits in the fourth.[3]

These are consistent with the hypothesis that low dividend yields forecast low returns, while high dividend yields forecast high returns. But the evidence against the hypothesis is almost as strong as the evidence for it; there are 31 false positives in the second cell and 31 false negatives in the third. The deviations of actual observations from those expected by chance alone are too small to be statistically significant. We can conclude only that dividend

TABLE 6.1 Relationship between Dividend Yields and Future Returns

	Below-Median Return	Above-Median Return
Below-median dividend yield	Positive hit	False positive
Above-median dividend yield	False negative	Negative hit

yields enable no statistically significant forecasts of returns in the following year. We also find no statistically significant relationship between dividend yields and returns in the following (nonoverlapping) two-year returns, as depicted in [Table 6.3].

The same is true for the relationship between P/Es and returns during the following year or during the following two (nonoverlapping) years, as depicted in Tables 6.4, 6.5, and 6.6.

For example, while high P/Es were followed by low returns in 32 years, high P/Es were followed by high returns in an equal 32 years. Low dividend yields are followed almost equally by low returns and high returns, and high dividend yields are followed almost equally by high returns and low returns. The same is true for high and low P/Es. Thus, dividend yields and P/Es are unreliable forecasters of shorter-term future returns because they provide so many bad forecasts along with the good ones.

TABLE 6.2 Relationship between Dividend Yields at Beginning of a Year and Stock Returns over Following Year, 1872 to 1999

	Below-Median Return	Above-Median Return	Total
Below-median dividend yield	33	31	64
Above-median dividend yield	31	33	64
Total	64	64	128

Chi-square = 0.03.

TABLE 6.3 Relationship between Dividend Yields at Beginning of Year and Stock Returns over Following (Nonoverlapping) Two Years 1872 to 1999

	Below-Median Return	Above-Median Return	Total
Below-median dividend yield	17	15	32
Above-median dividend yield	15	17	32
Total	32	32	64

Chi-square = 0.06.
Critical chi-square for 5 percent level of significance is 3.841.
Median dividend yield over 128 years (1872 to 1999) is 4.43 percent.
Median return during a year is 10.50 percent.

TABLE 6.4 Relationship between P/E Ratios and Future Returns

	Below-Median Return	Above-Median Return
Above-median P/E ratios	Positive hit	False positive
Below-median P/E ratios	False negative	Negative hit

TABLE 6.5 Relationship between P/E Ratios at Beginning of a Year and Stock Returns over Following Year 1872 to 1999

	Below-Median Return	Above-Median Return	Total
Above-median P/E ratios	32	32	64
Below-median P/E ratios	32	32	64
Total	64	64	128

Chi-square = 0.00.

TABLE 6.6 Relationship between P/E Ratios at Beginning of Year and Stock Returns over Following (Nonoverlapping) Two Years 1872 to 1999

	Below-Median Return	Above-Median Return	Total
Above-median P/E ratios	19	13	32
Below-median P/E ratios	13	19	32
Total	32	32	64

Chi-square = 1.56.
Median P/E ratio over 128 years (1872 to 1999) is 13.6 percent. Median return during a year is 10.50 percent.

DIAGNOSTIC TESTING

These questions are designed to detect cognitive errors stemming from confirmation bias. To complete the test, select the answer choice that best characterizes your response to each item.

Confirmation Bias Test

Question 1: Suppose you have invested in a security after some careful research. Now, you see a press release that states that the company you've invested in may have a problem with its main product line. The second paragraph, however, describes a completely new product that the company might debut later this year. What is your natural course of action?
  a. I will typically take notice of the new product announcement and research that item further.
  b. I will typically take notice of the problem with the company's product line and research that item further.

Question 2: Suppose you have invested in a security after some careful research. The investment appreciates in value but not for the reason you predicted (e.g., you were enticed by some buzz surrounding a new product, but resurgence by an older product line ultimately buoyed the stock). What is your natural course of action?

a. Since the company did well, I am not concerned. The shares I've selected have generated a profit. This confirms that the stock was a good investment.

b. Although I am pleased, I am concerned about the investment. I will do further research to confirm the logic behind my position.

Question 3: Suppose you decide to invest in a global emerging markets bond fund. You performed careful research to determine that this investment is a good way to hedge the dollar. Three months after you invest, you realize that the dollar hasn't depreciated much against the currencies of the bonds in the fund, but the investment seems to be doing well. This is not what you expected. How do you react?

a. I will just "go with it." The reason that an investment performs well is not important. What's important is that I made a good investment.

b. I will do research to try and determine why the fund is doing well. This will help me determine if I should remain invested in the fund.

Test Results Analysis

Question 1: People who select answer choice "a," indicating they would more readily research the new product line than the potential complications in the old product line, are likely to be susceptible to confirmation bias. They are avoiding information that might confirm—but, crucially, might also overrule—the previous decision to invest in the company.

Question 2: People who select "a" are more likely to exhibit confirmation bias than people who select "b." Rationalizing that only the company's recent performance is relevant, answer choice "a" implies that the respondent will avoid seeking out information that might contradict previously held beliefs regarding the quality of the (hypothetical) investment. Answer choice "b" is the more economically rational choice.

Question 3. Again, "a" is the response that signals susceptibility to confirmation bias. To "just go with it," in this instance, means adopting some arbitrary rationale just because it happens to confirm a previous conviction ("I made a good investment decision"). Answer choice "b," which entails further research, is unattractive to people suffering from confirmation bias. This is because further research might unearth information that contradicts a previous conviction ("I made a good investment decision").

ADVICE

The following advice corresponds to each of the four problem areas listed in this chapter.

General confirmation bias behavior. The first step toward overcoming confirmation bias is to recognize that the bias exists. Then people can mindfully compensate by making sure to seek out information that could contradict—not just confirm—their investment decisions. It is important to remember that the mere existence of contradictory evidence does not necessarily mean an investment was unwise. Rather, uncovering all available data simply facilitates informed decisions. Even the most precisely calculated judgments can go awry; however, when investors make sure to consider all available contingencies and perspectives, they are less likely to make mistakes.

Selection bias. When an investment decision is based on some preexisting criterion—such as a trend regarding stocks that break through 52-week highs—it is advisable to cross-verify the decision from additional angles. Fundamental research on a company, industry, or sector, for example, can often provide another informative dimension. This will help to ensure that investment selections don't blindly adhere to preconceived principles while ignoring practical considerations.

Company stock. Overconcentrating in company stock is inadvisable for numerous reasons. In guarding against confirmation bias, employees should monitor any negative press regarding their own companies and conduct research on any competing firms. While it is easy to become desensitized toward bad news regarding one's own company, remember: "Where there's smoke, there's (too often) fire." Employee investors should heed the warning signs—or risk getting burned.

Overconcentration. Company stock isn't the only investment with which people can become unduly enamored. People who demonstrate a disproportionate degree of commitment to any stock whatsoever should remember to seek out unfavorable data regarding that stock. This is especially true for investors whose portfolios concentrate discernibly in a favored investment.

NOTES

1. T. Gilovich, *How We Know What Isn't So: The Fallibility of Human Reason in Everyday Life* (New York: Free Press, 1993).
2. Meir Statman and Kenneth L. Fisher, "Cognitive Biases and Market Forecasts," *Journal of Portfolio Management* (Fall 2000).
3. Robert J. Prechter, *At the Crest of the Tidal Wave: A Forecast for the Great Bear Market* (New York: John Wiley & Sons, 1997).

CHAPTER 7

Representativeness Bias

Fit no stereotypes. Don't chase the latest management fads. The situation dictates which approach best accomplishes the team's mission.

—Colin Powell

BIAS DESCRIPTION

Bias Name: Representativeness
Bias Type: Cognitive
Subtype: Belief perseverance

General Description

In order to derive meaning from life experiences, people have developed an innate propensity for classifying objects and thoughts. When they confront a new phenomenon that is inconsistent with any of their preconstructed classifications, they subject it to those classifications anyway, relying on a rough best-fit approximation to determine which category should house and, thereafter, form the basis for their understanding of the new element. This perceptual framework provides an expedient tool for processing new information by simultaneously incorporating insights gained from (usually) relevant/analogous past experiences. It endows people with a quick response reflex that helps them to survive. Sometimes, however, new stimuli resemble—are *representative* of—familiar elements that have already been classified. In reality, these are drastically different analogues. In such an instance, the classification reflex leads to deception, producing an incorrect understanding of the new element that often persists and biases all our future interactions with that element.

Similarly, people tend to perceive probabilities and odds that resonate with their own preexisting ideas—even when the resulting conclusions drawn are statistically invalid. For example, the "Gambler's Fallacy" refers to the commonly held impression that gambling luck runs in streaks. However, subjective psychological dynamics, not mathematical realities, inspire this perception. Statistically, the streak concept is nonsense. Humans also tend to subscribe to something researchers call "the law of small numbers," which is the assumption that small samples faithfully represent entire populations. No scientific principle, however, underlies or enforces this "law."

Technical Description

Two primary interpretations of *representativeness bias* apply to individual investors.

1. *Base-Rate Neglect*. In base-rate neglect, investors attempt to determine the potential success of, say, an investment in Company A by contextualizing the venture in a familiar, easy-to-understand classification scheme. Such an investor might categorize Company A as a "value stock" and draw conclusions about the risks and rewards that follow from that categorization. This reasoning, however, ignores other unrelated variables that could substantially impact the success of the investment. Investors often embark on this erroneous path because it looks like an alternative to the diligent research actually required when evaluating an investment. To summarize this characterization, some investors tend to rely on *stereotypes* when making investment decisions.

2. *Sample-Size Neglect*. In sample-size neglect, investors, when judging the likelihood of a particular investment outcome, often fail to accurately consider the sample size of the data on which they base their judgments. They incorrectly assume that small sample sizes are *representative* of populations (or "real" data). Some researchers call this phenomenon the "law of small numbers." When people do not initially comprehend a phenomenon reflected in a series of data, they will quickly concoct assumptions about that phenomenon, relying on only a few of the available data points. Individuals prone to sample-size neglect are quick to treat properties reflected in such small samples as properties that accurately describe universal pools of data. The small sample that the individual has examined, however, may not be representative whatsoever of the data at large.

PRACTICAL APPLICATION

This section presents and analyzes two miniature case studies that demonstrate potential investor susceptibility to each variety of representativeness bias and then conducts a practical application research review.

Miniature Case Study Number 1: Base-Rate Neglect

Case Presentation. Suppose George, an investor, is looking to add to his portfolio and hears about a potential investment through a friend, Harry, at a local coffee shop. The conversation goes something like this:

George: Hi, Harry. My portfolio is really suffering right now. I could use a good long-term investment. Any ideas?

Harry: Well, George, did you hear about the new IPO [initial public offering] pharmaceutical company called PharmaGrowth (PG) that came out last week? PG is a hot new company that should be a great investment. Its president and CEO was a mover and shaker at an Internet company that did great during the tech boom, and she has PharmaGrowth growing by leaps and bounds.

George: No, I didn't hear about it. Tell me more.

Harry: Well, the company markets a generic drug sold over the Internet for people with a stomach condition that millions of people have. PG offers online advice on digestion and stomach health, and several Wall Street firms have issued "buy" ratings on the stock.

George: Wow, sounds like a great investment!

Harry: Well, I bought some. I think it could do great.

George: I'll buy some, too.

George proceeds to pull out his cell phone, call his broker, and place an order for 100 shares of PG.

Analysis. In this example, George displays base-rate neglect representativeness bias by considering this hot IPO is, necessarily, representative of a good long-term investment. Many investors like George believe that IPOs make good long-term investments due to all the up-front hype that surrounds them. In fact, numerous studies have shown that a very low percentage of IPOs actually turn out to be good long-term investments. This common investor misperception is likely due to the fact that investors in hot

IPOs usually make money in the first few days after the offering. Over time, however, these stocks tend to trail their IPO prices, often never returning to their original levels.

George ignores the statistics and probabilities by not considering that, in the long run, the PG stock will most likely incur losses rather than gains. This concept can be applied to many investment situations. There is a relatively easy way to analyze how an investor might fall prey to base-rate neglect. For example, what is the probability that person A (Simon, a shy, introverted man) belongs to Group B (stamp collectors) rather than Group C (BMW drivers)? In answering this question, most people typically evaluate the degree to which A (Simon) "represents" B or C; they might conclude that Simon's shyness seems to be more representative of stamp collectors than BMW drivers. This approach neglects base rates, however: Statistically, far more people drive BMWs than collect stamps.

Similarly, George, our hypothetical investor, has effectively been asked: What is the probability that Company A (PharmaGrowth, the hot IPO) belongs to Group B (stocks constituting successful long-term investments) rather than Group C (stocks that will fail as long-term investments)? Again, most individuals approach this problem by attempting to ascertain the extent to which A appears characteristically representative of B or C. In George's judgment, PG possesses the properties of a successful long-term investment rather than a failed one. Investors arriving at this conclusion, however, ignore the base-rate fact that IPOs are more likely to fail than to succeed.

Miniature Case Study Number 2: Sample-Size Neglect

Case Presentation. Suppose George revisits his favorite coffee shop the following week and this time encounters bowling buddy Jim. Jim raves about his stockbroker, whose firm employs an analyst who appears to have made many recent successful stock picks. The conversation goes something like this:

George: Hi, Jim, how are you?
Jim: Hi, George. I'm doing great! I've been doing superbly in the market recently.
George: Really? What's your secret?
Jim: Well, my broker has passed along some great picks made by an analyst at her firm.

George: Wow, how many of these tips have you gotten?

Jim: My broker gave me three great stock picks over the past month or so. Each stock is up now, by over 10 percent.

George: That's a great record. My broker seems to give me one bad pick for every good one. It sounds like I need to talk to your broker; she has a much better record!

Analysis: (As per Case Study 1.) As we'll see in a moment, this conversation exemplifies sample-size neglect representativeness bias. Jim's description has prompted George to arrive at a faulty judgment regarding the success rate of Jim's broker/analyst. George is impressed, but his assessment is based on a very small sample size; the recent, successful picks Jim cites are inevitably only part of the story. George concluded that Jim's broker is successful because Jim's account of the broker's and analyst's performances seems *representative* of the record of a successful team. However, George disproportionately weighs Jim's testimony, and if he were to ask more questions, he might discover that his conclusion draws on too small a sample size. In reality, the analyst that Jim is relying on happens to be one who covers an industry that is popular at the moment, and *every* stock that this analyst covers has enjoyed recent success. Additionally, Jim neglected to mention that last year, this same broker/analyst team made a string of three *losing* recommendations. Therefore, both Jim's and George's brokers are batting 50 percent. George's reasoning demonstrates the pitfalls of sample-size neglect representativeness bias.

Implications for Investors. Both types of representativeness bias can lead to substantial investment mistakes. In the following section, we list examples of behaviors, attributable to base-rate neglect and sample-size neglect, respectively, that can cause harm to an investor's portfolio. Advice on these four areas will come later.

RESEARCH REVIEW

In *Judgment under Uncertainty: Heuristics and Biases*, Daniel Kahneman, Paul Slovic, and Amos Tversky apply representativeness bias to the world of sports. The concepts brought forward in this book also translate easily to finance.

HARMFUL EFFECTS OF REPRESENTATIVENESS BIAS

Examples of the Harmful Effects of Sample-Size Neglect for Investors

1. Investors can make significant financial errors when they examine a money manager's track record. They peruse the past few quarters or even years and conclude, based on inadequate statistical data, that the fund's performance is the result of skilled allocation and/or security selection.
2. Investors also make similar mistakes when investigating track records of stock analysts. For example, they look at the success of an analyst's past few recommendations, erroneously assessing the analyst's aptitude based on this limited data sample.

Examples of the Harmful Effects of Base-Rate Neglect for Investors

1. What is the probability that Company A (ABC, a 75-year-old steel manufacturer that is having some business difficulties) belongs to group B (value stocks that will likely recover) rather than to Group C (companies that will go out of business)? In answering this question, most investors will try to judge the degree to which A is representative of B or C. In this case, some headlines featuring recent bankruptcies by steel companies make ABC Steel appear more representative of the latter categorization, and some investors conclude that they had best unload the stock. They are ignoring, however, the base-rate reality that far more steel companies survive or get acquired than go out of business.
2. What is the probability that AAA-rated Municipal Bond A (issued by an "inner city" and racially divided county) belongs to Group B (risky municipal bonds) rather than to Group C (safe municipal bonds)? In answering this question, most investors will again try to evaluate the extent to which A seems representative of B or C. In this case, Bond A's characteristics may seem representative of Group A (risky bonds) because of the county's "unsafe" reputation; however, this conclusion ignores the base-rate fact that, historically, the default rate of AAA bonds is virtually zero.

Abstract. *A game of squash can be played either to nine or to fifteen points. If you think you are a better player than your opponent, then which game—the shorter version, or lengthier version—provides you a higher probability of winning? Suppose, instead, that you are the weaker player. Which game is your best bet now? If you believe that you would favor the same game length in either case, then consider this theorem from probability theory: the larger the sample of rounds (i.e., fifteen rounds versus nine rounds), the greater likelihood of achieving the expected outcome (i.e., victory to the stronger player). So, if you believe you are the stronger player, then you should prefer the longer game; believing yourself to be the weaker player should produce a preference for the shorter game. Intuitively, though, victory over an opponent in either a nine-point or fifteen-point match would strike many people as equally representative of one's aptitude at squash. This is an example of sample-size neglect bias.*[1]

The concept of permitting the game "to go longer" in order to increase the probability that the stronger player wins can also apply to investing, where it is called time diversification, which refers to the idea that investors should spread their assets across ventures operating according to a variety of market cycles, giving their allocations plenty of time to work properly. Time diversification helps reduce the risk that an investor will be caught entering or abandoning a particular investment or category at a disadvantageous point in the economic cycle. It is particularly relevant with regard to highly volatile investments, such as stocks and long-term bonds, whose prices can fluctuate in the short term. Holding onto these assets for longer periods of time can soften the effects of such fluctuations. Conversely, if an investor cannot remain in a volatile investment over a relatively long time period, he or she should avoid the investment. Time diversification is less important when considering relatively stable investments, such as certificates of deposit, money market funds, and short-term bonds.

Time diversification also comes into play when investing or withdrawing large sums of money from a specified niche within an allocation. In general, it is best to move these amounts gradually over time, rather than all at once, to reduce risk. Borrowed from Kenneth Fisher and Meir Statman,[2] Figures 7.1 and 7.2 show a pair of graphic models illustrating expected average annual returns over a 1-year and a 30-year horizon, respectively.

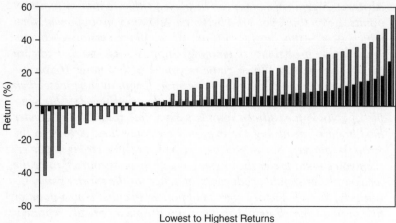

Lowest to Highest Returns
(means of 200 simulated returns in each group)

FIGURE 7.1   Returns Over a 1-Year Investment Horizon
Source: Kenneth Fisher and Meir Statman, "A Behavioral Framework for Time
Diversification," *Financial Analysts Journal* (May/June: 1999). Copyright
1999, CFA Institute. Reproduced and republished from *Financial Analysts
Journal* with permission from CFA Institute. All rights reserved.

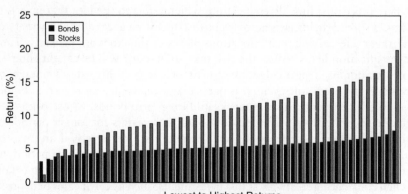

Lowest to Highest Returns
(means of 200 simulated returns in each group)

FIGURE 7.2   Annual Returns over a 30-Year Time Horizon
Note: Stock returns are CRSP+Value Weighted Index returns; bond returns are
five-year U.S. Treasury bond returns. Simulation is based on 10,000 random
drawings of realized 1926 to 1997 returns.
Source: Kenneth Fisher and Meir Statman, "A Behavioral Framework for Time
Diversification," *Financial Analysts Journal* (May/June: 1999). Copyright
1999, CFA Institute. Reproduced and republished from *Financial Analysts
Journal* with permission from CFA Institute. All rights reserved.

DIAGNOSTIC TESTING

This test will help to determine a client's susceptibility to both base-rate bias and sample-size neglect bias.

Base-Rate Neglect Representativeness Bias Test

Question 1: Jim is an ex-college baseball player. After he graduated from college, Jim became a physical education teacher. Jim has two sons, both of whom are excellent athletes. Which is more likely?
a. Jim coaches a local Little League team.
b. Jim coaches a local Little League team and plays softball with the local softball team.

Sample-Size Neglect Representativeness Bias Test

Question 2: Consider the two sequences of coin-toss results shown (Figure 7.3). Assume that an unbiased coin has been used. Which of the sequences pictured do you think is more likely: A or B?

Test Results Analysis

Question 1: Respondents who chose "b," which is the predictable answer, are likely to suffer from base-rate neglect representativeness bias. It is *possible* that Jim both coaches and plays softball, but it is *more likely* that he only coaches Little League. Figure 7.4 illustrates this.

Question 2: Most people ascertain Sequence A to be more likely, simply because it appears more "random." In fact, both sequences are

Sequence 1

Sequence 2

FIGURE 7.3 Sample-Size Neglect Diagnostic: Which Sequence of Coin Toss Results Appears Likelier?

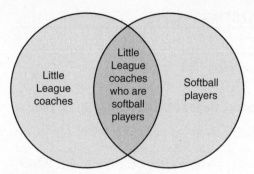

FIGURE 7.4   Softball Players Are Not Necessarily "Representative" of Little League Coaches

equally likely because a coin toss generates a 50:50 probability ratio of heads to tails. Therefore, respondents who chose Sequence B may be subject to sample-size neglect representativeness bias (also known in this case as Gambler's Fallacy, or the "Law of Small Numbers"). If six tosses of a fair coin all turn out to be heads, the probability that the next toss will turn up heads is still one-half. However, many people still harbor the notion that in coin tossing, a roughly even ratio of heads to tails should result and that a sequence of consecutive heads signals that a tails is overdue. Again, this is a case of representativeness bias. The law of large numbers, when applied to a small sample, will produce such biased estimates.

ADVICE

In both sample-size neglect and base-rate neglect, investors ignore the statistically dominant result in order to satisfy their need for patterns. Due to the fact that many examples of representativeniss bias exist, this advice tries to address two especially prevalent errors that representativeness-biased investors often commit. One of these mistakes falls in the base-rate neglect category, while the other exemplifies sample-size neglect.

Advice for Base-Rate Neglect

Earlier in the chapter, a very effective method for dealing with base-rate neglect was presented. When you or a client sense that base-rate neglect might be a problem, stop and perform the following analysis: "What is the probability that Person A (Simon, a shy, introverted man) belongs to Group B (stamp collectors) rather than Group C (BMW drivers)?"

Recalling this example will help you to think through whether you are erroneously assessing a particular situation. It will likely be necessary to go back and do some more research to determine if you have indeed committed an error (i.e., "Are there really more BMW drivers than stamp collectors?"). In the end, however, this process should prove conducive to better investment decisions.

Advice for Sample-Size Neglect

In the earlier example of sample-size neglect (George and Jim), an investor might conclude that a mutual fund manager possesses remarkable skill, based on the fund's performance over just the past three years. Viewed in the context of the thousands of investment managers, a given manager's three-year track record is just as likely an indication that the manager has benefited from luck as it is an indication of skill, right? Consider the following studies. The first is a study conducted by Vanguard Investments Australia, later released by Morningstar.[3] The five best-performing funds from 1994 to 2003 were analyzed. The results of the study were surprising to say the least:

- Only 16 percent of the top five funds make it to the following year's list.
- The top five funds average 15 percent lower returns the following year.
- The top five funds barely beat (by 0.3 percent) the market the following year.
- Of the top five funds, 21 percent ceased to exist within the following 10 years.

In the next study, Barras, Scaillet, and Wermers (2010) evaluate the skill of active managers. Their study was intended to make general statements about the mutual fund industry rather than about any single mutual fund. They evaluate performance over the full set of mutual funds and separate them into three categories—skilled (generating positive alpha), unskilled (generating negative alpha), and zero-alpha. They add to previous research by explicitly accounting for skill and luck. Earlier empirical work assumes either no luck or full luck, thus producing biased conclusions about the prevalence of truly skilled and truly unskilled fund managers. Barras et al. concluded that 75.4 percent of the 2,076 funds analyzed were zero-alpha funds over their lifetimes. Of the remainder, only 0.6 percent were skilled and 24.0 percent were unskilled. In sum, Barras et al. concluded that the majority of actively managed domestic equity mutual funds have generated at most zero alpha after adjusting for luck, trading costs, and fees.

The third study is DALBAR's 2008 Quantitative Analysis of Investor Behavior[4] which demonstrates that investors tend to invest in mutual funds at the wrong time: immediately following substantial price appreciation. They categorize the funds as good investments based on this recent information. These periods tend to precede a subsequent decline in the fund's performance. Then, when prices fall, investors sell their holdings and search for the next hot fund. Based on an analysis of actual investor behavior over 20 years ending on December 31, 2007, the average equity fund investor earned an annualized return of just 4.48 percent—underperforming the S&P 500 by more than 7 percent and outpacing inflation by a mere 1.44 percent. Fixed-income investors fared far worse, losing an average of 1.49 percent in purchasing power per year. Asset allocation fund investors did a bit better, beating inflation by 0.41 percent per year.[5]

These results are consistent with the fourth study we will review conducted by Bogle (2005). Bogle illustrates that returns earned by a group of investors must fall short of the reported market returns or mutual fund returns by the amount of the aggregate costs the investors incur. Thus, we can conclude that the additional costs of moving in and out of funds and lack of performance persistence will generally result in returns lower than those expected by investors. Moving in and out of investments based on categorizations that place undue reliance on recent performance and new information is likely to result in excessive trading and inferior performance results.

Prudent methods for identifying appropriate long-term investments exist., such as using an asset allocation strategy to increase the likelihood of better long-term portfolio returns, and investing in a diversified portfolio to meet financial goals, and sticking with it. The following questions should help investors avoid the futility of chasing returns and also help them select appropriate investments.

1. How does the fund under consideration perform relative to similarly sized and similarly styled funds?
2. What is the tenure of the managers and advisers at the fund?
3. Are the managers well-known and/or highly regarded?
4. Has the fund consistently pursued its strategy, or has its style drifted during different market conditions?

To counteract the effects of the representativeness bias when considering returns, many practitioners use what has become known as the "periodic table of investment returns," as shown in Figure 7.5.

	1999	2000	2001	2002	2003	2004	2005	2006	2007	2008
Highest Return	Emer. Mkts 66%	Commodity 32%	Small Value 14%	Commodity 26%	Int'l Small 58%	Real Estate 33%	Emer. Mkts 35%	Real Estate 36%	Emer. Mkts 40%	Fixed Inc. -3%
	Int'l Large 27%	Real Estate 31%	Real Estate 12%	Fixed Inc. 10%	Emer. Mkts 56%	Int'l Small 28%	Int'l Small 24%	Emer. Mkts 32%	Commodity 15%	Small Value -29%
	Commodity 24%	Small Value 23%	Fixed Inc. 10%	Real Estate 4%	Small Cap 47%	Emer. Mkts 26%	Commodity 21%	Int'l Large 27%	Int'l Large 12%	Small Cap -34%
	Small Cap 21%	Fixed Inc. 9%	Small Cap 2%	Emer. Mkts -6%	Small Value 46%	Small Value 22%	Int'l Large 14%	Small Value 23%	Fixed Inc. 6%	Commodity -36%
	S&P 500 21%	Large Value 7%	Emer. Mkts -2%	Diversified Port. -6%	Int'l Large 39%	Int'l Large 21%	Diversified Port. 13%	Large Value 22%	S&P 500 5%	Diversified Port. -36%
	Diversified Port. 18%	Diversified Port. 4%	Diversified Port. -4%	Int'l Small -10%	Diversified Port. 37%	Diversified Port. 19%	Real Estate 13%	Diversified Port. 20%	Diversified Port. 5%	Large Value -37%
	Int'l Small 18%	Small Cap -3%	Large Value -6%	Small Value -11%	Real Estate 36%	Small Cap 18%	Large Value 7%	Small Cap 18%	Int'l Small 2%	S&P 500 -37%
	Large Value 7%	Int'l Small -9%	S&P 500 -12%	Int'l Large -16%	Large Value 30%	Large Value 16%	S&P 500 5%	Int'l Small 17%	Large Value 0%	Real Estate -39%
	Fixed Inc. 0%	S&P 500 -9%	Int'l Small -14%	Large Value -16%	S&P 500 29%	S&P 500 11%	Small Cap 5%	S&P 500 16%	Small Cap -2%	Int'l Large -43%
	Small Value -1%	Int'l Large -14%	Commodity -20%	Small Cap -20%	Commodity 24%	Commodity 9%	Small Value 5%	Fixed Inc. 4%	Small Value -10%	Int'l Small -47%
Lowest Return	Real Estate -3%	Emer. Mkts -31%	Int'l Large -21%	S&P 500 -22%	Fixed Inc. 7%	Fixed Inc. 4%	Fixed Inc. 1%	Commodity 2%	Real Estate -18%	Emer. Mkts -53%

Source: Dimensional Fund Advisors and Thomson Financial

FIGURE 7.5 Sample of a Periodic Table of Investment Returns

Figure 7.5 shows that asset class returns are highly variable. Many investors fail to heed the advice offered by the chart—namely, that it is nearly impossible to accurately predict which asset class will be the best performer from one year to the next. Thus, diversification is prudent (note how the diversified portfolio consistently appears near the center of each column). Practitioners would be wise to present this chart when establishing asset allocations with new clients to emphasize the advantages of diversification over return chasing.

NOTES

1. Daniel Kahneman, Paul Slovic, and Amos Tversky (eds.), *Judgment under Uncertainty: Heuristics and Biases* (New York: Cambridge University Press, 1982).
2. Kenneth L. Fisher and Meir Statman, "A Behavioral Framework for Time Diversification," *Financial Analysts Journal* (May/June 1999).
3. See Morningstar web site: www.morningstar.com.
4. Russ Thornton. "*Quantitative Analysis of Investor Behavior 2008.*" Dalbar, Inc. (2008): 1–12. Accessed March 11, 2011. http://www.scribd.com/doc/13096471/DALBAR-QAIB-2008.
5. Ibid, pg. 3.

CHAPTER 8

Illusion of Control Bias

I claim not to have controlled events, but confess plainly that events have controlled me.

—Abraham Lincoln

BIAS DESCRIPTION

Bias Name: Illusion of control

Bias Type: Cognitive

Subtype: Belief perseverance

General Description

The *illusion of control bias,* another form of dissonant behavior, describes the tendency of human beings to believe that they can control or at least influence outcomes when, in fact, they cannot. This bias can be observed in Las Vegas, where casinos play host to many forms of this psychological fallacy. Some casino patrons swear that they are able to impact random outcomes such as the product of a pair of tossed dice. In the casino game "craps," for example, various research has demonstrated that people actually cast the dice more vigorously when they are trying to attain a higher number or when an "important" roll is happening. Some people, when successful at trying to predict the outcome of a series of coin tosses, actually believe that they are "better guessers," and some claim that distractions might diminish their performance at this statistically arbitrary task.

Technical Description

Ellen Langer, PhD, of Harvard University's psychology department, defines the illusion of control bias as the "expectancy of a personal success probability inappropriately higher than the objective probability would warrant."[1] Langer found that choice, task familiarity, competition, and active involvement can all inflate confidence and generate such illusions. For example, Langer observed that people who were permitted to select their own numbers in a hypothetical lottery game were also willing to pay a higher price per ticket than subjects gambling on randomly assigned numbers. Since this initial study, many other researchers have uncovered similar situations where people perceived themselves to possess more control than they did, inferred causal connections where none existed, or displayed surprisingly great certainty in their predictions for the outcomes of chance events.

A relevant analogy can be found in a humorous, hypothetical anecdote: In a small town called Smallville, a man marches to the town square every day at 6 p.m. carrying a checkered flag and a trumpet. When the man reaches an appointed spot, he brandishes the flag and blows a few notes on the trumpet. Then, he returns home to the delight of his family.

A police officer notices the man's daily display and eventually asks him, "What are you doing?"

The man replies, "Keeping the elephants away."

"But there aren't any elephants in Smallville," the officer replies.

"Well, then, I'm doing a fine job, aren't I?" At this, the officer rolls his eyes and laughs.

This rather absurd tale illustrates the fallacy inherent in the illusion of control bias.

PRACTICAL APPLICATION

When subject to illusion of control bias, people feel as if they can exert more control over their environment than they actually can. An excellent application of this concept was devised by Andrea Breinholt and Lynnette Dalrymple, two researchers at Westminster College in Salt Lake City, Utah. Their study entitled "The Illusion of Control: What's Luck Got to Do with It?"[2] illustrates that people often harbor unfounded illusions of control.

Breinholt and Dalrymple sought to examine subjects' susceptibility to illusions of control as determined by the intersection of two common impulses: the desire for control and the belief in good luck as a controllable attribute. Two hundred eighty-one undergraduate students participated in the study, and all rated themselves based on a "Desirability of Control Scale" and a "Belief in Luck Scale" immediately prior to the experiment. The subjects then participated in an online, simulated gambling task. Participants were randomly assigned either a high-involvement or a low-involvement condition and, also randomly, were rewarded with either a descending or a random sequence of outcomes.

All participants played 14 hands of "Red & Black," using four cards from a standard poker deck. Each card was presented facedown on the screen, and subjects were asked to wager as to whether a chosen card matched a selected, target color. Each player began with 50 chips. In each hand, participants could wager between zero and five chips; winning increased the participant's total stock of chips by the wagered amount. Likewise, following a lost hand, a player's supply of chips automatically decreased by the wagered amount. The odds of winning each hand were calibrated at 50:50.

Participants randomly assigned to the high-involvement condition were allowed to "shuffle" and "deal" the cards themselves. They could also choose, in each hand, the target color and the amount wagered. After the high-involvement participants chose their cards, the computer revealed each result accordingly. This sequence repeated over the course of 14 trials. The high-involvement condition was designed to maximize the participants' perception that they were controlling the game.

In the low-involvement condition, the computer shuffled and dealt the cards. The participants chose the amounts wagered, but the computer randomly selected the card on which the outcome of each hand would rest.

The descending outcome sequence was designed to maximize the illusion of control, letting the majority of successful outcomes occur during the first seven trials.[3] The descending sequence, for example, consisted of the outcomes depicted in Figure 8.1.

The random outcome sequence was designed to minimize the illusion of control by spacing the successful outcomes more evenly over the course of the 14 trials. Figure 8.2 demonstrates a sample distribution.

Ultimately, participants in the high-involvement condition tended to wager more chips on each hand than did participants in the low-involvement condition. Moreover, in the low-involvement condition, wagers did not differ reliably as a function of distributed feature composition (DFC)—in other words, participants receiving the descending sequence of outcomes

Win	Win	Lose	Win	Win	Win	Lose	Lose	Win	Lose	Lose	Lose	Win	Lose

FIGURE 8.1 A Sample Distribution of the Descending Outcome Sequence in "The Illusion of Control: What's Luck Got to Do with It?"
Source: Andrea Breinholt and Lynnette A. Dalrymple, "The Illusion of Control: What's Luck Got to Do with It?" *The Myriad: Westminster College Undergraduate Academic Journal* (Summer 2004).

| Win | Lose | Lose | Win | Win | Lose | Lose | Lose | Win | Lose | Win | Lose | Win | Win |

FIGURE 8.2 Sample Distribution of the Random Outcome Sequence in "The Illusion of Control: What's Luck Got to Do with It?"
Source: Andrea Breinholt and Lynnette A. Dalrymple, "The Illusion of Control: What's Luck Got to Do with It?" *The Myriad: Westminster College Undergraduate Academic Journal* (Summer 2004).

did not wager more or less, on average, than did participants allotted the random outcome sequence. In contrast, in the high-involvement condition, high-DFC participants wagered more than did low-DFC participants. These findings support the presence of an illusion of control phenomenon in the traditional sense.

This study clearly demonstrates the illusion of-control bias in practice. Investors are very much susceptible to this bias.

Implications for Investors

Below we list four primary behaviors that can lead to investment mistakes by investors who are susceptible to illusion of control bias.

ILLUSION OF CONTROL BIAS: BEHAVIORS THAT CAN CAUSE INVESTMENT MISTAKES

1. Illusion of control bias can lead investors to trade more than is prudent. Researchers have found that traders, especially online traders, believe themselves to possess more control over the outcomes of their investments than they actually do. An excess of trading results, in the end, in decreased returns.[4]
2. Illusions of control can lead investors to maintain underdiversified portfolios. Researchers have found that investors hold concentrated positions because they gravitate toward companies over whose fate they feel some amount of control. That control proves illusory, however, and the lack of diversification hurts the investors' portfolios.
3. Illusion of control bias can cause investors to use limit orders and other such techniques in order to experience a false sense of

control over their investments. In fact, the use of these mechanisms can often lead to an overlooked opportunity or, worse, a detrimental, unnecessary purchase based on the occurrence of an arbitrary price.

4. Illusion of control bias contributes, in general, to investor overconfidence. (Please see Chapter 18 for a detailed discussion of related pitfalls and compensation techniques.) In particular, investors who have been successful in business or other professional pursuits believe that they should also be successful in the investment realm. What they find is that they may have had the ability to shape outcomes in their vocation, but investments are a different matter altogether.

RESEARCH REVIEW

This section examines the results of a relatively new paper published in May 2004 by Gerlinde Fellner of the Max Planck Institute for Research into Economic Systems in Jena, Germany. In her work, "Illusion of Control as a Source of Poor Diversification: An Experimental Approach,"[5] Fellner explored the mechanics of this bias as they apply, specifically, to investing behavior. She hypothesized that the illusion of control bias accounts for systematic capital shifts toward investments (stocks) that offer investors the illusion of control. The paper investigated factors influencing individual portfolio allocations. The fundamental question asked was, "Do individuals invest more in a "lottery" (stocks) for which they can control the chance move?" Her hypothesis proved correct. In her words: "Results indicate that subjects invest more in an alternative when they can exercise control on its return and less in the alternative where they do not. This is especially pronounced when subjects can choose the investment alternative on which to exercise control."[6]

In summary, Fellner's research showed that investors prefer to make investments in which they believe they can control the outcome. Many practitioners know that investors have no control over the outcome of investments they make, only the decision to invest or not to invest (in rare cases, one individual may have influence over the outcome, but this is the exception, not the rule). Thus, practitioners need to be fully cognizant of this tendency to want to make "controlled" investments and dissuade investors of the notion that they have control over investment outcomes.

DIAGNOSTIC TESTING

This diagnostic test helps to determine whether people taking the test harbor illusions of control.

Illusion of Control Bias Test

Question 1: When you participate in games of chance that involve dice—such as backgammon, Monopoly, or craps—do you feel most in control when you roll the dice yourself?

a. I feel more in control when I roll the dice.

b. I am indifferent as to who rolls the dice.

Question 2: When returns to your portfolio increase, to what do you mainly attribute this turn of events?

a. The control that I've exercised over the outcome of my investments.

b. Some combination of investment control and random chance.

c. Completely random chance.

Question 3: When you are playing cards, are you usually most optimistic with respect to the outcome of a hand that you've dealt yourself?

a. A better outcome will occur when I am controlling the dealing of the cards.

b. It makes no difference to me who deals the cards.

Question 4: When and if you purchase a lottery ticket, do you feel more encouraged, regarding your odds of winning, if you choose the number yourself rather than using a computer-generated number?

a. I'm more likely to win if I control the numbers picked.

b. It makes no difference to me how the numbers are chosen.

Test Results Analysis

Question 1: People who feel more confident rolling the dice themselves, rather than allowing someone else to roll, are more likely to be susceptible to illusion of control bias.

Question 2: People who feel that they are able to exert control over their investments are likely to be susceptible to illusion of control bias.

Question 3: Question 3 parallels Question 1. People who perceive that they have more control over the outcome of a hand of cards when dealing the cards themselves are likely to be susceptible to illusion of control bias.

Question 4: Respondents selecting "a," indicating that they feel more optimistic when choosing their own lottery numbers instead of accepting randomized numbers, are likely to be susceptible to illusion of control bias.

ADVICE

Following are four advisories that investors can implement to stem the detrimental financial effects of illusions of control.

1. *Recognize that successful investing is a probabilistic activity.* The first step on the road to recovery from illusion of control bias is to take a step back and realize how complex U.S. and global capitalism actually is. Even the wisest investors have absolutely no control over the outcomes of the investments that they make.
2. *Recognize and avoid circumstances that trigger susceptibility illusions of control.* A villager blows his trumpet every day at 6 p.m., and no stampede of elephants ensues. Does the trumpet really keep the elephants away? Applying the same concept to investing, just because you have deliberately determined to purchase a stock, do you really control the fate of that stock or the outcome of that purchase? Rationally, it becomes clear that some correlations are arbitrary rather than causal. Don't permit yourself to make financial decisions on what you can logically discern is an arbitrary basis.
3. *Seek contrary viewpoints.* As you contemplate a new investment, take a moment to ponder whatever considerations might weigh against the trade. Ask yourself: Why am I making this investment? What are the downside risks? When will I sell? What might go wrong? These important questions can help you to screen the logic behind a decision before implementing that decision.
4. *Keep records.* Once you have decided to move forward with an investment, one of the best ways to keep illusions of control at bay is to maintain records of your transactions, including reminders spelling out the rationales that underlie each trade. Write down some of the important features of each investment that you make, and emphasize those attributes that you have determined to be in favor of the investment's success.

If you want proof that this fourth habit, in particular, pays off, look no further than renowned former Fidelity Magellan Fund manager Peter Lynch. Lynch was a meticulous record keeper, documenting his opinions on different companies at every opportunity. When I was a young analyst in Boston right out of college, I had the occasion to visit some colleagues at Fidelity and met Mr. Lynch in his office. What I saw was astounding. Lynch maintained an archive of notebooks filled with information. His office was literally wall-to-wall research papers. He expected his subordinates to be equally thorough. When analysts made a recommendation, Lynch would require a written presentation outlining the details and the basis of each recommendation. Average investors should strive to reach this standard.

FINAL THOUGHT

Rationally, we know that returns on long-term investment results aren't impacted by the immediate-term beliefs, emotions, and impulses that often surround financial transactions. Instead, success or lack thereof is usually a result of uncontrollable factors like corporate performance and general economic conditions. During periods of market turmoil, though, it can be difficult to keep this in mind. One of the best ways to prevent your biases from affecting your decisions is to keep the rational side of your brain engaged as often as possible. Success in investing ultimately is found by investors who can conquer these daily psychological challenges and keep a long-term perspective in view at all times. Also, if you habitually use limit orders, keep track of your successes and failures. Don't worry so much about overpaying by a quarter or an eighth to buy a stock. If you maintain your position for the long term, paying an extra quarter or eighth of a point will not impact your return. On the flip side, stop limit orders can help to limit losses if a bad decision has been made.

NOTES

1. Ellen Langer, "The Illusion of Control," *Journal of Personality and Social Psychology* 32 (1975): 311–328.
2. Andrea Breinholt and Lynnette A. Dalrymple, "The Illusion of Control: What's Luck Got to Do with It?" *The Myriad: Westminster College Undergraduate Academic Journal* (Summer 2004).
3. Ibid.
4. Terrance Odean, "Do Investors Trade Too Much?" *American Economic Review,* 89(5) (1999): 1279–1298.
5. Gerlinde Fellner, "Illusion of Control as a Source of Poor Diversification: An Experimental Approach," published by Max Planck Institute for Research into Economic Systems in Jena, Germany, May 2004.
6. Ibid.

CHAPTER 9

Hindsight Bias

Hindsight is a wonderful thing.
                    —David Beckham

BIAS DESCRIPTION

Bias Name: Hindsight bias

Bias Type: Cognitive

Subtype: Belief perseverance

General Description

Described in simple terms, *hindsight bias* is the impulse that insists: "I knew it all along!" This is perhaps the most pronounced version of belief perseverance biases. Once an event has elapsed, people afflicted with hindsight bias tend to perceive that the event was predictable—even if it wasn't. This behavior is precipitated by the fact that *actual* outcomes are more readily grasped by people's minds than the infinite array of outcomes that could have but didn't materialize. Therefore, people tend to overestimate the accuracy of their own predictions. This is not to say, obviously, that people cannot make accurate predictions, but merely that people may believe that they made an accurate prediction in hindsight. Hindsight bias has been demonstrated in experiments involving investing—a few of which will be examined shortly—as well as in other diverse settings, ranging from politics to medicine. Unpredictable developments bother people, since it's always embarrassing to be caught off-guard. Also, people tend to remember their own predictions of the future as more accurate than they actually were because they are biased by having knowledge of what actually happened. To alleviate the discomfort associated with the unexpected, people tend to view things that have already happened as being relatively inevitable and predictable. This view is often caused by the reconstructive nature of memory. When people look back, they do not have perfect memory; they tend to "fill in the gaps" with what they prefer to believe. In doing so, people may prevent themselves from learning from the past.

Technical Description

Hindsight bias is the tendency of people, with the benefit of hindsight following an event, to falsely believe that they predicted the outcome of that event in the beginning. Hindsight bias affects future forecasting. A person subject to hindsight bias assumes that the outcome he or she ultimately observes is, in fact, the only outcome that was ever possible. Thus, he or she underestimates the uncertainty preceding the event in question and underrates the outcomes that could have materialized but did not.

Baruch Fischhoff[1] described an experiment in which he asked subjects to answer general knowledge questions from almanacs and encyclopedias. Later, after revealing the correct answers, Fischhoff asked his subjects to recall their original responses from memory. The results are revealing: in general, people overestimated the quality of their initial knowledge and forgot their initial errors. Hindsight bias is a serious problem for market followers. Once an event is part of market history, there is a tendency to see the sequence that led up to it, making the event appear inevitable. As Richard Posner[2] noted, outcomes exert irresistible pressure on their own interpretations. In hindsight, blunders with happy results are described as brilliant tactical moves, and unfortunate results of choices that were well grounded in available information are described as avoidable blunders.

One detriment of hindsight bias is that it can prevent learning from mistakes. People with hindsight bias connected to another psychological bias, anchoring, find it difficult to reconstruct an unbiased state of mind—it is easier to argue for the inevitability of a reported outcome and convince oneself that it would not have turned out otherwise. In sum, hindsight bias leads people to exaggerate the quality of their foresight.

PRACTICAL APPLICATION

Many people have observed hindsight bias in the investment realm. They watch people fool themselves into thinking that they could have predicted the outcome of some financial gamble, but they achieve such crystal-clear insight only after the fact. Perhaps the most obvious example recalls the prevailing response by investors to the behavior of the U.S. stock market between 1998 and 2003. In 1998 and 1999, virtually nobody viewed the soaring market indexes as symptomatic of a short-lived "bubble" (or if they did harbor such misgivings, investors did not act on them). Above-average returns were the norm, though even a casual glance at historical business-cycle trends should have foretold that, eventually, the 1990s bull market had to recede. Still, sadly, even some of the most sophisticated investors succumbed to the fantasy: "It's different this time!" Similarly, in 2006, when the first edition of this book was published, it was inconceivable to most people that housing could be an unsafe "investment" and that a financial crisis of epic proportions was in the making. Now, in 2011, most people concede the reality of the housing and credit bubbles, the Internet stock bubble, and the subsequent meltdown in a distant memory or have forgotten altogether. In fact, chatting with most investors today, you'll get the impression that they expected the collapse of housing prices. The collapse of late 2000's prosperity was "clearly in the cards," or they comment: "Wasn't it obvious that we were in a bubble?" Giving in to hindsight bias can be very destructive because it leads investors to believe that they have better predictive powers than they actually do. Relying on these "powers" can invite poor decision making in the future.

Implications for Investors

Perhaps the hindsight bias's biggest implication for investors is that it gives investors a false sense of security when making investment decisions. This can manifest itself in excessive risk-taking behavior and place people's port-folios at risk. In the following, we review some common behaviors, rooted in hindsight bias that can cause investment mistakes.

RESEARCH REVIEW

This chapter's research review discusses hindsight bias in the context of fund manager selection. In their insightful paper entitled "On the Predictability of Stock Returns in Real Time," Michael Cooper of Purdue University, Roberto Gutierrez of Texas A&M University, and William Marcum of Wake Forest University argued that some money managers' track records are unduly criticized due to hindsight bias.[3]

The basic thrust of the argument is that money managers with long track records might be inordinately blamed for not outperforming a certain strategy that "worked" over a given time period. This happens when the researchers who are examining the track record of the fund manager are comparing the manager's track record to a strategy that has only recently been recognized as an accepted size or style strategy. For example, suppose a fund manager launched a fund in 1980 with the objective of finding undervalued stocks. Further suppose that from 1980 to 2004, the manager outperformed the Standard & Poor's (S&P) 500. Unfortunately, during the same time period, the manager lagged his benchmark, a value index. Is this lagging a valid criticism?

HINDSIGHT BIAS: BEHAVIORS THAT CAN CAUSE INVESTMENT MISTAKES

1. When an investment appreciates, hindsight-biased investors tend to rewrite their own memories to portray the positive developments as if they were predictable. Over time, this rationale can inspire excessive risk taking because hindsight-biased investors begin to believe that they have superior predictive powers, when, in fact, they do not. The bursting of the technology bubble is an example of this bias in action.

2. Hindsight-biased investors also "rewrite history" when they fare poorly and block out recollections of prior, incorrect forecasts in order to alleviate embarrassment. This form of self-deception, in some ways similar to cognitive dissonance, prevents investors from learning from their mistakes. A clear example of this bias took place in the early 1980s, when energy stocks generated over 20 percent of S&P 500 returns, and lots of investors were caught up in the boom. By the 1990s, though, the energy bubble subsided, and many stockholders lost money. Most now prefer, in hindsight, to not recognize that the speculative frenzy clouded their judgments.

3. Hindsight-biased investors can unduly fault their money managers when funds perform poorly. Looking back at what has occurred in securities markets, these investors perceive every development as inevitable. How, then, could a worthwhile manager be caught by surprise? In fact, even top-quartile managers who implement their strategies correctly may not succeed in every market cycle. Managers of small-cap value funds in the late 1990s, for example, drew a lot of criticism. However, these people weren't poor managers; their style was simply out of favor at the time.

4. Conversely, hindsight bias can cause investors to unduly praise their money managers when funds perform well. The clarity of hindsight obscures the possibility that a manager's strategy might simply have benefited from good timing or good fortune. Consider the wisdom attributed to managers of aggressive-growth tech funds in the late 1990s.

Cooper, Gutierrez, and Marcum argued implicitly that since true value indexes weren't created until after 1992, when Eugene Fama and Ken French came out with their now groundbreaking paper entitled "The Cross-Section of Expected Stock Returns" (*Journal of Finance,* 1992), the managers are being unduly criticized. In this example, the money manager would have no reason in 1980 to think that low price-to-book ratio stocks would out-perform the market because that was not a recognized strategy. Thus, this manager's track record should be compared to a value index only from 1992 to 2005 rather than from 1980 to 2005.

An analogy can be found in the sport of baseball. The concept of "relief pitching" did not appear until after the turn of the twentieth century. To make a point, assume that prior to 1900 pitchers only pitched complete games and that after 1900 relief pitching came into being. Also assume that immediately after relief pitching began, the idea of "earned run average" (ERA) began to be used (in actuality, there were some years in between these events, but this scenario approximates reality). For those unfamiliar with baseball, ERA is the number of earned runs a pitcher gives up per nine innings pitched.

Prior to 1900, pitchers were routinely expected to pitch complete games. Thus, the only way to measure their effectiveness was to look at their win-loss (W-L) record. After the ERA was introduced, pitchers were evaluated on both W-L and ERA. Suppose that a statistician went back and calculated the ERA for pitchers who pitched prior to 1900 and found that their ERAs were much higher (bad) than those who were evaluated after relief pitching was introduced. Evaluating the pre-1900 pitchers by ERA is unfair because ERA was not known prior to 1900 as a measure of effectiveness of a pitcher, as pitchers were forced to pitch complete games. This situation is analogous to the previous example of value managers prior to 1992.

From their paper, Cooper, Gutierrez, and Marcum noted:

> In this study, we address the ex ante predictability of the cross section of stock returns by investigating whether a real-time in-vestor could have used book-to-market equity, firm size, and one-year lagged returns to generate portfolio profits during the 1974–97 period. We develop variations on common recursive out-of-sample methods and demonstrate a marked difference between ex post and ex ante predictability, suggesting that the current notion of pre-dictability in the literature is exaggerated.[4]
>   —(There is much more to this article. At this writing, it can be found at http://lcb1.uoregon.edu/rcg/research/Realtime.pdf.)

A similar example lies with small-capitalization stocks. These man-agers should be judged from the early 1980s forward, when the idea of small-capitalization stocks outperforming large-capitalization stocks came into popularity. The point to be duly noted here is that before you criticize a fund manager's track record for any given asset class, make sure you know when his or her strategy gained popularity. Judge the track record from there.

DIAGNOSTIC TESTING

These questions are designed to detect cognitive errors caused by hindsight bias. To complete the test, select the answer choice that best characterizes your response to each item.

Hindsight Bias Test

Question 1: Suppose you make an investment, and it increases in value. Further suppose, though, that your reasons for purchasing the investment did not rely on the forces underlying its growth. How might you naturally react?

a. I do not concern myself with the reasons an investment does well. If it performs well, it means I did a good job as an investor, and doing well makes me more confident about the next investment I make.

b. Even though the stock went up, I'm concerned that the factors I thought were important didn't end up impacting its performance. In cases like this, I usually try to revisit the reasons that I bought the stock, and I also try to understand why it succeeded. Overall, I think I'd be more cautious the next time around.

Question 2: Suppose you make an investment and it goes down. What is your natural reaction to this situation?

a. Generally, I don't fault myself—if an investment doesn't work out, this may simply be due to bad luck. I'll sell the stock and move on, rather than pursuing the details of what went wrong.

b. I would want to investigate and determine why my investment failed. In fact, I'm very interested in finding out what went wrong. I put a lot of emphasis on the reasons behind my investment decisions, so I need to be aware of the reasons behind my investment's performance.

Question 3: Suppose you are investigating a money manager for inclusion in your portfolio. Your advisor suggests a large-cap value manager for you. What is your natural approach to examining the manager's performance?

a. I tend to look primarily at a manager's track record, comparing his or her performance to some relevant benchmark. I don't concern myself with the strategy that the manager employs. The results that a manager achieves are most important. If returns impress me, then I will select that manager; if I see a mediocre history, I'll pass.

b. I look at the returns, which are important, but I also look at the manager's strategy and try to determine what the manager was doing during the time frame I'm examining. In the case of the value manager, I will look, for example, at 2002—the manager was probably down, but by how much? Which companies did the manager invest in at the time? Evidence of a sound strategy makes me more likely to select this money manager.

Test Results Analysis

Questions 1, 2, and 3: Hindsight bias is a difficult bias to measure because people are rarely aware that they harbor it. So, few are likely to take a test like this and effectively respond: "Yes, I am susceptible to 'I-knew-it-all-along' behavior." Even people with reason to believe, objectively, that they might suffer from hindsight bias are unlikely to admit it to themselves. So, this diagnostic test looks for clues that might indicate *symptoms* of potential hindsight bias. For each item, respondents identifying with the rationale in "a" should be aware that they exhibit such symptoms and that they may suffer from hindsight bias.

ADVICE

In order to overcome hindsight bias, it is necessary, as with most biases, for the investors to understand and admit their susceptibility. Advisors should get their clients to understand that they are vulnerable and they counsel them on addressing specific problems that might arise. Here are some thoughts to help clients better deal with hindsight bias:

"Rewriting history"—predicting gains. When a client overestimates the degree to which some positive investment outcome was foreseeable, and you suspect this is due to hindsight bias, the best course of action is to gently point to the facts. Storytelling is a strategy that might help communicate your point without offending the client. You might make reference, for example, to the collapse of

the credit bubble in the 2008–2009 period, when risks fueled by excessive credit cost stockholders billions. In the face of rationales like "I knew that stock was going to go up! I told you so," a cautionary tale can highlight the pitfalls of overestimating one's own predictive powers.

"Rewriting history"—predicting losses. Advisors need to recognize that many people prefer to block recollections of poor investment decisions. Understanding why investments go awry, however, is critical to obtaining insight into markets and, ultimately, to finding investment success. Counsel clients to carefully examine their investment decisions, both good and bad. Encourage self-examination. This will help eliminate repeats of past investment mistakes.

Unduly criticizing money managers for poor performance. Clients need to understand that markets move in cycles and that, at certain times, an investment manager will underperform in his or her class, relative to other asset classes. Investors should understand that a good manager adheres to a consistent, valid style, through good times and bad. A manager is hired to do a job, and that job is to implement a defined investment strategy. Education is critical here. Just because many growth managers underperformed in the early 2000s, when values of many stocks were in a downward cycle, does not mean that growth managers are categorically unskilled. A similar case can be made today for managers of "quality" stocks (safe, large-capitalization companies).

Unduly praising a money manager for good performance. Using the same line of reasoning, counsel clients against becoming too giddy over the prospects offered by managers who happen to be in the right asset class at the right time. There are plenty of investment managers who benefit circumstantially from market cycles and still do not meet benchmarks. These are the managers to avoid. Again, education is critical; once clients understand the role that a manager plays in determining fund performance, hindsight bias can be curtailed.

NOTES

1. Baruch Fischhoff, "Hindsight/Foresight: The Effect of Outcome Knowledge on Judgment under Uncertainty," *Journal of Experimental Psychology: Human Perception and Performance* 1 (3): 288–299.

2. Richard Posner, "Rational Choice, Behavioral Economics, and the Law," *Stanford Law Review* 50 (1998): 1551–1575.

3. Michael Cooper, Roberto Gutierrez, and William Marcum, "On the Predictability of Stock Returns in Real Time," *Journal of Business* 78 (2) (April 2005): 469–499.

4. Ibid.

Three

Information Processing Biases Defined and Illustrated

OVERVIEW OF THE STRUCTURE OF CHAPTERS 10 THROUGH 16

In Chapters 4 to 23, 20 behavioral biases, both cognitive and emotional, are discussed. Two types of cognitive biases will be reviewed in Chapters 4 to 16. Belief perseverance cognitive biases are covered in Chapters 4 to 9 and information processing cognitive biases are covered now in Chapters 10 to 16. Emotional biases are covered in Chapters 17 to 23.

In the 20 bias chapters, the same basic format is used to discuss each bias, in order to promote greater accessibility. First, each bias is named, categorized as emotional or cognitive including sub-type (belief perseverance or information processing), and then generally described and technically described. This is followed by the all-important concrete practical application, in which it is demonstrated how each bias has been used or can be used in a practical situation. The practical application portion varies in content, either consisting of an intensive review of applied research or of a case study.

Implications for investors are then delineated. At the end of the practical application section is a research review of work directly applicable to each chapter's topic. A diagnostic test and test results analysis follow, providing a tool to indicate the potential bias of susceptibility. Finally, advice on managing the effects of each bias in order to minimize the effects of biases is offered.

CHAPTER 10

Mental Accounting Bias

There's no business like show business, but there are several businesses like accounting.
—David Letterman, Television Personality

BIAS DESCRIPTION

Bias Name: Mental accounting
Bias Type: Cognitive
Subtype: Information processing

General Description

First coined by University of Chicago professor Richard Thaler, *mental accounting* describes people's tendency to code, categorize, and evaluate economic outcomes by grouping their assets into any number of non-fungible (non-interchangeable) mental accounts.[1] A completely rational person would never succumb to this sort of psychological process because mental accounting causes subjects to take the irrational step of treating various sums of money differently based on where these sums are mentally categorized, for example, the way that a certain sum has been obtained (work, inheritance, gambling, bonus, etc.) or the nature of the money's intended use (leisure, necessities, etc.). Money is money, regardless of the source or intended use.

The concept of framing is important in mental accounting analysis. In framing, people alter their perspectives on money and investments according to the surrounding circumstances that they face. Thaler[2] performed an experiment in which he offered one group of people $30 and an accompanying choice: either pocket the money, no strings attached, or gamble on a coin toss, wherein a win would add $9 and a loss would subtract $9 from the initial $30 endowment. Seventy percent of the people offered this choice elected to gamble, because they considered the $30 to be "found" money—a little fortuitous windfall, not the sum of pennies meticulously saved and not the wages of hours spent slaving at some arduous task. So, why not have a little fun with this money? After all, what did these subjects really stand to lose?

A second group of people confronted a slightly different choice. Outright, they were asked: Would you rather gamble on a coin toss, in which you will receive $39 for a win and $21 for a loss? Or, would you rather simply pocket $30 and forgo the coin toss? The key distinction is that these people were not awarded $30, seemingly out of the blue, in the initial phase, as was the first group. Rather, at the outset of the exercise, the options were presented in terms of their ultimate payoffs. As you might expect, the second group reacted differently from the first. Only 34 percent of them chose to gamble, even though the economic prospects they faced were identical to those offered to group one. Sometimes people create mental accounts in order to justify actions that seem enticing but that are, in fact, unwise. Other times, people derive benefits from mental accounting; for example, earmarking money for retirement may prevent some households from spending that money prematurely. Such concepts will be explored at greater length later in this chapter.

Technical Description

Mental accounting refers to the coding, categorization, and evaluation of financial decisions. There are numerous interpretations of mental accounting, two of which will be reviewed here.

The first interpretation stems from Shefrin and Thaler's behavioral life-cycle theory, reviewed in the previous chapter, and submits that people mentally allocate wealth over three classifications: (1) current income, (2) current assets, and (3) future income. The propensity to consume is greatest from the current income account, while sums designated as future income are treated more conservatively.

Another interpretation of mental accounting describes how distinct financial decisions may be evaluated jointly (i.e., as though they pertain to the same mental account) or separately. For example, Kahneman and Tversky[3] conducted a study in which a majority of subjects declined to pay for a new theater ticket, which they were told would replace an identically priced ticket previously bought and lost. However, when the premise was altered and the subjects were told to imagine that they had not mislaid a previous ticket but, rather, an equivalent sum of cash—and so were contemplating the ticket purchase itself for the first time—a majority did decide to pay. Kahneman and Tversky concluded that subjects tended to evaluate the loss of a ticket and the purchase price of a new ticket in the same mental account; losing a ticket and shelling out for a new one would represent two losses incurred successively, debited from the same cluster of assets. The loss of actual cash, however, and the purchase of a ticket were debits evaluated separately. Therefore, the same aggregate loss felt less drastic when disbursed over two different accounts.

PRACTICAL APPLICATION

Marketing professors Drazen Prelec and Duncan Simester of Massachusetts Institute of Technology (MIT) brought mental accounting to life through an ingenious experiment.[4] Prelec and Simester organized a sealed-bid auction for tickets to a Boston Celtics game during the team's victorious Larry Bird era in the 1980s. Half the participants in the auction were told that whoever won the bidding would need to pay for the tickets in cash within 24 hours. The other half was informed that the winning bidder would pay by credit card. Prelec and Simester then compared the average bids put forth within each group. As predicted, bidders who thought that they were relying on their credit cards wagered, on average, nearly twice the average cash bid.

This experiment illustrated that people put money in separate "accounts" when presented with a financial decision. In this case, the auction participants value cash more highly than credit card remittances, even though both forms of payment draw, ultimately, from the participant's own money. People may allocate money to a "cash" (expenditures only paid in cash) account, while simultaneously placing additional funds in a "credit card" (expenditures only paid by credit card) account. Viewed in light of the life-cycle theory mentioned in the previous section, the cash might be more likely to represent a "current asset," and the credit card might represent "future income," which are two separate accounts. It probably goes without saying that this behavior touches on another bias previously reviewed: self-control.

Implications for Investors

Mental accounting is a deep-seated bias with many manifestations, and it can cause a variety of problems for investors. The most basic of these problems is the placement of investment assets into discrete "buckets" according to asset type, without regard for potential correlations connecting investments across categories. Tversky and Kahneman[5] contended that the difficulty individuals have in addressing interactions between investments leads investors to construct portfolios in a layered, pyramid format. Each tier addresses a particular investment goal independently of any additional investment goals. For example, when the objective is to preserve wealth, investors tend to target low-risk investments, like cash and money market funds. For income, they rely mostly on bonds and dividend-paying stocks. For a chance at a more drastic reward, investors turn to riskier instruments, like emerging market stocks and initial public offerings (IPOs). Combining different assets whose performances do *not* correlate with one another is an important consideration for risk reduction, but it is often neglected in this "pyramid" approach. As a result, investment positions held without regard to correlations might offset one another in a portfolio context, creating suboptimal inefficiencies. People quite often fail to evaluate a potential investment based on its contribution to overall portfolio return and aggregate portfolio risk; rather, they look only at the recent performance of the relevant asset layer. This common, detrimental oversight stems from mental accounting.

Below we review five investment mistakes that mental accounting can cause. Please note that this list is not exhaustive, as mental accounting bias is a vast, varied topic in application to private clients. Advice on each of the five potential pitfalls will follow in subsequent portions of this chapter.

MENTAL ACCOUNTING BIAS: BEHAVIORS THAT CAN CAUSE INVESTMENT MISTAKES

1. Mental accounting bias can cause people to imagine that their investments occupy separate "buckets," or accounts. These categories might include, for example, college fund or money for retirement. Envisioning distinct accounts to correspond with financial goals, however, can cause investors to neglect positions that offset or correlate across accounts. This can lead to suboptimal aggregate portfolio performance.
2. Mental accounting bias can cause investors to irrationally distinguish between returns derived from income and those derived from capital appreciation. Many people feel the need to preserve capital (i.e., principal) sums and prefer to spend interest. As a result, some investors chase income streams and can unwittingly erode principal in the process. Consider, for example, a high-income bond fund or a preferred stock that pays a high dividend yet, at times, can suffer a loss of principal due to interest rate fluctuations.

Mental accounting can make instruments like these appealing, but they may not benefit the investor in the long run.

3. Mental accounting bias can cause investors to allocate assets differently when employer stock is involved. Studies have shown that participants in company retirement plans that offer no company stock as an option tend to invest in a balanced way between equities and fixed-income instruments. However, when employer stock is an option, employees usually allocate a portion of contributions to company stock, with the remainder disbursed evenly over equity and fixed-income investments. Total equity allocation, then, could be too high when company stock was offered, causing these investors' portfolios to potentially be underdiversified. This can be a suboptimal condition because these investors do not fully comprehend the risk that exists in their portfolio.

4. In the same vein as anchoring bias, mental accounting bias can cause investors to succumb to the "house money" effect, wherein risk-taking behavior escalates as wealth grows. Investors exhibiting this rationale behave irrationally because they fail to treat all money as fungible. Biased financial decision making can, of course, endanger a portfolio. (In Research Review we will present some excellent research on the house money effect.)

5. Mental accounting bias can cause investors to hesitate to sell investments that once generated significant gains but, over time, have fallen in price. During the bull market of the 2000s, investors became accustomed to healthy, unrealized gains. When most investors had their net worth deflated by the market correction, they hesitated to sell their positions at the then-smaller profit margin. Many today still regret not reaping gains when they could; a number of investments to which people clung following the 1990s boom have become nearly worthless.

RESEARCH REVIEW

In their working paper entitled "An Experimental Examination of the House Money Effect in a Multi-Period Setting," Lucy F. Ackert, Narat Charupat, Bryan K. Church, and Richard Deaves cited evidence attesting to the influence exerted by prior monetary gains and losses over present-day risk-taking behavior. Their analysis confirmed that when endowed with "house money," people become more inclined to take risks. It is, incidentally, the first study to successfully employ an experimental methodology in corroborating the existence of "house money effect" in a dynamic, financial setting. The paper compared market outcomes across sessions that begin with participants benefiting from cash endowments at different levels (i.e., "low" versus "high" endowments). The study demonstrated that the traders' bids, their price predictions, and the market prices ultimately negotiated are all influenced by the level of the endowment that traders receive prior to trading. The paper carried significant implications for practitioners and investors: Namely, it implied that investors take more risks as wealth increases. This phenomenon, in turn, can endanger investors' portfolios. A rational investor should treat every dollar as "fungible"—of interchangeable value. However, if the value of each dollar decreases as the abundance of endowed dollars grows, then this assumption is clearly upset, and neoclassical theory no longer applies. Given the length and complexity of the paper, only one of the two main hypotheses will be reviewed. This hypothesis is that *market prices become higher when traders' endowments are larger.*

> *The purpose of the experiment is to test for a house money effect in a dynamic market setting. According to the house money effect, people are more willing to take risk after prior gains. To examine the impact of prior gains, we compare behavior across our low endowment (1 to 5) and high endowment (6 to 9) sessions. [Table 10.1] summarizes the experimental design. Across the sessions, we vary the initial endowment: low ($60) and high ($75). Each session*

TABLE 10.1   Experimental Design

Treatment	Session	Number of traders	Number of markets	Number of periods	Endowment of cash
Low endowment	1	8	6	3	$60
2	8	6	3	$60	
3	8	6	3	$60	
4	8	6	3	$60	
5	8	6	3	$60	
High endowment	6	8	8	3	$75
7	8	8	3	$75	
8	8	8	3	$75	
9	8	8	3	$75	

Source: Ackert, Charupat, Church, and Deaves (2003).

includes eight participants who bid to acquire a stock whose life is limited to a single period. Sessions include six or eight markets with three trading periods.

With larger monetary endowments, or more house money, market valuations will reflect greater risk taking. Traders with larger endowments will be more willing to gamble to acquire the stock, which translates into a higher market price for the stock. On this basis market prices are expected to differ across the two treatments. Hypothesis 1: The market price is higher when traders' endowments are larger. In testing hypothesis 1 we compare market prices across the low and high endowment treatments. Subsequent behavior is examined by looking at price changes in response to changes in market wealth. As a subset of the traders acquires the stock and the stock pays a positive dividend with a probability of 50 percent, incorporating the prior evolution of the market is important. Barberis, Huang, and Santos (2001)[6] assert that people are less risk averse as their wealth rises because prior gains cushion subsequent losses.

At the beginning of each session, participants receive a set of instructions and follow along as an experimenter reads aloud. Sessions 1 to 5 (6 to 9) consist of 6 (8) three-period markets. Participants are given tickets on which to record their bids for the stock. Prior to the beginning of each market period, participants are also asked to predict the purchase price of the stock for the upcoming period. Participants record their predictions on the confidential bid tickets. Participants are instructed that the roll of a die determines the dividend paid to asset holders at period end. If the roll of the die results in 1, 2, or 3, the dividend is $0, otherwise the dividend is $40, so that each dividend is equally likely. Participants are invited to examine the die at any time. The bidding procedure works as follows. All 8 participants submit sealed bids for the stock by recording the amount of money they are willing to pay for one share of stock. The four shares are allocated to the four highest bidders at the fifth highest bid. After the shares are allocated, one of the traders is specifically asked to observe the experimenter toss the die to ensure confidence that the dividend payment is randomly determined.

At the conclusion of the first period, the second period commences and four shares of an identical single-period stock are auctioned off in the exact same fashion. A trader's cash balance is carried forward across periods within a market. As before, subsequent to allocation with a Vickrey auction, a die roll determines *payout. A third period follows with identical procedures. The advantage of this approach is that it is possible to generate a reasonable number of identical dividend evolutions. Six or 8 markets are conducted in a similar manner bringing the session to a close. The traders' endowments are reinitialized at the beginning of each market. Subjects are told at the outset that they will be paid based on the results of only one of the markets, and this market is chosen by a die roll (or, in the case of sessions 6 to 9, by a card draw). Since ex ante the students have no way of knowing the identity of the payout market it is in their interest to treat all markets equally seriously. Participants' experimental earnings include their cash endowment, less payments to acquire stock, plus dividends earned on stock held in the one randomly selected market. In addition, the participant with the lowest absolute prediction error in the randomly selected market receives a bonus of $20. At the beginning of each period, participants are informed that the participant with the lowest sum of the three absolute prediction errors in the selected market will receive the bonus. At the conclusion of each session, participants compute the amount of cash they will receive and complete a post-experimental questionnaire. The purpose of the questionnaire is to collect general information about the participants and how they view the experiment. The average compensation across sessions 1 to 5 (6 to 9) is $66.75 ($79.66). Participants' responses on a post-experiment questionnaire indicate that they found the experiment interesting and the monetary incentives motivating.*

[Table 10.2] reports information concerning the prices, bids, and price predictions for each period in the low and high endowment treatments. Along with the number of observations (N), the table reports the mean, minimum, and maximum observed value. The final columns report the difference in means across the treatments and the p-value for a test of difference in means. The table reports the test results for hypothesis 1. The average initial price in the low endowment sessions is $17.10, while the average in the high endowment sessions is $20.37. Our results are consistent with a house money effect in a financial setting. Market prices are higher when traders have more found money. Further, the statistics reported in [Table 10.2] indicate that, compared to the low endowment sessions, average prices in the high endowment sessions are also significantly higher in periods 2 and 3 at $p < 0.05$. Thus, the house money effect persists over time.[7]

TABLE 10.2 Prices, Bids, and Predictions across Treatments

Period	Variable	Low Endowment Sessions				High Endowment Sessions					
		N	Mean	Min	Max	N	Mean	Min	Max	Difference in Mean	p-value
	Price	30	17.10	5.01	26.00	32	20.37	9.00	30.00	3.27	0.0336
1	Bid	240	19.70	0	60.00	256	24.95	0	75.00	5.25	0.0001
	Prediction	240	17.69	1.00	60.00	256	20.17	2.00	70.00	2.48	<0.0001
	Price	30	17.33	6.50	26.00	32	20.49	9.00	30.00	3.17	0.0334
2	Bid	240	19.97	0	87.25	256	22.10	0.01	92.00	2.13	0.0795
	Prediction	240	17.53	4.75	50.00	256	20.61	8.00	35.00	3.07	<0.0001
	Price	30	15.94	7.00	25.00	32	19.13	8.00	34.50	3.20	0.0296
3	Bid	240	19.13	0	99.01	256	22.13	0	100.00	3.00	0.0213
	Prediction	240	16.97	5.50	28.00	256	20.56	8.50	34.50	3.59	<0.0001

Source: Ackert, Charupat, Church, and Deaves (2003).

This excerpt is revealing because it describes, as experimentally observed, one of the irrational financial behaviors that can occur as a result of mental accounting. When people fail to consistently value their wealth—when, for example, their demonstrated risk aversion varies according to a criterion as arbitrary as endowment size—they distiniguish themseves sharply from Homo economicus. Moreover, they sometimes place their own financial security at risk.

DIAGNOSTIC TESTING

These questions are designed to detect signs of cognitive bias stemming from mental accounting. To complete the test, select the answer choice that best characterizes your response to each item.

Mental Accounting Bias Test

Question 1—Part A: Suppose that you are at a warehouse store, where you intend to purchase a flat screen television. The model you've selected is priced at $750, and you are about to pay. However, at the last minute, you notice a discarded advertising flier featuring the same television—at a price of $720. You retrieve the ad, examine it more closely, and discover that the offer is still valid. To receive the discount, you'll need to drive to a competing electronics outlet about 10 minutes away. Will you get into your car and travel to the other store to take advantage of the lower price?
a. Yes.
b. No.

Question 1—Part B: Now suppose that you are in the same warehouse store, this time to buy a mahogany table. The table that you want costs $4,000, and you are willing to pay. While you are waiting, you strike up a conversation with another store patron, who reveals that she's seen the same table available for $3,970 at a competing local furniture store about 10 minutes away. Will you get into your car and drive to the other store to obtain the lower price?
a. Yes.
b. No.

Question 2—Part A: Suppose that you have purchased a ticket to a concert by your favorite music artist. You arrive at the venue excited, but quickly panic as you realize that you have misplaced your ticket! You paid $100 for the ticket initially and discover that some similar seats are still available at the same price. What is the probability that you will purchase another $100 ticket in order to see the show?

a. 100 percent.

b. 50 percent.

c. 0 percent.

Question 2—Part B: Suppose that you have not purchased any concert tickets in advance but planned to buy one for $100 at the door. When you arrive at the box office to buy your ticket, you panic because you realize you've lost $100 on the subway en route to the show. There is an ATM close by, so you can still get cash and purchase a ticket. What is the probability that you will make a cash withdrawal and then purchase a ticket for $100 to see the show?

a. 100 percent.

b. 50 percent.

c. 0 percent.

Question 3—Part A: Suppose that you've taken half a day off work to shop for a new, ride-on lawn mower. You have a big yard, and trimming it with your current, push-propelled mower simply takes too long. You have been eyeing the Model A300, which offers all the features you require at a cost of $2,000. As luck would have it, you won $500 the previous evening playing bingo at your local Rotary Club. When you arrive at the lawn mower shop, you notice that they also stock Model A305, which has some fancy, desirable new options. This premium model costs $2,250. Considering the previous night's winnings, what is the probability that you will indulge yourself by purchasing the A305?

a. 100 percent.

b. 50 percent.

c. 0 percent.

Question 3—Part B: Suppose that your budget and your needs regarding the lawn mower are exactly as described in Question 3A and that again you've taken half a day off work to go buy the simpler-but-sufficient A300. However, imagine that while you've not been especially lucky at bingo, you do discover a $500 check in your jacket pocket. You recall that the money was a gift from your mother last year, something to be "put away for a rainy day." You apparently forgot that you put it in your jacket and have just come up on it. When you arrive at the lawn mower shop, you again notice the pricier A305 for $2,250, with its coveted, innovative mowing features. Considering the check you just found, what is the probability that you will go ahead and purchase the A305?

a. 100 percent.

b. 50 percent.

c. 0 percent.

Test Results Analysis

Question 1—Parts A and B: Most people would probably drive an extra 10 minutes to save $30 on the television but wouldn't go to the same trouble to save the same amount of money on the table. While both scenarios net a savings of $30, a typical mental accounting scheme doesn't envision things this way. So people who are more likely to go out of their way to receive a discount in Part A than in Part B are likely susceptible to mental accounting bias.

Question 2—Parts A and B: If the respondent is like most people, he or she answered "no" to the first question and "yes" to the second, even though both scenarios present the same prospect: an initial loss of $100, an additional $100 outlay for the ticket. Mental accounting causes people to perceive in the first scenario an aggregate cost of $200 for the show—two tickets, each costing $100. Conversely, for most people the loss of $100 cash and the additional $100 ticket price are somehow separate in the second scenario. Mentally, these sums are debited from two independent categories or accounts, meaning that no single, larger loss of $200 ever registers. In both cases, of course, the concert costs $200. If the respondent indicated a greater willingness to pay for a ticket in Part B than in Part A, then mental accounting bias is likely present.

Question 3—Parts A and B: Most people would answer "yes" in Part A and "no" in Part B. They would be willing to allocate the bingo winnings but not the check from mom toward the purchase of the premium lawn mower. This is because most people engage in mental accounting. In this instance, mental accounting values dollars obtained from different sources differently. However, money is indeed fungible. Responses demonstrate that this all-too-typical inconsistency between Parts A and B probably indicates mental accounting bias.

ADVICE

The following advice has been incremented to correspond to each of the five investment errors discussed in the box earlier. It is important to note that mental accounting is very common and that nearly everyone is susceptible to this bias in some way or another. Remember, moreover, that mental accounting can sometimes serve as a beneficial rather than as a harmful cognitive mechanism for investors. This section concludes with a special "bonus" discussion of the helpful aspects of mental accounting.

Correlations between Investment "Buckets"

The most effective method to prevent investors from viewing their money in terms of discrete investment buckets is demonstrating how investments identified with separate mental accounts can actually correlate with one another, impacting portfolio performance. A straightforward discussion of the harms of excessive correlation and the benefits of sufficient diversification ought to effectively refute the bucket rationale. Since mental accounting is a cognitive bias, education can often defeat it.

Total Returns as Priority

The best way to prevent mental accounting from weakening total returns is to remind your client that total returns are, after all, the number-one priority of any allocation. A renewed focus on global portfolio performance—not simply piecemeal aspects, such as principal or income—is often achievable. As clients become more conscious of total returns, they will likely recognize the pitfalls of excessive mental accounting, and the problem will remedy itself.

Company Stock and Diversification

Persuading clients to diversify away from company stock is indeed a theme that emerges again and again in contending with various behavioral biases. This problem arises once more with mental accounting. As in previous instances involving portfolios overly dominated by company stock, the client must be educated as to the benefits of a balanced, diversified portfolio. Excessive concentration in any stock is not good, but a variety of behavioral biases can crop up and cause investors to feel irrationally comfortable with their own companies' stocks.

House Money Effect

As the research review demonstrates, the house money effect is a manifestation of mental accounting that can cause people to take on more risk as their wealth increases. This specific bias is perhaps the most pernicious of any reviewed in this chapter; however, education can help clients overcome it. Gentle but straightforward reminders regarding the risk of a chosen investment or the fungibility of money in general can diminish the house money effect. The house money effect causes investors to devalue a dollar as aggregate dollars accumulate. Recall that this rationale causes investors to devalue individual dollars. They sense that they are now playing with the "house's" money, not their own. Remember, dollars won or found seem, for many people, irrationally expendable. When clients appear subject to the house money effect, it is crucial to stress the underlying truth that *a dollar equals a dollar*—no matter which mental account each dollar occupies.

Clinging to Formerly Gainful Investments

Mental accounting bias prevailed during the collapse of the tech boom in 2000 and 2001. Any investor who recalls those years should be somewhat inoculated against this behavior. Unfortunately, however, many people have short memories. If a company's prospects today do not look good and if it is still possible to divest from that company and capture a gain, then the client should evacuate the position immediately. The investment may have generated great profits in the past, but most clients should rationally grasp that the present-day outlook matters most. A convenient reminder is: "No one ever got hurt taking a profit."

Bonus Section: The Potential Benefits of Mental Accounting

It is important for practitioners to recognize that mental accounting can sometimes generate benefits. If clients regard college funds or retirement funds, for example, as sacrosanct, then they may be less inclined to disturb sound long-term investment plans by interfering with money stashed away. Of course, an instinct to preserve certain assets does not guarantee that those assets will be managed wisely. In the instance of a college fund, practitioners should recommend multiple shifts toward more conservative investments as the child's teen years approach. This will likely result in less resistance to change when reallocating funds.

Some financial advisors adhere to "goals-based planning," which leverages mental accounting for the benefit of the client. These practitioners argue that clients should set multiple, distinct investment goals, a practice that contrasts with many interpretations of traditional investment theory. Conventional approaches suggest that an allocation should be oriented toward total portfolio gains. Risk, in this view, is likewise managed at the global portfolio level, using an estimate of an investor's overall risk tolerance. Daniel Nevins argued that it is difficult to reconcile this single portfolio framework with the existence of separate mental accounts linked to specific investment goals.[8] An alternative to this traditional approach is to allow more than one strategy, as discussed also by Jean Brunel: "Each strategy is linked to a goal and managed according to the risk measures and risk tolerance that are most appropriate for that goal. This approach, which we call goals-based investing, is compatible with mental accounting. Another advantage is that it manages the risk of not achieving goals rather than relying on traditional risk measures."[9]

So, there are observable benefits of mental accounting. Practitioners, moreover, can often leverage this bias to the benefit of their clients. The next section outlines the practical application of an asset allocation strategy that can be used in this regard.

THE BEHAVIORAL FINANCE APPROACH TO ASSET ALLOCATION BASED ON MENTAL ACCOUNTING

Leveraging the power of mental accounting for the benefit of attaining financial goals, taking a behavioral finance or "goals-based" approach to asset allocation is helpful in order to keep financial goals in mind when creating a portfolio. I have found the following approach, outlined in Figure 10.1, and based on clients' tendencies to put money in separate mental accounts, to be of tremendous value. What advisors should aspire to do is to get their clients focused on their needs and obligations, and make sure that they have enough of their portfolio carved out in capital preservation assets to meet

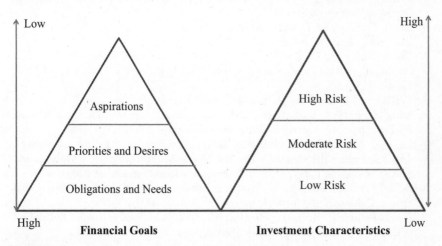

FIGURE 10.1 Behavioral Finance or Goals Based Approach to Asset Allocation

those needs and obligations. Next, if desired, more risk can be taken to attain one's priorities and expectations, and, even more risk to meet one's desires and aspirations. At the end of the process, advisors usually end up with a normal-looking, diversified portfolio, though it will likely differ from a portfolio based on traditional mean-variance framework. However, the components of the portfolio are individually justified based on needs and obligations versus priorities, and expectations versus desires and aspirations.

Financial advisers using this approach will typically first estimate how much should be invested in low-risk (capital preservation) assets to meet those needs and obligations. Next, riskier assets are considered to attain priorities and desires. Finally, even riskier assets are added to meet one's aspirational goals. Typically, investors will end up having a diversified portfolio using this approach, but the resulting portfolio may not be efficient from a traditional finance perspective. The lack of efficiency stems from the components of the portfolio being individually justified rather than based on modern portfolio theory that considers correlations between investments. However, investors may be better able to understand risk by using this methodology. As a result, investors may find it easier to adhere to investment decisions and portfolio allocations made.

NOTES

1. Richard H. Thaler, "Towards a Positive Theory of Consumer Choice," *Journal of Economic Behavior and Organization* 1 (1980): 39–60.
2. Richard H. Thaler, "Mental Accounting Matters," *Journal of Behavioral Decision Making* 12, no. 3: 183–206.
3. Amos Tversky and Daniel Kahneman, "Rational Choice and the Framing of Decisions," *Journal of Business* 59 (1986): S251–S278.
4. Drazen Prelec and Duncan Simester, "Always Leave Home without It: A Further Investigation of the Credit Card Effect on Willingness to Pay," *Marketing Letters* 12, no. 1: 5–12.
5. Tversky and Kahneman, "Rational Choice" (see 3).
6. Ming Hang, Nicholas Barberis, and Tano Santos, "Prospect Theory and Asset Prices," *Quarterly Journal of Economics* (February 2001).
7. Lucy F. Ackert, Narat Charupat, Bryan K. Church, and Richard Deaves, "An Experimental Examination of the House Money Effect in a Multi-Period Setting" (working paper, Federal Reserve of Atlanta, September 2003).
8. Daniel Nevins, "Goals-Based Investing: Integrating Traditional and Behavioral Finance," *Journal of Wealth Management* (Spring 2004): 8–23.
9. Jean L. P. Brunel, "Revisiting the Asset Allocation Challenge through a Behavioral Finance Lens," *Journal of Wealth Management* (Fall 2003): 10–20.

CHAPTER 11

Anchoring and Adjustment Bias

*To reach a port we must sail, sometimes with the wind, and
sometimes against it. But we must not drift or lie at anchor.*
—Oliver Wendell Holmes

BIAS DESCRIPTION

Bias Name: Anchoring and adjustment
Bias Type: Cognitive
Subtype: Information processing

General Description

When required to estimate a value with unknown magnitude, people generally begin by envisioning some initial, default number—an "anchor"—which
they then adjust up or down to reflect subsequent information and analysis.
The anchor, once fine-tuned and reassessed, matures into a final estimate.
Numerous studies demonstrate that regardless of how the initial anchors
were chosen, people tend to adjust their anchors insufficiently and produce
end approximations that are, consequently, biased. People are generally
better at estimating relative comparisons rather than absolute figures, which
the following example illustrates.

Suppose you are asked whether the population of Canada is greater than
or less than 20 million. Obviously, you will answer either above 20 million
or below 20 million. If you were then asked to guess an absolute population

value, your estimate would probably fall somewhere near 20 million, because you are likely subject to anchoring by your previous response.

Technical Description

Anchoring and adjustment is a psychological heuristic that influences the way people intuit probabilities. Investors exhibiting this bias are often influenced by purchase "points"—or arbitrary price levels or price indexes—and tend to cling to these numbers when facing questions like "Should I buy or sell this security?" or "Is the market overvalued or undervalued right now?" This is especially true when the introduction of new information regarding the security further complicates the situation. Rational investors treat these new pieces of information objectively and do not reflect on purchase prices or target prices in deciding how to act. Anchoring and adjustment bias, however, implies that investors perceive new information through an essentially warped lens. They place undue emphasis on statistically arbitrary, psychologically determined anchor points. Decision making therefore deviates from neoclassically prescribed "rational" norms.

PRACTICAL APPLICATION

This chapter reviews one miniature case study and provides an accompanying analysis and interpretation that will demonstrate investor potential for anchoring and adjustment bias.

Miniature Case Study: Anchoring and Adjustment Bias

Case Presentation   Suppose Alice owns stock in Corporation ABC. She is a fairly astute investor and has recently discovered some new information about ABC. Her task is to evaluate this information for the purpose of deciding whether she should increase, decrease, or simply maintain her holdings in ABC. Alice bought ABC two years ago at $12, and the stock is now at $15. Several months ago, ABC reached $20 after a surprise announcement of higher-than-expected earnings, at which time Alice contemplated selling the stock but did not. Unfortunately, ABC then dropped to $15 after executives were accused of faulty accounting practices. Today, Alice feels as though she has "lost" 25 percent of the stock's value, and she would prefer to wait and sell her shares in ABC once it returns to its recent $20 high.

Alice has a background in accounting, and she does some research that leads her to conclude that ABC's methods are indeed faulty, but not extremely so. However, Alice cannot entirely gauge the depth of the problem and realizes that holding ABC contains risk, but ABC is also a viable corporate entity with good prospects. Alice must make a decision. On one hand, she has confirmed that ABC does have an accounting problem, and she is unsure of how severe the problem might become. On the other hand, the company has a solid business, and Alice wants to recoup the 25 percent that she feels she lost. What should Alice do?

Analysis Most investors have been confronted with situations similar to this one. They decide to invest in a stock; the stock goes up and then declines. Investors become conflicted and must evaluate the situation to determine whether to hold on to the stock. A rational investor would examine the company's financial situation; make an objective assessment of its business fundamentals; and then decide to buy, hold, or sell the shares. Conversely, some irrational investors—even after going through the trouble of performing the aforementioned rational analysis—permit cognitive errors to cloud their judgment. Alice, for example, may irrationally disregard the results of her research and "anchor" herself to the $20 figure, refusing to sell unless ABC once again achieves that price. This type of response reflects an irrational behavioral bias and should be avoided.

Implications for Investors A wide variety of investor behaviors can indicate susceptibility to anchoring and adjustment bias. Below we highlight some important examples of which investors and advisors should be aware.

Some excellent research into the effects of anchoring and adjustment was performed in 1987 by University of Arizona researchers Gregory Northcraft and Margaret Neale.[1] Their study asked a group of real estate professionals to value a property after being given a proposed selling price quoted by the researchers at the outset of the experiment. The agents were also given 20 minutes to examine the premises before being asked to estimate its worth. Specifically, the study asked each researcher to provide the appraised value of the property, the value of the property should it be put up for sale, the price that a potential buyer should be advised to regard as reasonable, and the minimum offer that the seller should be advised to accept. Table 11.1 summarizes the results with respect to the first two categories—appraised value and salable value (the remaining estimates followed patterns similar to those evidenced here).

During the experiment, the real estate agents were divided into two groups. Each group received a guided tour of the home, a 10-page packet of information describing the home, and a list price for the property. The two trials proceeded identically but with one twist: The first group of agents was quoted a list price higher than that quoted to the second group (for details, please see Table 11.1). When both groups subsequently appraised the

RESEARCH REVIEW

ANCHORING AND ADJUSTMENT BIAS: BEHAVIORS THAT CAN CAUSE INVESTOR MISTAKES

1. Investors tend to make general market forecasts that are too close to current levels. For example, if the Dow Jones Industrial Average (DJIA) is at 10,500, investors are likely to forecast the index in a way narrower than what might be suggested by historical fluctuation. For example, an investor subject to anchoring might forecast the DJIA to fall between 10,000 and 11,000 at year-end, versus making an absolute estimate based on historical standard deviation (rational) analysis.

2. Investors (and securities analysts) tend to stick too closely to their original estimates when new information is learned about a company. For example, if an investor determines that next year's earnings estimate is $2 per share and the company subsequently falters, the investor may not readjust the $2 figure enough to reflect the change because he or she is "anchored" to the $2 figure. This is not limited to downside adjustments—the same phenomenon occurs when companies have upside surprises. (At the end of the chapter, we will review a behaviorally based investment strategy leveraging this concept that has proven to be effective at selecting investments.)

3. Investors tend to make a forecast of the percentage that a particular asset class might rise or fall based on the current level of returns. For example, if the DJIA returned 10 percent last year, investors will be anchored on this number when making a forecast about next year.

4. Investors can become anchored on the economic states of certain countries or companies. For example, in the 1980s, Japan was an economic powerhouse, and many investors believed that they would remain so for decades. Unfortunately for some, Japan stagnated for years after the late 1980s. Similarly, IBM was a bellwether stock for decades. Some investors became anchored to the idea that IBM would always be a bellwether. Unfortunately for some, IBM did not last as a bellwether stock.

TABLE 11.1 Estimates by Real Estate Agents in Northcraft and Neale's 1987 Study

Real Estate Agent Group 1	Real Estate Agent Group 2
Given asking price = $119,900	Given asking price = $149,900
Predicted appraisal value = $144,202	Predicted appraisal value = $128,752
Listing price = $117,745	Listing price = $130,981
Purchase price = $111,454	Purchase price = $127,316
Lowest acceptable offer = $111,136	Lowest acceptable offer = $111,136

Reprinted from Gregory Northcroft and Margaret Neale, "Experts, Amateurs, and Real Estate: An Anchoring-and-Adjustment Perspective on Property Pricing Decisions," *Organizational Behavior and Human Decision Processes* 39(1) (1987): 84–97. Copyright © 1987, with permission from Elsevier.

property, anchoring and adjustment theory held: other things held constant, the higher proposed list price was determined to have led to higher appraisal estimates. The appraisals, then, did not necessarily reflect the objective characteristics of the property. Rather, they were influenced by the initial values on which the agents "anchored" their estimates.

This study clearly demonstrated that anchoring is a very common bias, applying to many areas of finance and business decision making. Wealth management practitioners need to be keenly aware of this behavior and its effects.

Any time someone fixates on a fact or figures that should not rationally factor in at the anticipated decision juncture, that decision becomes potentially subject to the adverse effects of anchoring. The observations recorded in Table 11.1 regarding the real estate study are anchored by reference points that have no bearing on the future prospects of the property in question. Real-life investors likewise need to guard against the natural human tendency toward anchoring, lest their calculations become similarly swayed.

DIAGNOSTIC TESTING

In this section, we outline a hypothetical decision-making problem and discuss how and why various reactions to this problem may or may not indicate susceptibility to anchoring and adjustment bias.

Anchoring and Adjustment Bias Test

Scenario: Suppose you have decided to sell your house and downsize by acquiring a townhouse that you have been eyeing for several years. You do not feel extreme urgency in selling your house, but the associated taxes are eating into your monthly cash flow, and you want to unload the property as soon as possible. Your real estate agent, whom you have known for many years, prices your home at $900,000—you are shocked. You paid $250,000 for the home only 15 years ago, and the $900,000 figure is almost too thrilling to believe. You place the house on the market and wait a few months, but you don't receive any nibbles. One day, your real estate agent calls, suggesting that the two of you meet right away. When he arrives, he tells you that PharmaGrowth, a company that moved into town eight years ago in conjunction with its much-publicized initial public offering (IPO), has just declared Chapter 11 bankruptcy. Now, 7,500 people are out of work. Your agent has been in meetings all week with his colleagues, and together they estimate that local real estate prices have taken a hit of about 10 percent across the board. Your agent tells you that you must decide the price at which you want to list your home, based on this new information. You tell him that you will think it over and get back to him shortly.

> **Question:** Assume your house is at the mean in terms of quality and salability. What is your likeliest course of action?
> 1. You decide to keep your home on the market for $900,000.
> 2. You decide to lower your price by 5 percent, and ask $855,000.
> 3. You decide to lower your price by 10 percent, and ask $810,000.
> 4. You decide to lower your price to $800,000 because you want to be sure that you will get a bid on the house.

Test Results Analysis

A tendency toward either of the first two responses probably indicates susceptibility of the subject to anchoring and adjustment bias. Remember that real estate prices here have declined 10 percent. If the subject wants to sell his or her home, he or she clearly must lower the price by 10 percent. Resistance to an adequate adjustment in price can stem, however, from being anchored to the $900,000 figure. Anchoring bias impairs the subject's ability to incorporate updated information. This behavior can have significant impact in the investment arena and should be counseled extensively.

ADVICE

Before delving into specific strategies for dealing with anchoring and adjustment, it's important and, perhaps, uplifting to note that you can actually exploit this bias to your advantage. Understanding anchoring and adjustment can, for example, be a powerful asset when negotiating. Many negotiation experts suggest that the participants communicate radically strict initial positions, arguing that an opponent subject to anchoring can be influenced even when the anchor values are extreme. If one party begins a negotiation by offering a given price or condition, then the other party's subsequent counteroffer will likely reflect that anchor. So, when negotiating, it is wise to start with an offer much less generous than reflects your actual position (beware, however, of overdoing this). When presenting someone with a set of options, state first the options that you would most prefer that the other party select. Conversely, if a rival negotiator makes a first bid, do not assume that this number closely approximates a potential final price.

From the investment perspective, awareness is the best countermeasure to anchoring and adjustment bias. When you are advising clients on the sale of a security, encourage clients to ask themselves: "Am I analyzing the situation rationally, or am I holding out to attain an anchored price?" When making forecasts about the direction or magnitude of markets or individual securities, ask yourself: "Is my estimate rational, or am I anchored to last year's performance figures?" Taking these sorts of actions will undoubtedly root out any anchoring and adjustment bias that might take hold during asset sales or asset reallocation.

Finally, when considering a recommendation by a securities analyst, delve further into the research and ask yourself: "Is this analyst anchored to some previous estimate, or is the analyst putting forth an objective rational response to a change in a company's business fundamentals?" Investment professionals are not immune to the effects of anchoring and adjustment bias. In fact, there is an investment strategy that can leverage this behavior, which will be discussed in the "bonus discussion."

BONUS DISCUSSION: INVESTMENT STRATEGIES THAT LEVERAGE ANCHORING AND ADJUSTMENT BIAS

An awareness of the mechanics of anchoring and adjustment can actually serve as a fundamental tenet of a successful investment strategy. Some finance professionals leverage anchoring and adjustment bias by observing patterns in securities analyst earnings upgrades (downgrades) on various stocks and then purchasing (selling) the stocks in response. The behavioral aspect of this strategy is that it takes advantage of the tendency exhibited by securities analysts to underestimate, both positively and negatively, the magnitudes of earnings fluctuations due to anchoring and adjustment bias.

As previously noted, when issuing upgrades and downgrades, analysts anchor on their initial estimates, which can be exploited. If an analyst is anchored to an earnings estimate and earnings are rising, this is an opportunity for investors to win, as it is likely that the analyst is underestimating the magnitude of the earnings upgrades. Conversely, if an analyst is anchored to an earnings estimate and earnings are falling, this is an opportunity to lose, so it's best to sell immediately on the first earnings downgrade, as it is likely that the analyst is underestimating the magnitude of the earnings downgrades.

In sum, we have learned that we need to be aware of the tendency toward anchoring and adjustment bias and the ill effects it can have on our portfolios. At the same time, we can leverage it to our advantage in certain cases, such as in negotiation and in the investment strategy just reviewed.

NOTES

1. Gregory Northcraft and Margaret Neale, "Experts, Amateurs, and Real Estate: An Anchoring-and-Adjustment Perspective on Property Pricing Decisions," *Organizational Behavior and Human Decision Processes* 39 (1987): 84–97.

CHAPTER 12

Framing Bias

You better cut the pizza in four pieces, because I'm not hungry enough to eat six.

—Yogi Berra

BIAS DESCRIPTION

Bias Name: Framing bias

Bias Type: Cognitive

Subtype: Information processing

General Description

Framing bias notes the tendency of decision makers to respond to various situations differently, based on the context in which a choice is presented (framed). This can happen in a number of contexts, including how word problems are described, how data is presented in tables and charts, and how figures are illustrated. For example, take a look at Figure 12.1. Which line is longer?

People subject to visual framing bias experience an optical illusion, which leads them to insist that the line on the bottom is longer. The graphic is reproduced, however, in Figure 12.2, this time with vertical marks added in as a guide. Which line is longer?

With the framing effect of the "arrow" detail neutralized, it becomes clear that the line on the top and the line on the bottom are equal in length.

In the context of everyday evidence of framing bias, we can look at how retailers price their products. Many grocers, for example, will price items in multiples: "2 for $2" or "3 for $7."

143

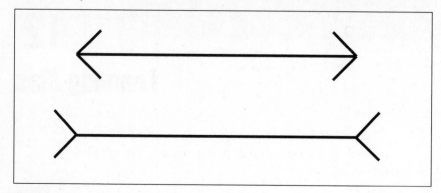

FIGURE 12.1 Which Line Is Longer?

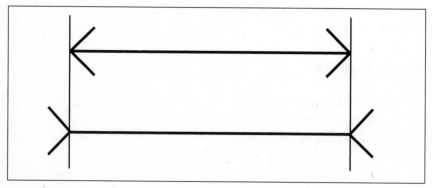

FIGURE 12.2 Which Line Is Longer?

This doesn't necessarily imply, however, that any kind of bulk discount is being offered. Have you ever found an item priced at "3 for $7" also available at a unit price of $2.33? This isn't unusual. Shopping represents a rudimentary rational choice problem ("How many oranges should I buy?"), and good salespeople try to frame a solution for a buyer that benefits the store. "Don't buy oranges in units of one," suggests the price policy. "Buy them in multiples of three." This takes advantage of people's susceptibility to framing. Applications to investing will follow later in the chapter.

Technical Description

A decision frame is the decision maker's subjective conception of the acts, outcomes, and contingencies associated with a particular choice. The frame that a decision maker adopts is controlled partly by the formulation of the problem and partly by the norms, habits, and personal characteristics of the decision maker.

It is often possible to frame a given decision problem in more than one way. Framing effects occur when preferences change as a function of some variation in framing. For example, one prospect can be formulated in two ways: as a gain ("25 percent of crops will be saved if they are provided with fertilizer XYZ") or as a loss ("75 percent of crops will die without fertilizer XYZ"). Most people in the first case will adopt a gain frame, which generally leads to risk-averse behavior. In the second case—75 percent of crops will die—most people will adopt a loss frame and thereby become more likely to engage in risk-seeking behavior.

Framing bias also encompasses a sub-categorical phenomenon known as *narrow framing,* which occurs when people focus too restrictively on one or two aspects of a situation, excluding other crucial aspects and thus compromising their decision making. For example, take the case of a lawnmower purchase. A consumer working within too narrow a frame of reference might shop for a mower that is fast, while overlooking blade width, fuel economy, and other factors that affect the length of time required to mow a lawn.

PRACTICAL APPLICATION

Decision frames are quite prevalent in the context of investor behavior. Building on the definitions outlined in the preceding section, we can now use our newly acquired insights into framing bias as we consider a typical investor risk tolerance questionnaire. This will demonstrate how framing bias is applied in practice and how advisors should be aware of its effects.

Suppose that an investor completes a risk tolerance questionnaire for the purpose of determining the "risk category" into which he or she falls. The responses the investor selects are highly relevant because the risk category outcome will determine the types of investments that are selected for this individual's portfolio. Ideally, question phrasing and framing—elements uncorrelated with the investor's actual level of risk tolerance—should not be factors that affect the questionnaire's results. Let's examine some of the material that might appear on a typical risk tolerance questionnaire.

First, suppose that the items on the questionnaire refer to a hypothetical securities portfolio, Portfolio ABC. Over a 10-year period, ABC has historically returned an annual average of 10 percent, with a standard deviation of 15 percent. (Recall that standard deviation quantifies the amount of expected variation in an investment's performance from year to year.) Basic statistics dictate that 67 percent of ABCs returns will fall within one standard deviation of the mean, or annual average, return that ABC generates.

Similarly, 95 percent of returns will fall within two standard deviations, and 99.7 percent within three standard deviations of the mean. So, if ABC's mean return was 10 percent and its standard deviation was 15 percent, then two-thirds of all returns produced by ABC would equal 10 percent plus-or-minus no more than 15 percent; that is, 67 percent of the time, ABC's return will likely be somewhere between −5 percent and 25 percent. It follows that 95 percent of ABC's returns will fall between −20 percent and 40 percent and that 99.7 percent will fall somewhere between −35 percent and 55 percent.

Now, imagine that one, but not both, of the following questions is to appear on an investor's risk tolerance questionnaire. Both concern Portfolio ABC, and both try to measure an investor's comfort level with ABC, given its average returns, volatility, and so on. However, the two questions frame the situation very differently. As you compare questions 1 and 2, try to imagine how an average investor, probably subject to a few common behavioral biases, might respond to each respective frame. Do you think most investors' answers would be identical in each instance?

1. Based on Table 12.1, which investment portfolio seems like the best fit, bearing in mind your own risk tolerance as well as your desire for long-term return?
   a. Portfolio XYZ
   b. Portfolio DEF
   c. Portfolio ABC
2. Assume that you own Portfolio ABC and that it lost 15 percent of its value over the past year, despite previous years of good performance. This loss is consistent with the performance of similar funds during the past year. What is your reaction to this situation?
   a. Sell all Portfolio ABC shares.
   b. Sell some, but not all, Portfolio ABC shares.
   c. Continue to hold Portfolio ABC shares.
   d. Increase investment in Portfolio ABC.

TABLE 12.1 Portfolio Selection: Which Portfolio Seems Best?

Portfolio Number	95% Probability Gain/Loss Range	Long-Term Return
XYZ	2% to 4%	3%
DEF	−6% to 18%	6%
ABC	−20% to 40%	10%

There is a chance that a person will select similar answers for both questions. However, there is also a significant probability that inconsistent framing will generate inconsistent responses from many investors. Specifically, respondents might reject Portfolio ABC in Question 1, yet decide to proceed with ABC in Question 2.

In Question 1, "95 Percent Probability Gain/Loss Range" refers (in Table 12.1) to an interval of two standard deviations above and below the mean. In 95 percent of all cases, ABC returned 10 percent plus-or-minus 30 percent; its standard deviation is 15 percent.

In Question 2, ABC produced a return that, in two-thirds of all cases, would have been the worst return imaginable: It returned one standard deviation below the mean. However, because Question 2 employs one standard deviation rather than two, readers are less likely to consider the one-third of all cases in which ABC could lose more than 5 percent of its value (entering into the 95 percent, rather than the 67 percent, probable gain/loss range).

Like the method employed by grocers (pricing produce in multiples), which subtly suggests some arbitrary, benchmark quantity of oranges for purchase, Question 1 similarly invites people to more intuitively consider the rarer, heavier losses Portfolio ABC could incur if returns breached the 67 percent confidence interval. Here, the implications of framing are important: Inconsistent responses to Questions 1 and 2 could make the questionnaire inconsistent and an inaccurate measure of investor risk tolerance (the questionnaire's outcome would be, accordingly, a flawed basis for structuring an allocation). Practitioners need to be acutely aware of how framing can affect the outcome of various investment choices.

Implications for Investors

An individual's willingness to accept risk can be influenced by how questions/scenarios are framed—positively or negatively. Recall, for example, the subjective difference between "25 percent of crops will be saved" and "75 percent of crops will die." The same optimism or pessimism in framing can affect investment decision making. For example, suppose that Mrs. Smith chooses to invest in either Portfolio A or Portfolio B. Further suppose that Portfolios A and B are identical in every respect. Mrs. Smith learns that Portfolio A will offer her a 70 percent chance of attaining her financial goals, whereas Portfolio B offers Mrs. Smith a 30 percent chance of not attaining her financial goals. If Mrs. Smith is like most people, she will choose Portfolio A, because its performance prospects were more attractively framed.

Another key point to keep in mind is that framing bias and loss aversion bias can and do work together. When people have suffered losses, they may view losses as the right time to embark on risk-taking behavior; when people have gained, they may feel threatened by options that entail additional risk. For example, an investor who has just suffered a net loss is likely to seek risk with his or her investments. Someone who has gained, however, is more likely to opt for a sure thing.

In the following we review four investor mistakes caused by framing bias.

RESEARCH REVIEW

In their 1984 paper entitled "Choices, Values, and Frames," Daniel Kahneman and Amos Tversky[1] studied framing bias in a sample population of physicians, posing the following question to each participating doctor:

> *Imagine that the U.S. is preparing for the outbreak of an unusual Asian disease, which is expected to kill 600 people. Two alternative programs to combat the disease have been proposed. Assume that the exact scientific estimates of the consequences of the programs are as follows: If program A is adopted, 200 people will be saved. If program B is adopted, there is a one-third probability that 600 people will be saved and a two-thirds probability that no people will be saved. Which of the two programs would you favor?*

FRAMING BIAS: BEHAVIORS THAT CAN CAUSE INVESTMENT MISTAKES

1. Depending on how questions are asked, framing bias can cause investors to communicate responses to questions about risk tolerance that are either unduly conservative or unduly aggressive. For example, when questions are worded in the "gain" frame, a risk-averse response is more likely. When questions are worded in the "loss" frame, risk-seeking behavior is the likely response.
2. The optimistic or pessimistic manner in which an investment or asset allocation recommendation is framed can affect people's willingness or lack of willingness to invest. Optimistically worded questions are more likely to garner affirmative responses, and optimistically worded answer choices are more likely to be selected than pessimistically phrased alternatives. Framing contexts are often arbitrary and uncorrelated and therefore shouldn't impact investors' judgments ... but, they do.

3. *Narrow framing,* a subset of framing bias, can cause even long-term investors to obsess over short-term price fluctuations in a single industry or stock. This behavior works in concert with myopic loss aversion (see Chapter 17): The risk here is that by focusing only on short-term market fluctuations, excessive trading may be the result. This trading behavior has proven to be less than optimal for investors.

4. Framing and loss aversion can work together to explain excessive risk aversion. An investor who has incurred a net loss becomes likelier to select a riskier investment, whereas a net gainer feels predisposed toward less risky alternatives.

As previously noted, people answer questions differently based on how the questions are framed—either positively or negatively. Notice that the preceding dilemma is positively framed, focusing on the expected number of "lives saved" in each scenario. When the question was framed in this manner, 72 percent of physicians chose "A," the safe-and-sure strategy: only 28 percent preferred to accept the risks inherent in option "B."

Another statistically identical population of physicians was posed the same basic question. In this trial, however, the scenario was framed negatively:

Imagine that the U.S. is preparing for the outbreak of an unusual Asian disease, which is expected to kill 600 people. Two alternative programs to combat the disease have been proposed. Assume that the exact scientific estimates of the consequences of the programs are as follows: If program C is adopted, 400 people will die. If program D is adopted, there is a one-third probability that nobody will die and a two-thirds probability that 600 people will die. Which of the two programs would you favor?

As you can see, the two scenarios examine an identical dilemma. Saving 200 of 600 infected people, after all, implies that the remaining 400 of 600 are lost. However, when the question was framed negatively and physicians were concentrating on losses rather than gains, they voted in a dramatically different fashion. In the second trial, 22 percent of the physicians elected the conservative strategy ("400 will die"), and 72 percent felt more comfortable with the more volatile set of possible outcomes. This is almost a perfect, symmetric reversal of the breakdown that prevailed with positive framing.

Advisors need to be aware of how they ask questions. It does matter!

DIAGNOSTIC TESTING

These questions are designed to detect signs of cognitive bias stemming from framing. Instead of one test, however, this section contains two shorter tests designed to be taken in tandem. Would you respond differently to the same dilemma if its framing were altered? Answer the following items and find out.

Framing Bias Mini-Test 1

Question 1: Suppose that you have the opportunity to invest in a mutual fund called MicroTrend. Over the past 10 years, MicroTrend has had an average annual return of 6 percent, with a standard deviation of 10 percent. So if MicroTrend continues to perform consistently, you can expect two-thirds of all returns to fall between −4 percent and 16 percent. How comfortable would you feel about investing in MicroTrend?

a. Comfortable
b. Somewhat comfortable
c. Uncomfortable

Question 2: Suppose that you have the opportunity to invest in a fund called MicroTrend. Over the past 10 years, MicroTrend has had an average annual return of 6 percent, with a standard deviation of 10 percent. So if MicroTrend continues to perform consistently, you can expect 95 percent of all returns to fall between −14 percent and 26 percent. How comfortable would you feel about investing in MicroTrend?

a. Comfortable
b. Somewhat comfortable
c. Uncomfortable

Framing Bias Mini-Test 2

Question 1: Suppose you are preparing for retirement. You need $50,000 annually to live comfortably, but you could take care of basic needs at about $40,000 and could even survive on a minimum of $30,000 if necessary. Further assume that there is no inflation. Now, imagine that you are choosing between two hypothetical investment options. Option 1 guarantees you an income of $40,000 per year—offering you a chance at a risk-free lifestyle. Option 2 offers you a 50 percent chance at $50,000 and a 50 percent chance at receiving $30,000 each year. Which option would you choose?

a. Option 1
b. Option 2

Question 2: Suppose you are preparing for retirement. You need $50,000 to live comfortably, but could take care of basic needs at about $40,000, and could even survive on a minimum of $30,000 if necessary. Further assume that there is no inflation. Now, imagine that you are choosing between two hypothetical investment options. Option 1 guarantees you enough income to cover your needs, but it will never provide you a comfortable lifestyle. With Option 2, you have the opportunity for a better lifestyle. With a probability of 50 percent, you might be limited to your bare minimum acceptable income. But with a corresponding probability of 50 percent, you would enjoy the comfortable lifestyle you desire and an income of $50,000. Which option do you choose?

a. Option 1
b. Option 2

Test Results Analysis

Mini-Test 1: People who answer the second question differently from the first are likely subject to framing bias. If you are a practitioner and your client answers in this fashion, then you should remain mindful of the manner in which you present information to the client—because subjective details can have a dramatic impact. Typically, investors susceptible to framing bias choose the riskier strategy in Question 2.

Mini-Test 2: This test can't be interpreted too rigidly because lifestyle preferences are not black and white. However, people subject to framing bias will probably prefer an assured income in Question 1 and a riskier strategy in Question 2. This is because Question 1 is framed in a relatively positive fashion, focusing on the attribute "safe" lifestyle offered from the guarantee in Option 1. The framing in Question 2, however, is less upbeat; it reminds you that neither investment option offers you a reliably pleasurable standard of living. When framing intersects with loss aversion, this type of response pattern is especially likely to result.

ADVICE

Financial markets don't just reflect financial realities. Investors' beliefs, perceptions, and desires exert a tremendous influence on most instruments and indexes. When investor and advisor expectations regarding portfolio performance fail to complement one another, the advisory relationship can deteriorate quickly. So it's important that a practitioner accurately gauge a client's mind-set; this doesn't just mean listening carefully when the client answers important questions. Sometimes, the formulation of the question itself also matters because framing determines reference points and defines expectations. Each investor has the right to express his or her personal financial objectives and should expect investment plans to be created relative to these desires. The advisor needs to ask the right questions and to make sure to understand the client's answers. Assessing investor risk tolerance is a process wherein framing can be particularly influential; so practitioners and clients should make sure to carve out a precise, shared understanding of what constitutes risk and should decide exactly how much risk is tolerable. Ultimately, question framing can and does determine appropriate information elicitation.

This section offers advice on each of the specific investor errors outlined in the preceding feature box.

> *Narrow framing.* Investors engaging in narrow framing may become preoccupied with short-term price oscillations in an isolated stock or industry, or they may favor certain asset classes while remaining oblivious to others. Advisors should encourage clients to keep the big picture in mind: overall wealth accumulation and long-term financial goals. Clients should work on building balanced asset allocations and focus on ensuring that those allocations are helping them meet their financial goals.

> *Framing and loss aversion.* Investors who feel that they've been faring poorly will seek out risks, while those pleased with their recent returns tend to play it safe. Advisors should encourage clients to isolate from their ongoing decision making any references to gains or losses incurred in a prior period. Advisors should also try to ask questions that are less likely to elicit biased answers. Finally, an emphasis on education, diversification, and proper portfolio management can help to neutralize these biases.

> *Unintended investment choices based on incorrectly framed questions.* Risk tolerance questionnaires are critical in assessing client goals and selecting appropriate investments. Advisors, therefore, need

to be thoroughly familiar with question wording and need to understand—and remain alert for—biases that can be awakened when options are formulated in certain ways. Remember, clear communication ensures the success of the advisory relationship.

Positive and negative frames. We've observed the considerable influence that positive and negative framing can exert. The lesson for practitioners is to present facts and choices to clients as neutrally and uniformly as possible. This reduces the likelihood of a biased client response and should help you to help your investors achieve their financial goals.

NOTES

1. Daniel Kahneman and Amos Tversky, "Choices, Values, and Frames," *American Psychologist* 39 (1984): 341–50. Reprinted as Chapter 1 in Daniel Kahneman and Amos Tversky, eds., *Choices, Values, and Frames* (New York: Cambridge University Press and the Russell Sage Foundation, 2000).

CHAPTER 13

Availability Bias

It is ironic that the greatest stock bubble coincided with the greatest amount of information available. I always thought this would be a good thing, but maybe it was not so good.
         —James J. Cramer, financial news analyst for CNBC

BIAS DESCRIPTION

Bias Name: Availability bias
Bias Type: Cognitive
Subtype: Information processing

General Description

The *availability bias* is a rule of thumb, or mental shortcut, that causes people to estimate the probability of an outcome based on how prevalent or familiar that outcome appears in their lives. People exhibiting this bias perceive easily recalled possibilities as being more likely than those prospects that are harder to imagine or difficult to comprehend.

One classic example cites the tendency of most people to guess that shark attacks more frequently cause fatalities than airplane parts falling from the sky do. However, as difficult as it may be to comprehend, the latter is actually 30 times more likely to occur. Shark attacks are probably assumed to be more prevalent because sharks invoke greater fear or because shark attacks receive a disproportionate degree of media attention. Consequently, dying from a shark attack is, for most respondents, easier to imagine than death by falling airplane parts. In sum, the availability rule of thumb underlies judgments about the likelihood or frequency of an occurrence based on readily available information, not necessarily based on complete, objective, or factual information.

Technical Description

People often inadvertently assume that readily available thoughts, ideas, or images represent unbiased indicators of statistical probabilities. People estimate the likelihoods of certain events according to the degree of ease with which recollections or examples of analogous events can be accessed from memory. Impressions drawn from imagination and past experience combine to construct an array of conceivable outcomes, whose real statistical probabilities are, in essence, arbitrary. There are several categories of availability bias, of which the four that apply most to investors are: (1) *retrievability*, (2) *categorization*, (3) *narrow range of experience*, and (4) *resonance*. Each category will be described and corresponding examples given.

1. *Retrievability*. Ideas that are *retrieved* most easily also seem to be the most credible, though this is not necessarily the case. For example, Daniel Kahneman, Paul Slovic, and Amos Tversky performed an experiment in which subjects were read a list of names and then were asked whether more male or female names had been read.[1] In reality, the majority of names recited were unambiguously female; however, the subset of male names contained a much higher frequency of references to celebrities (e.g., "Richard Nixon"). In accordance with availability theory, most subjects produced biased estimates indicating, mistakenly, that more male than female names populated the list.

2. *Categorization*. In Chapter 5, "Representativeness Bias," we discussed how people's minds comprehend and archive perceptions according to certain classification schemes. Here, we will discuss how people attempt to categorize or summon information that matches a certain reference. The first thing that their brains do is generate a set of search terms, specific to the task at hand, that will allow them to efficiently navigate their brain's classification structure and locate the data they need. Different tasks require different search sets, however; and when it is difficult to put together a framework for a search, people often mistakenly conclude that the search simply references a more meager array of results. For example, if a French person simultaneously tries to come up with a list of high-quality U.S. vineyards and a corresponding list of French vineyards, the list of U.S. vineyards is likely to prove more difficult to create. The French person, as a result, might predict that high-quality U.S. vineyards exist with a lower probability than famous French vineyards, even if this is not necessarily the case.

3. *Narrow range of experience.* When a person possesses an overly restrictive frame of reference from which to formulate an objective estimate, then *narrow range of experience bias* often results. For example, assume that a very successful college basketball player is drafted by a National Basketball Association (NBA) team, where he proceeds to enjoy several successful seasons. Because this person encounters numerous other successful former college basketball players on a daily basis in the NBA, he is likely to overestimate the relative proportion of successful college basketball players that go on to play professionally. He will, likewise, probably underestimate the relative frequency of failed college basketball players, because most of the players he knows are those who have gone on to reap great rewards from their undergraduate basketball careers. In reality, only an extremely small percentage of college basketball players will ever graduate to the NBA.

4. *Resonance.* The extent to which certain, given situations *resonate* vis-à-vis individuals' own, personal situations can also influence judgment. For example, fans of classical music might be likely to overestimate the portion of the total population that also listens to classical music. Those who dislike classical music would probably underestimate the number of people who listen to classical music.

PRACTICAL APPLICATION

Each variation of the availability bias just outlined has unique implications in personal finance, both for advisory practitioners and for clients. Let's explore these now.

1. *Retrievability.* Most investors, if asked to identify the "best" mutual fund company, are likely to select a firm that engages in heavy advertising, such as Fidelity or Schwab. In addition to maintaining a high public relations profile, these firms also "cherry pick" the funds with the best results in their advertising, which makes this belief more "available" to be recalled. In reality, the companies that manage some of today's highest-performing mutual funds undertake little to no advertising. Consumers who overlook these funds in favor of more widely publicized alternatives may exemplify retrievability/availability bias.

2. *Categorization.* Although this is changing, most Americans, if asked to pinpoint one country, worldwide, that offers the best investment prospects, would designate their own: the United States. Why? When conducting an inventory of memories and stored knowledge regarding "good investment opportunities" in general, the country category that

most Americans most easily recall is the United States. However, to dismiss the wealth of investment prospects abroad as a result of this phenomenon is irrational. In reality, over 50 percent of equity market capitalization exists outside the United States. People who are unduly "patriotic" when looking for somewhere to invest often suffer from availability bias.

3. *Narrow range of experience.* Assume that an employee of a fast-growing, high-tech company is asked: "Which industry generates the most successful investments?" Such an individual, who probably comes into contact with other triumphant tech profiteers each and every day, will likely overestimate the relative proportion of corporate successes stemming from technologically intensive industries. Like the NBA star who got his start in college and, therefore, too optimistically estimates the professional athletic prospects of college basketball players, this hypothetical high-tech employee demonstrates narrow range of experience availability bias.

4. *Resonance.* People often favor investments that they feel match their personalities. A thrifty individual who discount shops, clips coupons, and otherwise seeks out bargains may demonstrate a natural inclination toward value investing. At the same time, such an investor might not heed the wisdom of balancing value assets with more growth-oriented ventures, owing to a reluctance to front the money and acquire a quality growth stock. The concept of value is easily available in such an investor's mind, but the notion of growth is less so. This person's portfolio could perform suboptimally as a result of resonance availability bias.

A Classic Example of Availability Bias

In the period 1927 to 1999, which political party's leadership has correlated with higher stock market returns? Many Wall Street professionals are known to lean Republican, so a lot of people, given this readily available information, might speculate that the markets benefit from Republican political hegemony. After all, why would so many well-informed individuals, whose livelihoods depend on the success of the stock market, vote for Republicans if Democrats produced higher returns? According to a study done by University of California at Los Angeles professors Pedro Santa-Clara and Rossen Valkanov,[2] the 72-year period between 1927 and 1999 showed that a broad stock index, similar to the Standard & Poor's (S&P) 500, returned approximately 11 percent more a year on average under a Democratic president than safer, three-month Treasury bonds (T-bonds). By comparison, the index returned 2 percent a year more than the T-bonds when Republicans were in office. If your natural reaction was to answer "Republican" to this question, you may suffer from availability bias.

Implications for Investors

In the following we summarize the primary implications for investors of susceptibility to availability bias in each of the four forms we've reviewed. In all such instances, investors ignore potentially beneficial investments because information on those investments is not readily available, or they make investment decisions based on readily available information, avoiding diligent research.

AVAILABILITY BIAS: BEHAVIORS THAT CAN CAUSE INVESTMENT MISTAKES

1. *Retrievability.* Investors will choose investments based on information that is available to them (advertising, suggestions from advisors, friends, etc.) and will not engage in disciplined research or due diligence to verify that the investment selected is a good one.

2. *Categorization.* Investors will choose investments based on categorical lists that they have available in their memory. In their minds, other categories will not be easily recalled and, thus, will be ignored. For example, U.S. investors may ignore countries where potentially rewarding investment opportunities may exist because these countries may not be an easily recalled category in their memory.

3. *Narrow range of experience.* Investors will choose investments that fit their narrow range of life experiences, such as the industry they work in, the region they live in, and the people they associate with. For example, investors who work in the technology industry may believe that only technology investments will be profitable.

4. *Resonance.* Investors will choose investments that resonate with their own personality or that have characteristics that investors can relate to their own behavior. Taking the opposite view, investors ignore potentially good investments because they can't relate to or do not come in contact with characteristics of those investments. For example, thrifty people may not relate to expensive stocks (high price/earnings multiples) and potentially miss out on the benefits of owning these stocks.

RESEARCH REVIEW

A 2002 working paper by Terrance Odean and Brad Barber, entitled "All That Glitters: The Effect of Attention and News on the Buying Behavior of Individual and Institutional Investors,"[3] asks a simple question: how do investors choose the stocks that they buy? Odean and Barber tested the proposition that individual investors buy stocks that happen to catch their attention. In this work, Odean and Barber pointed out that when buying stocks, investors are faced with a formidable decision task because there are over 7,000 U.S. common stocks from which to choose. They proposed that investors manage the search problem by limiting their search to stocks that have recently caught their attention. They tested the hypothesis that individual investors are more likely to be net buyers of attention-grabbing stocks than are institutional investors by looking at three indications of how likely stocks are to catch investors' attention: (1) daily abnormal trading volume, (2) daily returns, and (3) daily news. They examined the buying and selling behavior associated with abnormal trading volume for four samples of investors:

1. Investors with accounts at a large discount brokerage.
2. Investors at a smaller discount brokerage firm that advertises its trade execution quality.
3. Investors with accounts at a large retail brokerage.
4. Professional money managers.

As news agencies routinely report the prior day's big winners and big losers, stocks that soar or dive catch people's attention. As predicted, Odean and Barber found that individual investors tend to be net buyers on high attention days: Investors at the large discount brokerage made nearly twice as many purchases as sales of stocks experiencing unusually high trading volume (e.g, the highest 5 percent). They also found that attention-driven investors tend to be net buyers of companies on days that those companies are in the news (see Figure 13.1).

Odean and Barber also found that professional investors are less likely to indulge in attention-based purchases. With more time and resources, professionals are able to continuously monitor a wider range of stocks and they are unlikely to consider only attention-grabbing stocks. Furthermore, many professionals may solve the problem of searching through too many stocks by concentrating on a particular sector or on stocks that have passed an initial screen. Perhaps the most important and relevant finding is that

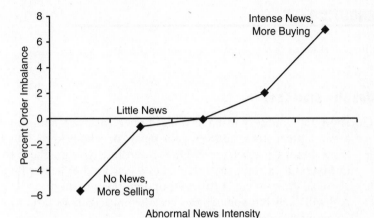

FIGURE 13.1 Order Imbalance as a Function of News Intensity Reprinted with permission from Brad M. Barber and Terrance Odean, "All That Glitters: The Effect of Attention and News on the Buying Behavior of Individual and Institutional Investors" (working paper, University of California-Berkeley, 2002).

investors who engage in attention-based buying do not benefit from doing so. Abnormal volume and extreme return analysis that Odean and Barber performed showed that attention-grabbing stocks do not outperform the market.

In this paper, Odean and Barber illustrated a direct practical application of availability bias in individual finance: people tend to deviate from rationally prescribed economic behavior because, in this instance, they lack the capacity to process the utterly massive quantities of data that ought to contextualize a truly "rational" stock purchase. Information that is literally available to investors—information that is published on a daily basis—simply isn't always cognitively available. When pertinent information isn't available in this latter, practical sense, decisions are ultimately flawed.

DIAGNOSTIC TEST

This brief test helps detect investor availability bias.

Availability Bias Test

Question 1: Suppose you have some money to invest and you hear about a great stock tip from your neighbor who is known to have a good stock market sense. He recommends you purchase shares in Mycrolite, a company that makes a new kind of lighter fluid for charcoal grills. What is your response to this situation?
   a. I will likely buy some shares because my neighbor is usually right about these things.
   b. I will likely take it under advisement and go back to my house and do further research before making a decision.

Question 2: Suppose that you are planning to buy stock in a generic drug maker called "Generics Plus." Your friend Marian sent you a report on the company and you like the story, so you plan to purchase 100 shares. Right before you do, you hear on a popular financial news show that "GN Pharmaceuticals," another generic drug maker, just reported great earnings and the stock is up 10 percent on the news. What is your response to this situation?
   a. I will likely take this information as confirmation that generics are a good area to be in and proceed with my purchase of Generics Plus.
   b. I will pause before buying Generics Plus and request research on GN prior to proceeding with the purchase of Generics Plus.
   c. I will purchase GN rather than Generics Plus because GN appears to be a hot stock and I want to get in on a good thing.

Question 3: Which claims more lives in the United States?
   a. Lightning.
   b. Tornadoes.

Test Results Analysis

Question 1: Respondents choosing "a" are likely to be susceptible to availability bias.

Question 2: Respondents choosing "c" are likely to be susceptible to availability bias.

Question 3: Respondents choosing "b" are likely to be susceptible to availability bias. More Americans are killed annually by lightning than by tornadoes. Media attention, drills, and other publicity, however, make tornado fatalities memorable and therefore more "available" for people.[4]

ADVICE

Generally speaking, in order to overcome availability bias, investors need to carefully research and contemplate investment decisions before executing them. Focusing on long-term results, while resisting chasing trends, are the best objectives on which to focus if availability bias appears to be an issue. Be aware that everyone possesses a human tendency to mentally overemphasize recent, newsworthy events; refuse to let this tendency compromise you. The old axiom that "nothing is as good or as bad as it seems" offers a safe, reasonable recourse against the impulses associated with availability bias.

When selecting investments, it is crucial to consider the effects of the availability rule of thumb. For example, stop and consider how you decide which investments to research before making an investment. Do you frequently focus on companies you've read about in *Business Week* or the *Wall Street Journal* or on investments that have been mentioned on popular financial news programs? A Cornell University researcher named Christopher Gadarowski in 2001 investigated the relationship between stock returns and press coverage. He found that the stocks receiving the most press coverage actually went on to underperform the market in the two years following their exposure in the news.[5]

It is also important to keep in mind that people tend to view things that occur more than a few years ago as past history. For example, if you got a speeding ticket last week, you will probably reduce your speed over the course of the next month or so. However, as time passes, you are likely to revert to your old driving habits. Likewise, availability bias causes investors to overreact to present-day market conditions, whether they are positive or negative. The tech bubble of the late 1990s provided a superb illustration of this phenomenon. Investors, swept up in the euphoria of the "new economy," disregarded elementary risks. When the market corrected itself, these same investors lost confidence and overfocused on the short-term, negative results that they were experiencing.

Another significant problem is that much of the information investors receive is inaccurate and is based on insufficient information and multiple opinions. Furthermore, the information can be outdated or confusingly presented. Availability bias causes people to attribute disproportionate degrees of credibility to such information when it arrives amid a flurry of media attention. Many investors, suffering from information overload, overlook the fact that they often lack the training, experience, and objectivity to filter or interpret this deluge of data. As a result, investors often believe themselves to be more accurately informed than is, ultimately, the case. Because availability bias is a cognitive bias, often it can be corrected with updated information.

NOTES

1. Daniel Kahneman, Paul Slovic, and Amos Tversky, eds., *Judgment under Uncertainty: Heuristics and Biases* (New York: Cambridge University Press, 1982).
2. Pedro Santa-Clara and Rossen Valkanov, "The Presidential Puzzle: Political Cycles and the Stock Market," *Journal of Finance* 58(5) (October 2003): 1841–1872.
3. Brad M. Barber and Terrance Odean, "All That Glitters: The Effect of Attention and News on the Buying Behavior of Individual and Institutional Investors" (working paper, University of California-Berkeley, 2002).
4. See Paul Slovic, Baruch Fischoff, and Sarah Lichtenstein, "Facts versus Fiction: Understanding Public Fears," in Daniel Kahneman, Paul Slovic, and Amos Tversky, eds., *Judgment under Uncertainty: Heuristics and Biases* (New York: Cambridge University Press, 1982), 463–491.
5. Christopher Gadarowski, "Financial Press Coverage and Expected Stock Returns" (working paper, Cornell University, 2001).

CHAPTER 14

Self-Attribution Bias

Heads I win, tails it's chance.

—Ellen Langer and Jane Roth, 1975

BIAS DESCRIPTION

Bias Name: Self-attribution bias
Bias Type: Cognitive
Subtype: Information processing

General Description

Self-attribution bias (or self-serving attribution bias) refers to the tendency of individuals to ascribe their successes to innate aspects, such as talent or foresight, while more often blaming failures on outside influences, such as bad luck. Students faring well on an exam, for example, might credit their own intelligence or work ethic, while those failing might cite unfair grading. Similarly, athletes often reason that they have simply performed to reflect their own superior athletic skills if they win a game, but they might allege unfair calls by a referee when they lose a game.

Technical Description

Self-attribution is a cognitive phenomenon by which people attribute failures to situational factors and successes to dispositional factors. Self-serving bias can actually be broken down into two constituent tendencies or subsidiary biases.

1. *Self-enhancing bias* represents people's propensity to claim an irrational degree of credit for their successes.
2. *Self-protecting bias* represents the corollary effect—the irrational denial of responsibility for failure.

Self-enhancing bias can be explained from a cognitive perspective. Research has shown that if people intend to succeed, then outcomes in accordance with that intention—successes—will be perceived as the result of people acting to achieve what they've originally intended. Individuals, then, will naturally accept more credit for successes than failures, since they intend to succeed rather than to fail. Self-protecting bias can also be partially explained from an emotional perspective. Some argue that the need to maintain self-esteem directly affects the attribution of task outcomes because people will protect themselves psychologically as they attempt to comprehend their failures. Because these cognitive and emotional explanations are linked, it can be difficult to ascertain which form of the bias is at work in a given situation.

PRACTICAL APPLICATION

Dr. Dana Dunn, a professor of psychology at Moravian College in Bethlehem, Pennsylvania, has done some excellent work regarding self-serving bias. She observed that her students often have trouble recognizing self-serving attributional bias in their own behaviors. To illustrate this phenomenon, she performs an experiment in which she asks students to take out a sheet of paper and draw a line down the middle of the page. She then tells them to label one column "strengths" and the other "weaknesses" and to list their personal strengths and weaknesses in the two columns. She finds that students consistently list more strengths than weaknesses.[1]

Dunn's result suggests that her students tend to suffer from self-serving attributional bias. Investors are not immune from this behavior. The old Wall Street adage "Don't confuse brains with a bull market" is relevant here. When an investor who is susceptible to self-attribution bias purchases an investment and it goes up, then it was due, naturally, to their business and investment savvy. In contrast, when an investor who is susceptible to self-attribution bias purchases an investment and it goes down, then it was due, naturally, to bad luck or some other factor that was not the fault of the investor. People's strengths, generally, consist of personal qualities that they believe empower them to succeed, whereas weaknesses are traits they possess that predispose them to fail. Investors subject to self-attribution bias perceive that investment successes are more often attributable to innate characteristics and that investment failures are due to exogenous factors.

Implications for Investors

Irrationally attributing successes and failures can impair investors in two primary ways. First, people who aren't able to perceive mistakes they've made are, consequently, unable to learn from those mistakes. Second, investors who disproportionately credit themselves when desirable outcomes do arise can become detrimentally overconfident in their own market savvy. Below we describe the pitfalls of self-serving behavior that often lead to financial mistakes.

RESEARCH REVIEW

A very pertinent discussion of self-serving bias is "Learning to Be Overconfident," written by Terrance Odean and Simon Gervais.[2] They developed a model that describes how novice traders who exhibit susceptibility to self-serving bias end up unjustifiably confident in their investment skills because they tend to take inadequate degrees of responsibility for losses they've incurred. Self-attribution teaches investors to unwittingly take on inappropriate degrees of financial risk and to trade too aggressively, amplifying personal market volatility. This study revealed that while the novice investors are consistently overconfident that they can outperform the market, most fail to do so.

Gervais and Odean developed three hypotheses that are all backed by statistical data.

1. Periods of general prosperity are usually followed by periods of higher-than-expected trading volume, a trend signifying the impact of overconfidence on investor decision making.
2. During periods in which overconfidence increases trading volume, lower-than-average profits are the result.
3. Traders who are both young and successful tend to trade the most and demonstrate the most overconfidence.

SELF-ATTRIBUTION BIAS: BEHAVIORS THAT CAN CAUSE INVESTMENT MISTAKES

1. Self-attribution investors can, after a period of successful investing (such as one quarter or one year) believe that their success is due to their acumen as investors rather than to factors out of their control. This behavior can lead to taking on too much risk, as the investors become too confident in their behavior.
2. Self-attribution bias often leads investors to trade more than is prudent. As investors believe that successful investing (trading) is attributed to skill versus luck, they begin to trade too much, which has been shown to be "hazardous to your wealth."
3. Self-attribution bias leads investors to "hear what they want to hear." That is, when investors are presented with information that confirms a decision that they made to make an investment, they will ascribe "brilliance" to themselves. This may lead to investors making a purchase or holding an investment that they should not.
4. Self-attribution bias can cause investors to hold underdiversified portfolios, especially among investors that attribute the success of an company's performance to their own contribution, such as corporate executives, board members, and so on. Often, the performance of a stock is not attributed to the skill of an individual person, but rather many factors, including chance; thus, holding a concentrated stock position can be associated with self-attribution and should be avoided.

Gervais and Odean, in an excerpt from "Learning to Be Overconfident," summarized their approach and their findings:

In assessing his ability, the trader takes too much credit for his successes. This leads him to become overconfident. A trader's expected level of overconfidence increases in the early stages of his career. Then, with more experience, he comes to better recognize his own ability. An overconfident trader trades too aggressively, thereby increasing trading volume and market volatility while lowering his own expected profits. Though a greater number of successes indicate greater probable ability, a more successful trader may actually have lower expected profits in the next period than a less success-ful trader due to his greater overconfidence. Since overconfidence is generated by success, overconfident traders are not the poorest traders. Their survival in the market is not threatened. Overconfidence does not make traders wealthier, but the process of becoming wealthy can make traders overconfident.[3]

DIAGNOSTIC TESTING

This diagnostic quiz can help to detect susceptibility to self-attribution bias.

Self-Attribution Test

Question 1: Suppose you make an investment and it does well, but not for the reason you thought it would. You are feeling good about yourself for making the investment. Which of the following would most accurately describe your feelings:

   a. Your keen eye for a good investment is alive and well.

   b. Even though the investment did well for the wrong reason, it was still a great investment.

   c. Actually, I'm not feeling that great even though I made money because the reason I thought the investment would go up did not occur; I got lucky.

Question 2: When returns to your portfolio increase, to what do you believe the change in performance is mainly due?

   a. Your investment skill.

   b. A combination of investment skill and luck.

   c. Luck.

Question 3: After you make a successful trade, how likely are you to put your profits to work in a quick, subsequent trade, rather than letting the money idle until you're sure you've located another good investment?

   a. When I sell a profitable investment, I usually invest the money again right away because I might be on a hot streak.

   b. I will usually wait until I find something I really like before making a new investment.

   c. Some combination of choices A and B.

Question 4: Relative to other investors, how good an investor are you?

   a. Below average

   b. Average

    c. Above average

    d. Well above average

Test Results Analysis

Question 1: People whose response indicates that their keen eye for investments is alive and well are likely to suffer from self-attribution bias. This is so because an investment success in this case was due not to good decision making, but to good luck.

Question 2: Attributing financial success to skill tends to indicate susceptibility to self-attribution bias.

Question 3: Investors who roll over their money immediately without carefully plotting their next move are, often, disproportionately attributing their successes to their own market savvy. Therefore, they are likely to suffer from self-attribution bias.

Question 4: Investors who rate themselves as "above average" or "well above average" in skill are likely to suffer from self-attribution bias.

ADVICE

Recall again the old Wall Street adage that perhaps provides the best warning against the pitfalls of self-attribution bias: "Don't confuse brains with a bull market."

Often, when financial decisions pan out well, investors like to congratulate themselves on their shrewdness. When things don't turn out so profitably, however, they can console themselves by concluding that someone or something else is at fault. In many cases, neither explanation is entirely correct. Winning investment outcomes are typically due to any number of factors, a bull market being the most prominent; stocks' decline in value, meanwhile, can be equally random and complex. Sometimes, the fault does lie in arenas well beyond an investor's control, such as fraud or mismanagement.

One of the best things investors can do is view both winning and losing investments as objectively as possible. However, most people don't take the time to analyze the complex confluence of factors that helped them realize profit or to confront the potential mistakes that aggravated a loss. Postanalysis is one of the best learning tools at any investor's disposal. It's understandable but, ultimately, irrational to fear an examination of one's past mistakes. The only real, grievous error is to continue to succumb to overconfidence and, as a result, to repeat the same mistakes!

Advisors and individual investors should perform a postanalysis of each investment: Where did you make money? Where did you lose money? Mentally separate your good, money-making decisions from your bad ones. Then, review the beneficial decisions and try to discern what, exactly, you did correctly: Did you purchase the stock at a particularly advantageous time? Was the market, in general, on an upswing? Similarly, you should review the decisions that you've categorized as poor: What went wrong? Did you buy stocks with poor earnings? Were those stocks trading at or near their recent price highs when you purchased them, or did you pick up the stocks as they were beginning to decline? Did you purchase a stock aptly and simply make an error when it came time to sell? Was the market, in general, undergoing a correction phase?

When reviewing unprofitable decisions, look for patterns or common mistakes that perhaps you were unaware of making. Note any such tendencies that you discover, and try to remain mindful of them by, for example, brainstorming a rule or a reminder such as: "I will not do X in the future" or "I will do Y in the future." Being conscious of these rules will help you overcome any bad habits that you may have acquired and can also reinforce your reliance on the strategies that have served you well.

Remember: Being humble and learning from your past mistakes is the best way to become a smarter, better, and more successful investor!

NOTES

1. Dana S. Dunn, "Demonstrating a Self-Serving Bias," *Teaching of Psychology* 16 (1989): 21–22.
2. Simon Gervais and Terrance Odean, "Learning to Be Overconfident," *Review of Financial Studies* 14 (1): 1–27.
3. Ibid.

CHAPTER 15

Outcome Bias

Insanity is doing the same thing in the same way and expecting a different outcome.

—Old Chinese Proverb

BIAS DESCRIPTION

Bias Name: Outcome bias

Bias Type: Cognitive

Subtype: Information processing

General Description

Outcome bias refers to the tendency of individuals to decide to do something—such as make an investment in a mutual fund—based on the outcome of past events (such as returns of the past five years) rather than by observing the process by which the outcome came about (the investment process used by the mutual fund manager over the past five years). An investor might think, "This manager had a fantastic five years, I am going to invest with her," rather than understanding how such great returns were generated or why the returns generated by other managers might not have had good results over the past five years.

Technical Description

In the name of attempting to make better decisions themselves, people are prone to evaluating the decisions others make (and subsequent results of those decisions). We do this because it helps people, for example, to determine who they want to lead their country, who they want to be thier local judges and officials, who they wish to associate with personally, and who they want to manage their money. However, in evaluating someone else's decisions after they have made them, observers possess information that the decision makers may not have had while they made their decisions (such as what kind of impact their decision had on us and other outside or big picture information), and it is possible that we judge others too kindly or too harshly. As Baron states in his work, "...Reasonable decisions are criticized by Monday morning quarterbacks who think they might have decided otherwise, and decision makers end up being punished for their bad luck."[1] Similarly, people who make flawed decisions that turn out okay should not necessarily be judged on the outcome, however good it was, but rather on the process they used during the decision making process.

Information that becomes available only after a decision is made should not be considered in judging the quality of someone's decision, since having knowledge of the information after the fact does not help to teach the decision maker any valuable lessons. That is, because decision makers do not know what the outcome of their decision may be, but outcome information is available to those who evaluate the decisions afterwards, decisions are often unfairly judged since outcome information is never available while making decisions. In the context of investing, it is therefore important when evaluating the results of a money manager to not only consider their results, however good or bad, but rather the decision-making process by which they achieved their results.

Practical Application: Outcome Bias

Jonathan Baron and John C. Hershey of the University of Pennsylvania administered several experiments on outcome bias.[2] Subjects were given descriptions of decisions made by others under conditions of uncertainty, together with outcomes of those decisions. Some decisions were medical decisions made by a physician or a patient, and others were decisions about monetary gambles. Subjects rated the quality of thinking that went into the decisions, the competence of the decision maker, or their willingness to let the decision maker act on their behalf. Subjects understood that all relevant information was available to the decision maker. Subjects rated the thinking as better (i.e., rated the decision maker as more competent, or indicated greater willingness to yield the decision) when the outcome was favorable than when it was unfavorable. In monetary gambles, subjects rated the thinking as better when the outcome of the option *not* chosen turned out poorly than when it turned out positively. When asked, subjects felt that they should not take outcomes into account in making these evaluations. However, they did exactly that. In part, the effect of outcome knowledge on evaluation may be explained in terms of its effect on the salience of arguments for each side of the choice.

Baron and Hershey's results suggest that subjects suffer from outcome bias. Investors are not immune to this behavior. For example, when investors who are susceptible to outcome bias make mutual fund investments, they may be doing so because they are focused on the outcome of a past investment experience related to this decision—such as their manager's track record or the asset class performance of that particular investment—and are not focused on *how* the returns were generated or why they should be investing in that asset class. On the contrary, when investors who are not susceptible to outcome bias make investments, they may not make an investment with that manager or asset class (well, they might, but for different reasons) because they may see that the manager took too much risk to obtain a given set of returns or the asset class is overvalued and should be avoided. Investors subject to outcome bias are not focusing on the process, but rather the result—and this can be dangerous.

Implications for Investors

Irrationally attributing successes and failures can impair investors in two primary ways. First, people who aren't able to perceive the mistakes that they have made are, consequently, unable to learn from those mistakes. Secondly, investors who disproportionately credit themselves when desirable outcomes do arise can become detrimentally overconfident in their own market savvy. The following points describe the pitfalls of self-serving behavior that can often lead to financial losses:

1. Investors may invest in funds that they should not because they are focused on the outcome of a prior action, such as the performance record of the manager, rather than on the process by which the manager achieved the results. This may cause investors to subject themselves to excessive risk if the source of the performance was a risky strategy.
2. Investors may avoid investing in funds that they should not because they are focused on the outcome of a prior action, such as the performance record of the manager, rather than on the process by which the manager achieved the results. Investors may avoid a manager based on a bad outcome while ignoring the potentially sound process by which the manager made the decision.
3. Investors may invest in overvalued asset classes based on recent outcomes, such as strong performance in gold or housing prices, and not pay heed to valuations or past price history of the asset class in question, thereby exposing them to the risk that the asset class may be peaking, which can be "hazardous to one's wealth."

Research Review: Assignment of Responsibility Elaine Walster of the University of Hawaii[3] presents an interesting example of outcome bias through her research on the attributions of responsibility for doing harm. Walster presented subjects with information about a hypothetical person and a description of an accident in which the person was involved. Some subjects were informed that the person's parked car rolled a short distance down a hill and struck a tree stump, resulting in minor damage. Others were informed that the car rolled all the way down the hill and struck a tree, resulting in considerable damage. Whether or not the hypothetical person and other people were or could have been injured also varied. Results revealed that subjects attributed more responsibility for the accident to the stimulus person when the consequences of the accident were severe rather than mild. From an investment perspective, we can extrapolate this example. Investors tend to ascribe more meaning to more drastic outcomes (either positive or negative) than they do to mild ones. This means that investors can irrationally avoid or be drawn to managers who have dramatic moves in their returns as opposed to those who do not, rather than focusing on the process by which the outcome arose.

DIAGNOSTIC

This section contains a diagnostic quiz that can help to detect susceptibility to outcome bias. In the Advice section that follows, you will find guidelines for scoring responses to this quiz, along with corresponding suggestions for managing outcome bias.

> **Question 1:** You are contemplating making an investment in small-cap U.S. equities. Before proceeding with an investment, you decide to research the track record of a mutual fund manager that has outperformed her index, the Russell 2000, by 600 basis points per annum over the past five years. How likely would you be to then seek information to understand what strategy was used and what kinds of risks were taken to achieve this result before investing (i.e., you might not invest if you think the manager might be taking too much risk)?
> a. Very unlikely
> b. Unlikely
> c. Likely
> d. Very likely

Question 2: You are contemplating making an investment in emerging markets equities. Before making an investment, you decide to research the track record of a mutual fund manager that has underperformed his index, the MSCI EM Index, by 300 basis points per annum over the past five years. How likely would you be to then seek information to understand what strategy was used and what kinds of risks were taken to achieve this result (i.e., you might actually invest if you understand why the manager underperformed)?
   a. Very unlikely
   b. Unlikely
   c. Likely
   d. Very likely

Diagnostic Quiz: Review

Let's begin by reviewing the logic employed in the preceding diagnostic quiz. First, here are a few scoring and assessment guidelines, broken down by question/item. Afterwards, we will discuss some overall tactics that can help to prevent people from sustaining financial harm as a result of self-attribution bias.

Question 1: Often, investors examine the track record of a mutual fund, see terrific performance over three or five years, and decide to invest. This can be a mistake if returns were achieved by taking too much risk or in a single strategy. For example, the Russell 2000 manager might have achieved her returns by concentrating the portfolio in 15 names, and hit two grand slam home runs and picked four substantially losing investments. This might have been a case of luck versus skill, but the track record doesn't show that. Also, what was the annualized standard deviation? If it was markedly higher than the index, this is a red flag. Investors need to focus not only on the outcome but also the process.

Question 2: Similarly, in Question 2, the emerging markets manager may have made a conscious decision to avoid a certain country or a group of countries that performed exceptionally well but unexpectedly so. (By the way, this is the case for indexing—you never need to worry about substrategies that you do not own performing well because you own them all.) Suppose your thesis now is that China and India will outperform and this manager is well positioned in these markets. You may want to invest after all, even though this manager has underperformed. You need to look not only at the outcome, but also at the process that drove the outcome.

Advice

One of the most basic mistakes in investing is focusing on the investment outcome without regard to the process used to create the outcome. A closely related concept is when a great amount of risk is used to create the returns. It is not a positive thing when inordinate amounts of risk are used to generate returns. When analyzing investment managers, it is critical to understand how the managers are creating returns, especially if they are above their stated benchmarks. How many positions are in the fund, and how does this compare to the benchmark? How many names in the portfolio created returns? What is the tracking error and R-squared to the benchmark? Sometimes you will find that a manager with a solid strategy has simply been unlucky and underperformed even though his strategy is quite sound. Numerous studies have shown that managers who have strong 10-year track records will underperform for one, two, or even three years in a row only to have the manager revert back to strong outperformance. One of the best things investors can do is dig deep into the details of the contemplated strategies and learn how returns were generated. Ex-post analysis is one of the best learning tools at any investor's disposal.

NOTES

1. Jonathan Baron & John C. Hershey, "Outcome Bias in Decision Evaluation," *Journal of Personality and Social Psychology* 54 (2008): 569–579.
2. Jonathan Baron & John C. Hershey, "Outcome Bias in Decision Evaluation," *Journal of Personality and Social Psychology* 54 (2008): 569.
3. Elaine Walster, "Assignment of Responsibility for an Accident," *Journal of Personality and Social Psychology* 3 (1966): 73–79.

CHAPTER 16

Recency Bias

The present is never our goal; the past and present are our means, the future alone is our goal.
> —Blaise Pascal (1623 to 1662), French mathematician
> and philosopher

BIAS DESCRIPTION

Bias Name: Recency bias

Bias Type: Cognitive

Subtype: Information processing

General Description

Recency bias is a cognitive predisposition that causes people to more prominently recall and emphasize recent events and observations than those that occurred in the near or distant past. Suppose, for example, that a cruise passenger peering off the observation deck of a ship spots precisely equal numbers of green boats and blue boats over the duration of the trip. However, if the green boats pass by more frequently toward the end of the cruise, with the passing of blue boats dispersed evenly or concentrated toward the beginning, then recency bias would influence the passenger to recall, following the cruise, that more green than blue boats sailed by.

Technical Description

In order to best understand the technical description of recency bias, it is helpful to examine human memory recall testing, the two main components of which are primacy effect and the recency effect.

When studying human memory, psychologists use a paradigm called free recall. In a free recall task, a subject is presented a list of to-be-recalled items, one after another. For example, an experimenter might read off a list of 15 words, presenting a new word to the test taker every 5 seconds. When the experimenter has read the entire list, the subject is asked to recall as many of the listed items as possible (e.g., by writing them down). This is known as a *free recall task* because the subject is free to recall the items in any order that he or she desires.

The results of a free recall task are plotted on something called a *serial position curve,* which is normally U-shaped. The serial position curve is graphed on a basic, coordinate plane, in which the x axis plots the serial position of to-be-remembered items in the list (e.g., the first item, the second item, the third item, and so on). The y axis, meanwhile, indicates the probability of recalling the item, which is based on the average frequency of recall across a number of subjects in a given trial. The serial position curve, once constructed, tends to exhibit both a recency and a primacy effect.

The primacy effect describes the left portion of the U shape, that is, the elevated portion at the beginning of the curve, which precedes the concavity at the middle. The primacy effect dictates that, in a free recall experiment like the one just described, articles presented at the beginning of a list of to-be-remembered items are remembered better than ones presented in the middle of the list. The primacy effect appears to result from subjects recalling items directly from semantic memory—a type of memory that might be thought of as the "hard drive" of a computer brain. The first items inscribed in a given session onto this hard drive are more precisely retained and are easier to access than items inscribed later on.

The recency effect describes the right portion of the serial position curve. When the recency effect appears in a free recall experiment, it means that subjects recall items appearing toward the end of the to-be-remembered list better than they remember items appearing in the middle. The effect is named in such a way because the observations comprising the right-hand tail of the serial position curve correspond to the items the subjects heard most recently prior to the recall challenge. Recency bias is the result of subjects recalling items directly from short-term memory. In continuing the computer analogy, if semantic memory represents a portion of your brain's long-term memory, or "hard drive," then short-term memory is like random access memory (RAM), which contains data that your computer can access dynamically during a session, but which it may also lose after rebooting. Short-term memory stores only limited quantities of information over limited periods of time. Therefore, while the primacy effect results from the extra-long-term memory rehearsal accorded to primary items on a list, the recency effect occurs because the items the subject heard most recently are more likely to persist in short-term memory than previous, "older" items that have been discarded.

The technical description of recency bias refers to the errors people make when the recency effect prejudices their recollections. Recency bias privileges information recently retained and neglects events and observations not as fresh in the mind.

PRACTICAL APPLICATION

One of the most obvious and most pernicious manifestations of recency bias among investors pertains to their misuse of investment performance records for mutual funds and other types of funds. Investors track managers who produce temporary outsized returns during a one-, two-, or three-year period and then make investment decisions based only on such recent experiences. These investors do not pay heed to the cyclical nature of asset class returns, and so, for them, funds that have performed spectacularly in the very recent past appear unduly attractive. To counteract the effects of this bias, many practitioners wisely use what has become known as the "periodic table of investment returns," an adaptation of scientists' periodic table of chemical elements (see Table 16.1).

As the periodic table of investment returns in Table 16.1 demonstrates, asset class returns are highly variable. Many investors fail to heed the advice offered by the chart—namely, that it is nearly impossible to accurately predict which asset class will be the best performer from one year to the next. Thus, diversification is prudent (note how the diversified portfolio consistently appears near the center of each column). Practitioners would be wise to present this chart when establishing asset allocations with new clients to emphasize the advantages of diversification over return chasing.

Implications for Investors

As many wealth managers know, recency bias ran rampant during the bull market period between 2004 and 2007. Many investors implicitly presumed, as they have during other cyclical peaks, that the market would continue its enormous gains forever. They all but forgot the fact that bear markets can and do occur. Investors, who based decisions on their own subjective short-term memories, hoped that near-term history would continue to repeat itself. Intuitively, they insisted that evidence gathered from recent experience narrowed the range of potential outcomes and thus enabled them to project future returns. All too often, this behavior creates misguided confidence and becomes a catalyst for error.

TABLE 16.1 Sample of a Periodic Table of Investment Returns

1995	1996	1997	1998	1999	2000	2001	2002	2003
Large-Cap Value 38.35%	Real Estate 37.04%	Large-Cap Value 35.19%	Large-Cap Growth 38.70%	Small-Cap Growth 43.10%	Commodities 31.84%	Small-Cap Value 14.02%	Commodities 25.91%	Small-Cap Growth 48.54%
Large-Cap Growth 37.19%	Commodities 23.16%	Small-Cap Value 31.80%	International Stocks 20.34%	Large-Cap Growth 33.16%	Real Estate 31.04%	Real Estate 12.36%	Long-Term Bonds 16.79%	Small-Cap Value 46.035
Small-Cap Growth 31.04%	Large-Cap Growth 23.11%	Large-Cap Growth 30.48%	Large-Cap Value 15.65%	International Stocks 27.31%	Small-Cap Value 22.80%	Interm-Term Bonds 8.44%	Interm-Term Bonds 10.26%	International Stocks 39.17%
Long-Term Bonds 30.69%	Large-Cap Value 21.64%	Real Estate 19.66%	Long-Term Bonds 13.52%	Commodities 24.35%	Long-Term Bonds 20.27%	Short-Term Bonds 8.30%	Foreign Bonds 7.01%	Large-Cap Value 30.03%
Small-Cap Value 25.74%	Small-Cap Value 21.37%	Long-Term Bonds 15.08%	Foreign Bonds 12.09%	Large-cap Value 7.34%	Interm-Term Bonds 11.63%	Foreign Bonds 6.05%	Short-Term Bonds 5.76%	Large-Cap Growth 29.75%
High-Yield Bonds 20.46%	Foreign Bonds 12.16%	High-Yield Bonds 13.27%	Interm-Term Bonds 8.69%	Cash 4.74%	Foreign Bonds 9.71%	High-Yield Bonds 4.48%	Real Estate 3.60%	High-Yield Bonds 28.15%

Real Estate 27.75%	Cash 1.70%	Long-Term Bonds 4.21%	Short-Term Bonds 8.00%	Short-Term Bonds 3.06%	Short-Term Bonds 7.00%	Small-Cap Growth 12.95%	High-Yield Bonds 11.27%	Interm-Term Bonds 18.47%
Commodities 23.93%	High-Yield Bonds −1.89%	Cash 4.09%	Large-Cap Value 7.02%	High-Yield Bonds 2.51%	Cash 5.06%	Foreign Bonds 11.32%	Small-Cap Growth 11.26%	Foreign Bonds 18.24%
Interm-Term Bonds 4.10%	Small-Cap Value −11.42%	Large-Cap Value −5.59%	Cash 5.95%	Foreign Bonds 2.48%	High-Yield Bonds 2.95%	Interm-Term Bonds 9.65%	International Stocks 6.36%	Commodities 15.21%
Long-Term Bonds 2.48%	Large-Cap Value −15.52%	Small-Cap Growth −9.23%	High-Yield Bonds −5.12%	Interm-Term Bonds −0.82%	Small-Cap Growth 1.24%	Short-Term Bonds 6.66%	Cash 5.25%	Real Estate 12.24%
Foreign Bonds 1.98%	International Stocks −15.64%	Commodities −19.51%	International Stocks −13.95%	Small-Cap Value −1.49%	Small-Cap Value −6.43%	Cash 5.25%	Short-Term Bonds 4.98%	International Stocks 11.55%
Short-Term Bonds 1.90%	Large-Cap Growth −27.89%	Large-Gap Growth −20.42%	Large-Cap Growth −22.43%	Real Estate −2.57%	Real Estate −17.00%	International Stocks 2.06%	Interm-Term Bonds 3.63%	Short-Term Bonds 11.00%
Cash 1.07%	Small-Cap Growth −30.27%	International Stocks −21.21%	Small-Cap Growth −22.44%	Long-Term Bonds −8.74%	Commodities −27.03%	Commodities −3.39%	Long-Term Bonds −0.87%	Cash 5.76%

When studying the market, good investors analyze large data samples to determine probabilities. By doing so, solid conclusions can be scientifically obtained. Recency bias causes investors to place too much emphasis on data recently gathered, rather than examining entire, relevant bodies of information, which often span much more extensive intervals of time. Investors need to be advised to look at underlying value and not just recent performance. If prices have just risen strongly, for example, then assets may be approaching or may have exceeded their fair value. This should imply that there are, perhaps, better investment opportunities elsewhere. In what follows we summarize investment mistakes that can stem from recency bias.

RESEARCH REVIEW

James Montier's February 2003 paper entitled "Irrational Pessimism and the Road to Revulsion"[1] developed a model using recency bias. This is an outstanding real-world application of behavioral finance, as it lets practitioners observe how recency bias, in combination with anchoring bias, creates false intuition regarding market trajectories.

To proxy investors' expectations, Montier draws on two main behavioral biases: (1) anchoring and (2) recency. Recall, from Chapter 11, that anchoring is the term used to describe an investor's adherence to some arbitrary benchmark, often such that related calculations become skewed. Recency bias occurs when more recent events tend to remain more prominent in decision making than events that occurred further in the past. Montier uses both of these biases as the basis for his model of investor expectations regarding equity returns. Anchoring is represented in the model via a dependence of expectations on the long-run real return from U.S. equities (i.e., the long-run return of just over 7 percent is given a weight of 0.75 in this model of expectations).

RECENCY BIAS: BEHAVIORS THAT CAN CAUSE INVESTMENT MISTAKES

1. Recency bias can cause investors to extrapolate patterns and make projections based on historical data samples that are too small to ensure accuracy. Investors who forecast future returns based too extensively on only a recent sample of prior returns are vulnerable to purchasing at price peaks. These investors tend to enter asset classes at the wrong times and end up experiencing losses.

2. Recency bias can cause investors to ignore fundamental *value* and to focus only on recent upward price performance. When a return cycle peaks and recent performance figures are most attractive, human nature is to chase promise of a profit. Asset classes can and do become overvalued. By focusing only on price performance and not on valuation, investors risk principal loss when these investments revert to their mean or long-term averages.

3. Recency bias can cause investors to utter the words that many market veterans consider the most deceptive and damning of all: "It's different this time." In 1998 and 1999, for example, the short-term memory of recent gains influenced some investors so strongly as to overrule, in their minds, historical facts regarding rational valuations and the bubbles, peaks, and valleys that naturally occur. If your client ever seems to be yielding to this rationale, then it is time for a reality check.

4. Recency bias can cause investors to ignore proper asset allocation. Professional investors know the value of proper asset allocation, and they rebalance when necessary in order to maintain proper allocations. Recency bias can cause investors to become infatuated with a given asset class that, for example, appears in vogue. They often concentrate their holdings accordingly. Proper asset allocation is crucial to long-term investment success.

The recency effect is captured by giving the geometric 10-year annual price return a weight of 0.25 in the model. The two models are compared in Figures 16.1 and 16.2. Figure 16.1 shows the absolute level of expectations. The rational model shows that investors should expect no more than 5 percent real returns over the long run. Montier's irrational model shows that investors are looking for a return of over 8 percent annually in the long run.

Figure 16.2 shows the measure of the scope for disappointment. This is calculated as the difference between the irrational and rational models. The graph shows the irrational pessimism that gripped the market in the 1970s and early 1980s.

DIAGNOSTIC TESTING

These questions are designed to detect cognitive errors stemming from recency bias. To complete the test, select the answer choice that best characterizes your response to each item.

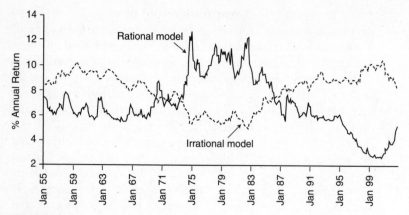

FIGURE 16.1 Irrational Exuberance versus Irrational Pessimism: Expected Annual Returns in the United States (%)

Recency Bias Test

Note that while most of the tests in this book are primarily intended to be administered by practitioners to their clients, they can, in general, be self-administered. This test, however, does require that someone other than the respondent administer the rest (i.e., it contains free recall memory exercises, etc.).

> **Question 1:** Suppose you are asked to select a mutual fund for your portfolio based only on the fund's performance record. What is your most likely course of action?
> **a.** I will look at the 1- to 3-year record of the fund to see how the fund has done recently.

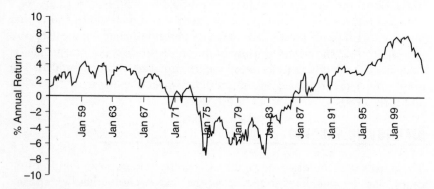

FIGURE 16.2 Scope for Disappointment: Irrational Model Minus Rational Model

b. I will look at the 5-year track record of the fund, as this time period showcases some elements of recent performance, but also historical performance.

c. I will look at the 10-year track record, even though it doesn't focus on the fund's most recent performance.

Question 2: Read the following list of names to the respondent. Then ask: Did the list contain more male or female names?

1. Sally
2. Mark
3. Amy
4. Annette
5. Jim
6. Barbara
7. Steven
8. David
9. Michael
10. Donna

Test Results Analysis

Question 1: People who select response "a" or "b" are likely subject to recency bias.

Question 2: This list actually contains an equal number of male and female names. The male names, however, are concentrated toward the end of the list. Therefore, people who suffer from recency bias are more likely to recall that the list was dominated by male names.

ADVICE

We have listed some errors that investors often commit when they are subject to recency bias. These corresponding strategies can be employed by practitioners who want to attempt to moderate recency bias in their clients.

Sample size and extrapolating trends. Investors afflicted with recency bias often make projections based only on recent data—based on a data sample too narrowly drawn to be accurately informative with regard to future market trends. This behavior is relatively easy to overcome, as investors can often be persuaded by data when it is presented to them. Often, clients simply don't have immediate access to the data they need in order to make good decisions; other times, they lack the patience for undertaking a careful analysis. Education is critical to overcoming this aspect of recency bias.

Price versus value. Human nature is to chase "hot money," and investors subject to recency bias often fixate on price performance while neglecting value indicators. Advisors need to demonstrate that out-of-favor, undervalued asset classes can make for very wise investments. The periodic table of investment returns is often a very persuasive visual aid and can help sway the recency-biased client toward a balanced allocation.

"It's different this time." Most practitioners recognize that an uninhibited, spontaneous critique of a client's every investment whim would probably hurt the relationship. Many advisors instead take an "advisory piggy bank" approach, saving up (i.e., holding back) some sentiments with regard to certain clients' ideas about their portfolios. Practitioners of this mind-set rationalize that the number of blatant criticisms (e.g., "How can you be so overconcentrated in XYZ stock?!") that advisory relationships can endure is probably limited. So, they should try to "withdraw from the piggy bank" only on the important occasions. If you're an advisor who utilizes the piggy bank approach and your client utters, "It's different this time," then you may need to make a substantial piggy bank withdrawal. Point to historical evidence until your client understands that it won't be different this time. It never is.

Unbalanced portfolio. Proper asset allocation and diversification are crucial to long-term investment success. Educating clients on these principles is essential to helping them reach their financial goals. Do not let your clients become enamored with one certain stock and let that stock dominate a portfolio. The stock could tumble, and your client could lose money. Education is critical to demonstrating why recency bias can be so dangerous. It might, perhaps, go without saying that in these situations, nothing can replace the benefit of objective advice.

NOTES

1. James Montier, "Irrational Pessimism and the Road to Revulsion" (research report, Dresdner Kleinwort Wasserstein, February 2003).

Four

Emotional Biases Defined and Illustrated

In Chapters 4 through 23, twenty behavioral biases, both cognitive and emotional, are discussed. Two types of cognitive biases were reviewed in Chapters 4 through 16. Belief perseverance cognitive biases were covered in Chapters 4 through 9, and information processing cognitive biases were covered in Chapters 10 through 16. Emotional biases are now covered in Chapters 17 through 23.

In each of the 20 bias chapters, the same basic format is used to discuss each bias, in order to promote greater accessibility. First, each bias is named, categorized as emotional or cognitive including subtype (belief perseverance or information processing), and then generally described and technically described. Note that in Chapters 17 through 23, which are the emotional biases, there are no subtypes. This is followed by the all-important concrete practical application, where it is demonstrated how each bias has been used or can be used in a practical situation. The practical application portion varies in content, consisting of either an intensive review of applied research or a case study. Implications for investors are then delineated. At the end of the practical application section is a research review of work directly applicable to each chapter's topic. A diagnostic test and test results analysis follow, providing a tool to indicate the potential bias of susceptibility. Finally, advice on managing the effects of each bias in order to minimize the effects of biases is offered.

CHAPTER 17

Loss Aversion Bias

Win as if you were used to it, lose as if you enjoyed it for a change.
—Ralph Waldo Emerson

BIAS DESCRIPTION

Bias Name: Loss aversion bias

Bias type: Emotional

General Description

Loss aversion bias was developed by Daniel Kahneman and Amos Tversky in 1979 as part of the original prospect theory;[1] specifically, in response to prospect theory's observation that people generally feel a stronger impulse to avoid losses than to acquire gains. A number of studies on loss aversion have given birth to a common rule of thumb: psychologically, the possibility of a loss is, on average, twice as powerful a motivator as the possibility of making a gain of equal magnitude; that is, a loss-averse person might demand, at minimum, a $2 gain for every $1 placed at risk. In this scenario, risks that don't "pay double" are unacceptable.

Loss aversion can prevent people from unloading unprofitable investments, even when they see little to no prospect of a turnaround. Some industry veterans have coined a diagnosis of "get-even-itis" to describe this widespread affliction, whereby a person waits too long for an investment to rebound following a loss. Get-even-itis can be dangerous because, often, the best response to a loss is to sell the offending security and to redeploy those assets. Similarly, loss aversion bias can make investors dwell excessively on risk avoidance when evaluating possible gains, since dodging a loss is a more urgent concern than seeking a profit. When their investments do begin to succeed, loss-averse individuals hasten to lock in profits, fearing that, otherwise, the market might reverse itself and rescind their returns. The problem here is that divesting prematurely to protect gains limits upside potential. In sum, loss aversion causes investors to hold their losing investments and to sell their winning ones, leading to suboptimal portfolio returns.

Technical Description

The technical definition of loss aversion comes from prospect theory, wherein Kahneman and Tversky don't explicitly mention concrete, relative preferences (e.g., "I prefer avoiding a loss to realizing a gain"). Rather, they discuss loss aversion in the context of the S-shaped, utility representative value function that models the entire evaluation stage in prospect theory. According to Kahneman and Tversky, people weigh all potential gains and losses in relation to some benchmark reference point (the point of origin on the graph in Figure 17.1).

The value function that passes through this point is asymmetric; and its profile implies, given the same variation in absolute value, a bigger impact of losses than of gains. The result is that risk-seeking behavior prevails in the domain of losses (below the x axis), while risk-averse behavior prevails in the domain of gains (above the x axis). An important concept embedded

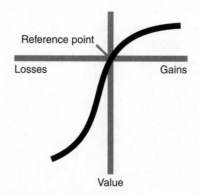

FIGURE 17.1 The Value Function—a Key Tenet of Prospect Theory
Source: The Econometric Society. Reprinted by permission.

in this utility representation is Hersh Shefrin and Meir Statman's disposition effect.[2] The disposition effect is the desire to hold losing investments too long (risk-seeking behavior) and to sell winning investments too quickly (risk-avoidance behavior).

PRACTICAL APPLICATION

Loss aversion bias, observed in practice as the *disposition effect,* is seen often by wealth management practitioners. Investors open up the monthly statements prepared by their advisors, skim columns of numbers, and usually notice both winners and losers. In classic cases of loss aversion, clients dread selling the securities that haven't performed well. Get-even-itis takes hold, and the instinct is to hold onto a losing investment until, at the very least, it rebounds enough for the client to break even. Often, however, research into a losing investment would reveal a company whose prospects don't forecast a rebound. Continuing to hold stock in that company actually adds risk to an investor's portfolio (hence, the client's behavior is risk seeking, which accords with the path of the value function in Figure 17.1).

Conversely, when the monthly statement indicates that profits are being made, the loss-averse client is gripped by a powerful urge to "take the money and run," rather than to assume continued risk. Of course, frequently, holding on to a winning stock isn't a risky proposition, if the company is performing well; that is, profitable investments that the loss-averse investor wants to sell might actually be improving the portfolio's risk/return profile. Therefore, selling deteriorates that risk/return profile and eliminates the potential for further gains. When the increased risks associated with holding on to losing investments are considered in combination with the prospect of losing future gains that occur when selling winners, the degree of overall harm that a loss-averse investor can suffer begins to become clear.

A final thought on taking losses: Some investors, remarking on losing investments that haven't yet been sold, rationalize that "it's only a paper loss." In one sense, yes, this is true. Inasmuch as the investment is still held, a loss has technically not been triggered for tax purposes.

In reality, though, this kind of rationale covers up the fact that a loss has taken place. If you went to the market to sell, having just incurred a "paper loss," the price you would obtain for your investment would be lower than the price you paid—effecting a very "real" loss indeed. Thus, if holding on to a losing investment does not objectively enhance the likelihood of recouping a loss, then it is better to simply realize the loss, which won't remain on paper forever.

Implications for Investors

Loss aversion is a bias that simply cannot be tolerated in financial decision making. It instigates the exact opposite of what investors want: increased risk, with lower returns. Investors should take risk to increase gains, not to mitigate losses. Holding losers and selling winners will wreak havoc on a portfolio. The following inset summarizes some common investment mistakes linked to loss aversion bias.

LOSS AVERSION BIAS: BEHAVIORS THAT CAN CAUSE INVESTMENT MISTAKES

1. Loss aversion causes investors to hold losing investments too long. This behavior is sometimes described in the context of a debilitating disease: *get-even-itis*. This is the affliction in which investors hold losing investments in the hope that they get back what they lost. This behavior has seriously negative consequences by depressing portfolio returns.
2. Loss aversion can cause investors to sell winners too early, in the fear that their profit will evaporate unless they sell. This behavior limits upside potential of a portfolio, and can lead to too much trading, which has been shown to lower investment returns.
3. Loss aversion can cause investors to unknowingly take on more risk in their portfolio than they would if they simply eliminated the investment and moved into a better one (or stayed in cash).
4. Loss aversion can cause investors to hold unbalanced portfolios. If, for example, several positions fall in value and the investor is unwilling to sell due to loss aversion, an imbalance can occur. Without proper rebalancing, the allocation is not suited to the long-term goals of the client, leading to suboptimal returns.

RESEARCH REVIEW

Over the course of the twentieth century, one investment enigma lingered: Given the respective risk elements of the two asset classes, why had equity returns so markedly and consistently exceeded fixed income returns over time? In 1985, Rajnish Mehra and Edward C. Prescott wrote a paper entitled "The Equity Premium: A Puzzle," which demonstrated that the *equity premium*—the gap between the average rate of return on stocks and the lower, average rate of return on riskless Treasury bills (T-bills)—had steadily averaged 6.18 percent over the preceding century.[3] A more recent study has since observed that, from 1900 to 2002, U.S. stocks earned a 5.3 percent annual premium over T-bills.[4] So, why don't investors reject low-paying bonds and purchase equities instead? Mehra and Prescott quantified the conundrum using coefficients of relative risk aversion.

Professors Shlomo Benartzi and Richard Thaler[5] suggested a solution to the equity risk premium puzzle based on what they call "myopic loss aversion." Their explanation is grounded in two behavioral concepts: loss aversion and myopia. Loss-averse investors are more sensitive to losses than gains, with losses estimated to be two times more influential than gains of the same size. Myopia denotes shortsightedness. When loss aversion is combined with myopia, investors who evaluate their portfolios most frequently are also the most likely to experience losses and, hence, to suffer from loss aversion. It follows that myopic, loss-averse investors would invest in bonds.

Benartzi and Thaler argued that most investors evaluate their portfolios in a relatively shortsighted way and that, as loss aversion implies, they are highly sensitive to losses that have occurred over the examined time period. Using a number of simulation approaches, the evaluation time period implied in their model (consistent with the realized equity risk premium) is about one year. Benartzi and Thaler demonstrated that nonmyopic investors (investors with long time horizons who don't give in to the temptation to evaluate their portfolios frequently) are more willing to invest in risky assets than are short-term investors (people who evaluate their portfolios more often). In this case, then, an asset's value depends on an investor's time horizon.

Practitioners need to be sensitive to the fact that many clients will evaluate their portfolios myopically and, as a result, may become loss averse. Stress the long-term benefits of asset allocation, and counsel clients not to pay too much attention to short-term market fluctuations.

DIAGNOSTIC TESTING

These questions are designed to detect signs of emotional bias stemming from loss aversion. To complete the test, select the answer choice that best characterizes your response to each item.

Loss Aversion Bias Test

Question 1: Suppose you make a plan to invest $50,000. You are presented with two alternatives. Which scenario would you rather have?

a. Be assured that I'll get back my $50,000, at the very least—even if I don't make any more money.

b. Have a 50 percent chance of getting $70,000 and a 50 percent chance of getting $35,000.

Question 2: Suppose you make a plan to invest $70,000. You are presented with two alternatives. Which scenario would you rather have?
   a. Know that I'll only be repaid $60,000, for sure.
   b. Take a 50-50 gamble, knowing that I'll get back either $75,000 or $50,000.

Question 3: Choose one of these two outcomes:
   a. An assured gain of $475.
   b. A 25 percent chance of gaining $2,000 and a 75 percent chance of gaining nothing.

Question 4: Choose one of these two outcomes:
   a. An assured loss of $725.
   b. A 75 percent chance of losing $1,000 and a 25 percent chance of losing nothing.

Test Results Analysis

Question 1: People who are loss averse are most likely to select "a," even though "b" offers a larger potential return on the upside.

Question 2: Increased initial endowment aside, this is basically the same question as Question 1. Most people, however, would probably select "b," because most people tend to be loss averse. Loss-averse investors are willing to gamble and risk an even greater loss rather than to admit a loss ("a"). However, this isn't simply a matter of an unconditional penchant for gambling. Most investors (that is, loss-averse investors) prefer the assurance of breaking even over the opportunity to gain a profit in Question 1.

Question 3: The rational response is "b," but loss-averse investors are likely to opt for the assurance of a profit in "a."

Question 4: The rational response is "a." Loss-averse investors are more likely to select "b."

ADVICE

Get-even-itis. Beware: Holding losing stocks for too long is harmful to your investment health. One symptom of get-even-itis is that a client's decision making regarding some investments seems to be dependent on the original price paid for that investment. One effective remedy is a stop-loss rule. You may, for example, agree to sell a security immediately if it ever incurs a 10 percent loss. However, it's best to consider an investment's normal, expected levels of volatility when devising a stop-loss rule. You don't want to be forced to sell if an investment's price is just exhibiting its customary ups and downs.

Take the money and run. Loss aversion can cause investors to sell winning positions too early, fearing that that their profits will evaporate otherwise. This behavior limits the upside potential of a portfolio and can lead to overtrading (which also reduces returns). Just as stop-loss rules can help to combat get-even-itis, it is often helpful to institute rules for selling appreciating investments. As with stop-loss rules, price-appreciation rules work best when tailored to reflect details related to fundamentals and valuation. The goal is to let gains run. Remember, too, that in a taxable account, you should avoid paying taxes on appreciations as long as possible.

Taking on excessive risk. Loss aversion can cause investors to hold onto losing investments even in companies that are in serious trouble. In such a case, it may be helpful to educate clients about an investment's risk profile—taking time to discuss items like standard deviation, credit rating, buy/sell/hold ratings, and so on. The investor will then, hopefully, make the right decision to protect the overall portfolio and jettison the risky, poorly performing investment.

Unbalanced portfolios. Loss aversion can cause investors to hold unbalanced portfolios. Education about the benefits of asset allocation and diversification is critical, yet it may be insufficient if an investor holds a concentrated stock position with emotional strings attached. A useful question in this situation is: "If you didn't own any XYZ stock today, would you still want to pick up as many shares as you own right now?" If and when the answer is "no," some leeway for maneuvering emerges. Tax considerations, such as low cost basis, sometimes factor in, but certain strategies can be employed to manage this cost.

NOTES

1. Daniel Kahneman and Amos Tversky, "Prospect Theory: An Analysis of Decision under Risk," *Econometrica* 47 (1979): 263–291.
2. Hersh Shefrin and Meir Statman, "The Disposition to Sell Winners Too Early and Ride Losers Too Long: Theory and Evidence," *Journal of Finance* 40 (1985): 77–90.

3. Rajnish Mehra and Edward C. Prescott, "The Equity Premium: A Puzzle," *Journal of Monetary Economics* 15 (March 1985): 145–161.

4. Shlomo Benartzi and Richard H. Thaler, "Myopic Loss Aversion and the Equity Premium Puzzle," *Quarterly Journal of Economics* (February 1995): 73–92. See http://gsbwww.uchicago.edu/fac/richard.thaler/research/myopic.pdf.

5. Ibid.

CHAPTER 18

Overconfidence Bias

Too many people overvalue what they are not and undervalue what they are.

—Malcolm S. Forbes

BIAS DESCRIPTION

Bias Name: Overconfidence

Bias Type: Emotional

General Description

In its most basic form, *overconfidence* can be summarized as unwarranted faith in one's intuitive reasoning, judgments, and cognitive abilities. Although the concept of overconfidence derives from psychological experiments and surveys in which subjects overestimate both their own predictive abilities and the precision of the information they've been given (essentially cognitive weaknesses), these faulty cognitions lead to emotionally charged behavior, such as excessive risk taking, and therefore overconfidence is classified as an emotional rather than cognitive bias. In short, people think they are smarter and have better information than they actually do. For example, they may get a tip from a financial advisor or read something on the Internet, and then they're ready to take action, such as making an investment decision, based on their perceived knowledge advantage.

Technical Description

Numerous studies have shown that investors are overconfident in their investing abilities. Specifically, the confidence intervals that investors assign to their investment predictions are too narrow. This type of overconfidence can be called *prediction overconfidence*. For example, when estimating the future value of a stock, overconfident investors will incorporate far too little leeway into the range of expected payoffs, predicting something between a 10 percent gain and decline, while history demonstrates much more drastic standard deviations. The implication of this behavior is that investors may underestimate the downside risks to their portfolios (being, naturally, unconcerned with "upside risks"!).

Investors are often also too certain of their judgments. We will refer to this type of overconfidence as certainty overconfidence. For example, having resolved that a company is a good investment, people often become blind to the prospect of a loss and then feel surprised or disappointed if the investment performs poorly. This behavior results in the tendency of investors to fall prey to a misguided quest to identify the "next hot stock." Thus, people susceptible to certainty overconfidence often trade too much in their accounts and may hold portfolios that are not diversified enough.

PRACTICAL APPLICATION

Prediction Overconfidence

Roger Clarke and Meir Statman demonstrated a classic example of prediction overconfidence in 2000 when they surveyed investors on the following question: "In 1896, the Dow Jones Average, which is a price index that does not include dividend reinvestment, was at 40. In 1998, it crossed 9,000. If dividends had been reinvested, what do you think the value of the DJIA would be in 1998? In addition to that guess, also predict a high and low range so that you feel 90 percent confident that your answer is between your high and low guesses."[1] In the survey, few responses reasonably approximated the potential 1998 value of the Dow, and no one estimated a correct confidence interval. (If you are curious, the 1998 value of the Dow Jones Industrial Average [DJIA], under the conditions postulated in the survey, would have been 652,230!)

A classic example of investor prediction overconfidence is the case of the former executive or family legacy stockholder of a publicly traded company such as Johnson & Johnson, ExxonMobil, or DuPont. These investors often refuse to diversify their holdings because they claim "insider knowledge" of, or emotional attachment to, the company. They cannot contextualize these stalwart stocks as risky investments. However, dozens of once-iconic names in U.S. business—AT&T, for example—have declined or vanished.

Certainty Overconfidence

People display certainty overconfidence in everyday life situations, and that overconfidence carries over into the investment arena. People tend to have too much confidence in the accuracy of their own judgments. As people find out more about a situation, the accuracy of their judgments is not likely to increase, but their confidence does increase, as they fallaciously equate the quantity of information with its quality. In a pertinent study, Baruch Fischhoff, Paul Slovic, and Sarah Lichtenstein gave subjects a general knowledge test and then asked them how sure they were of their answer. Subjects reported being 100 percent sure when they were actually only 70 percent to 80 percent correct.[2] A classic example of certainty overconfidence occurred during the technology boom of the late 1990s. Many investors simply loaded up on technology stocks, holding highly concentrated positions, only to see these gains vanish during the meltdown.

Implications for Investors

Both prediction and certainty overconfidence can lead to making investment mistakes. Below we list four behaviors, resulting from overconfidence bias, that can cause harm to an investor's portfolio. Advice on overcoming these behaviors follows the diagnostic test later in the chapter.

RESEARCH REVIEW

Numerous studies analyze the detrimental effects of overconfidence by investors, but the focus here is on one landmark work that covers elements of both prediction and certainty overconfidence. Professors Brad Barber and Terrance Odean, when at the University of California at Davis, studied the 1991 to 1997 investment transactions of 35,000 households, all holding accounts at a large discount brokerage firm, and they published their results in a 2001 paper, "Boys Will Be Boys: Gender, Overconfidence, and Common Stock Investment."[3] Barber and Odean were primarily interested in the relationship between overconfidence as displayed by both men and women and the impact of overconfidence on portfolio performance.

OVERCONFIDENCE BIAS: BEHAVIORS THAT CAN CAUSE INVESTMENT MISTAKES

1. Overconfident investors overestimate their ability to evaluate a company as a potential investment. As a result, they can become blind to any negative information that might normally indicate a warning sign that either a stock purchase should not take place or a stock that was already purchased should be sold.
2. Overconfident investors can trade excessively as a result of believing that they possess special knowledge that others don't have. Excessive trading behavior has proven to lead to poor returns over time.
3. Because they either don't know, don't understand, or don't heed historical investment performance statistics, overconfident investors can underestimate their downside risks. As a result, they can unexpectedly suffer poor portfolio performance.
4. Overconfident investors hold underdiversified portfolios, thereby taking on more risk without a commensurate change in risk tolerance. Often, overconfident investors don't even know that they are accepting more risk than they would normally tolerate.

Overconfident investors overestimate the probability that their personal assessments of a security's value are more accurate than the assessments offered by others. Disproportionate confidence in one's own valuations leads to differences of opinion, which influences trading. Rational investors only trade and purchase information when doing so increases their expected utility. Overconfident investors decrease their expected utilities by trading too much; they hold unrealistic beliefs about how high their returns will be and how precisely these returns can be estimated; and, they expend too many resources obtaining investment information (see Figure 18.1).

Odean and Barber noted that overconfident investors overestimate the precision of their information and thereby the expected gains of trading. They may even trade when the true expected net gains are negative. Models of investor overconfidence predict that because men are more overconfident than women, men will trade more and perform worse than women. Both men and women in Barber and Odean's study would have done better, on average, if they had maintained their start-of-the-year portfolios for the entire year.

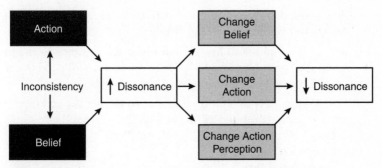

FIGURE 18.1 Trading Is Hazardous to Your Wealth
Source: Reprinted with permission by Blackwell Publishing, from Brad
M. Barber and Terrance Odean, "Trading Is Hazardous to Your
Wealth," *Journal of Finance* (April 2000).

In general, the stocks that individual investors sell go on to earn greater returns than the stocks with which investors replace them. The stocks men chose to purchase underperformed those they chose to sell by 20 basis points per month. For women, the figure was 17 basis points per month. In the end, Barber and Odean summarized overconfidence as a factor that is "hazardous to your wealth." They concluded that "individuals turn over their common stock investments about 70 percent annually." Mutual funds have similar turnover rates. Yet, those individuals and mutual funds that trade most earn lowest returns. They believe that there is a simple and powerful explanation for the high levels of counterproductive trading in financial markets: overconfidence.[4]

DIAGNOSTIC TESTING

This is a diagnostic test for both prediction overconfidence and certainty overconfidence. If you are an investor, take the test and then interpret the results. If you are an advisor, ask your client to take these tests and then discuss the results with you. After analyzing the test results in the next section, we will offer advice on how to overcome the detrimental effects of overconfidence.

Prediction Overconfidence Bias Test

Question 1: Give high and low estimates for the average weight of an adult male sperm whale (the largest of the toothed whales) in tons.

Choose numbers far enough apart to be 90 percent certain that the true answer lies somewhere in between.

Question 2: Give high and low estimates for the distance to the moon in miles. Choose numbers far enough apart to be 90 percent certain that the true answer lies somewhere in between.

Question 3: How easy do you think it was to predict the collapse of the housing and credit bubbles of 2008–2009?
a. Easy
b. Somewhat easy
c. Somewhat difficult
d. Difficult

Question 4: From 1926 through 2010, the compound annual return for equities was approximately 9 percent. In any given year, what returns do you expect on *your* equity investments to produce?
a. Below 9 percent
b. About 9 percent
c. Above 9 percent
d. Well above 9 percent

Certainty Overconfidence Bias Test

Question 5: How much control do you believe you have in picking investments that will outperform the market?
a. Absolutely no control
b. Little if any control
c. Some control
d. A fair amount of control

Question 6: Relative to other drivers on the road, how good a driver are you?
a. Below average
b. Average
c. Above average
d. Well above average

Question 7: Suppose you are asked to read this statement: "Capetown is the capital of South Africa." Do you agree or disagree?

Now, check how confident are you that you are correct?
a. 100 percent
b. 80 percent
c. 60 percent
d. 40 percent
e. 20 percent

Question 8: How would you characterize your personal level of investment sophistication?
   a. Unsophisticated
   b. Somewhat sophisticated
   c. Sophisticated
   d. Very sophisticated

Prediction Overconfidence Bias Test Results Analysis

Question 1: In actuality, the average weight of a male sperm whale is approximately 40 tons. Respondents specifying too restrictive a weight interval (say, "10 to 20 tons") are likely susceptible to prediction overconfidence. A more inclusive response (say, "20 to 100 tons") is less symptomatic of prediction overconfidence.

Question 2: The actual distance to the moon is 240,000 miles. Again, respondents estimating too narrow a range (say, "100,000 to 200,000 miles") are likely to be susceptible to prediction overconfidence. Respondents naming wider ranges (say, "200,000 to 500,000 miles") may not be susceptible to prediction overconfidence.

Question 3: If the respondent recalled that predicting the rupture of the credit and housing bubbles in 2008–2009 seemed easy, then this is likely to indicate prediction overconfidence. Respondents describing the collapse as less predictable are probably less susceptible to prediction overconfidence.

Question 4: Respondents expecting to significantly outperform the long-term market average are likely to be susceptible to prediction overconfidence. Respondents forecasting returns at or below the market average are probably less subject to prediction overconfidence.

Certainty Overconfidence Bias Test Results Analysis

Question 5: Respondents professing greater degrees of control over their investments are likely to be susceptible to certainty overconfidence. Responses claiming little or no control are less symptomatic of certainty overconfidence.

Question 6: The belief that one is an above-average driver correlates positively with certainty overconfidence susceptibility. Respondents describing themselves as average or below-average drivers are less likely to exhibit certainty overconfidence.

Question 7: If the respondent agreed with the statement and reported a high degree of confidence in the response, then susceptibility to certainty overconfidence is likely. If the respondent disagreed with the statement, and did so with 50 to 100 percent confidence, then susceptibility to certainty overconfidence is less likely. If respondents agree but with low degrees of confidence, then they are unlikely to be susceptible to certainty overconfidence. Confidence in one's knowledge can be assessed, in general, with questions of the following kind:

Which Australian city has more inhabitants—Sydney or Melbourne?

How confident are you that your answer is correct? Choose one: 50 percent, 60 percent, 70 percent, 80 percent, 90 percent, 100 percent.

If you answer 50 percent, then you are guessing. If you answer 100 percent, then you are absolutely sure of your answer.

Two decades of research into this topic have demonstrated that in all cases wherein subjects have reported 100 percent certainty when answering a question like the Australia one, the relative frequency of correct answers has been about 80 percent. Where subjects have reported, on average, that they feel 90 percent certain of their answers, the relative frequency of correct answers has averaged 75 percent. Subjects reporting 80 percent confidence in their answers have been correct about 65 percent of the time, and so on.

Question 8: Respondents describing themselves as sophisticated or highly sophisticated investors are likelier than others to exhibit certainty overconfidence. If the respondent chose "somewhat sophisticated" or "unsophisticated," susceptibility is less likely.

ADVICE

Overconfidence is one of the most detrimental biases that an investor can exhibit. This is because underestimating downside risk, trading too frequently and/or trading in pursuit of the "next hot stock," and holding an under-diversified portfolio all pose serious "hazards to your wealth" (to borrow from Barber and Odean's phrasing). Prediction and certainty overconfidence have been discussed and diagnosed separately, but the advice presented here deals with overconfidence in an across-the-board, undifferentiated manner. Investors susceptible to either brand of overconfidence should be mindful of all four of the detrimental behaviors identified in the feature box. None of these tendencies, of course, is unavoidable, but each occurs with high relative frequency in overconfident investors.

This advice is organized according to the specific behavior it addresses. All four behaviors are "wealth hazards" resulting frequently from overconfidence.

1. *Unfounded belief in own ability to identify companies as potential investments.* Many overconfident investors claim above-average aptitudes for selecting stocks, but little evidence supports this belief. The Odean study showed that after trading costs (but before taxes), the average investor underperformed the market by approximately 2 percent per year.[5] Many overconfident investors also believe they can pick mutual funds that will deliver superior future performance, yet many tend to trade in and out of mutual funds at the worst possible times because they chase unrealistic expectations. The facts speak for themselves: from 1984 through 1995, the average stock mutual fund posted a yearly return of 12.3 percent, whereas the average investor in a stock mutual fund earned 6.3 percent.[6]

   An advisor whose client claims an affinity for predicting hot stocks should consider asking the investor to review trading records of the past two years and then calculate the performance of the client's trades. More often than not, the trading activity will demonstrate poor performance (if it doesn't, go back further in time).

2. *Excessive trading.* In Odean and Barber's landmark study, "Boys Will Be Boys," the average subject's annual portfolio turnover was 80 percent (slightly less than the 84 percent averaged by mutual funds).[7] The least active quintile of participants, with an average annual turnover of 1 percent, earned 17.5 percent annual returns, outperforming the 16.9 percent garnered by the Standard & Poor's index during this period. The most active 20 percent of investors, however, averaged a *monthly* turnover of over 9 percent, and yet realized pretax returns of only 10 percent annually. The authors of the study do indeed seem justified in labeling trading as hazardous.

   When a client's account shows too much trading activity, the best advice is to ask the investor to keep track of each and every investment trade and then to calculate returns. This exercise will demonstrate the detrimental effects of excessive trading. Since overconfidence is a cognitive bias, updated information can often help investors to understand the error of their ways.

3. *Underestimating downside risks.* Overconfident investors, especially those who are prone to prediction overconfidence, tend to underestimate downside risks. They are so confident in their predictions that they do not fully consider the likelihood of incurring losses in their portfolios. For an advisor whose client exhibits this behavior, the best course of action is twofold. First, review trading or other investment

holdings for potentially poor performance, and use this evidence to illustrate the hazards of overconfidence. Second, point to academic and practitioner studies that show how volatile the markets are. The investor often will get the picture at this point, acquiring more cautious respect for the vagaries of the markets.

4. *Portfolio underdiversification.* As in the case of the retired executive who can't relinquish a former company's stock, many overconfident investors retain underdiversified portfolios because they do not believe that the securities they traditionally favored will ever perform poorly. The reminder that numerous, once-great companies have fallen is, oftentimes, not enough of a reality check. In this situation, the advisor can recommend various hedging strategies, such as costless collars, puts, and so on. Another useful question at this point is: "If you didn't own any XYZ stock today, would you buy as much as you own today?" When the answer is "no," room for maneuvering emerges. Tax considerations, such as low cost basis, sometimes factor in; but certain strategies can be employed to manage this cost.

A FINAL WORD ON OVERCONFIDENCE

One general implication of overconfidence bias in any form is that overconfident investors may not be well prepared for the future. For example, most parents of children who are high school aged or younger claim to adhere to some kind of long-term financial plan and thereby express confidence regarding their long-term financial well-being. However, a vast majority of households do not actually save adequately for educational expenses, and an even smaller percentage actually possess any "real" financial plan that addresses such basics as investments, budgeting, insurance, savings, and wills. This is an ominous sign, and these families are likely to feel unhappy and discouraged when they do not meet their financial goals. Overconfidence can breed this type of behavior and invite this type of outcome. Investors need to guard against overconfidence, and financial advisors need to be in tune with the problem. Recognizing and curtailing overconfidence is a key step in establishing the basics of a real financial plan.

NOTES

1. Roger G. Clarke and Meir Statman, "The DJIA Crossed 652,230," *Journal of Portfolio Management* 26 (Winter 2000): 89–93.

2. Sarah Lichtenstein, Baruch Fischhoff, and L. D. Phillips, "Calibration of Probabilities: The State of the Art to 1980," in David Kahneman, Paul Slovic, and Amos Tversky, eds., *Judgment under Uncertainty: Heuristics and Biases* (New York: Cambridge University Press, 1982), 306–334.
3. Brad M. Barber and Terrance Odean, "Boys Will Be Boys: Gender, Overconfidence, and Common Stock Investment," *Quarterly Journal of Economics* 116(1) (February 2001): 261–292.
4. Terrance Odean, "Do Investors Trade Too Much?" *American Economic Review* 89(5) (December 1999): 1279–1298.
5. Ibid.
6. Ibid.
7. See note 3.

CHAPTER 19

Self-Control Bias

Self-reverence, self-knowledge, self-control—these three alone lead to power.

—Alfred, Lord Tennyson (1880)

BIAS DESCRIPTION

Bias Name: Self-control bias

Bias Type: Emotional

General Description

Simply put, *self-control bias* is a human behavioral tendency that causes people to fail to act in pursuit of their long-term, overarching goals because of a lack of self-discipline. Money is an area in which people are notorious for displaying a lack of self-control. Attitudes toward paying taxes provide a common example. Imagine that you, a taxpayer, estimate that your income this year will cause your income tax to increase by $3,600, which will be due one year from now. In the interest of conservatism, you decide to set money aside. You contemplate two choices: Would you rather contribute $300 per month over the course of the next 12 months to some savings account earmarked for tax season? Or would you rather increase your federal income tax withholding by $300 each month, sparing you the responsibility of writing out one large check at the end of the year? Rational economic thinking suggests that you would prefer the savings account approach because your money would accrue interest and you would actually net more than $3,600. However, many taxpayers choose the withholding option because they realize that the savings account plan might be complicated in practice by a lack of self-control (i.e., one might overspend and then the tax money might not be there when one needs it.)

Self-control bias can also be described as a conflict between people's overarching desires and their inability, stemming from a lack of self-discipline, to act concretely in pursuit of those desires. For example, a college student desiring an "A" in history class might theoretically forgo a lively party to study at the library. An overweight person desperate to shed unwanted pounds might decline a tempting triple fudge sundae. Reality demonstrates, however, that plenty of people do sabotage their own long-term objectives for temporary satisfaction in situations like the ones described.

Investing is no different. The primary challenge in investing is saving enough money for retirement. Most of this chapter will focus on the savings behaviors of investors and how best to promote self-control in this often-problematic realm. Perhaps the best framework for understanding how to advise clients on self-control bias is done in the context of life-cycle hypothesis, a rational theory of savings behavior.

Technical Description

The technical description of self-control bias is best understood in the context of the *life-cycle hypothesis,* which describes a well-defined link between the savings and consumption tendencies of individuals and those individuals' stages of progress from childhood, through years of work participation, and finally into retirement. The foundation of the model is the *saving decision,* which directs the division of income between consumption and saving. The saving decision reflects an individual's relative preferences over present versus future consumption. Because the life-cycle hypothesis is firmly grounded in expected utility theory and assumes rational behavior, an entire lifetime's succession of optimal saving decisions can be computed given only an individual's projected household income stream vis-à-vis the utility function.

The income profile over the life cycle starts with low income during the early working years, followed by increasing income that reaches a peak prior to retirement. Income during retirement, based on assumptions regarding pensions, is then substantially lower. To make up for the lower income during retirement and to avoid a sharp drop in utility at the point of retirement, individuals will save some fraction of their income when they're still working, spending it later during retirement. The main prediction, then, of the life-cycle hypothesis is a lifetime savings profile characterized by a "hump"-shaped curve, with savings building gradually, maxing out, and finally declining again as a function of time.

Two common tendencies of individuals underlie spending patterns, according to the life-cycle hypothesis:

1. Most people prefer a higher standard of living to a lower standard of living; that is, people want to maximize consumption spending in the present.
2. Most people prefer to maintain a relatively constant standard of living throughout their lives. They dislike volatility and don't desire abrupt intervals of feast interspersed with famine.

Basically, the life-cycle hypothesis envisions that people will try to maintain the highest, smoothest consumption paths possible.

Now that we have an understanding of the life-cycle hypothesis, we can integrate behavioral concepts that account for real-world savings behavior. In 1998, Hersh Shefrin and Richard Thaler introduced a behaviorally explained life-cycle hypothesis,[1] which is a descriptive model of household savings in which self-control plays a key role. The key assumption of the behavioral life-cycle theory is that households treat components of their wealth as "nonfungible" or noninterchangeable even in the absence of credit rationing. Specifically, wealth is assumed to be divided into three "mental" accounts: (1) current income, (2) current assets, and (3) future income. The temptation to spend is assumed to be greatest for current income and least for future income.

Considerable empirical evidence supporting the behavioral life-cycle theory exists. In a survey of students' expectations of future consumption, Shefrin and Thaler obtained direct support for the tenets of behavioral life-cycle theory. Specifically, they found that subjects envisioning themselves to be the beneficiaries of some financial windfall predicted that they would consume, immediately, a greater portion of that windfall during the same year if the money was coded as current income rather than current assets. Subjects said that they would consume the smallest portions of income coded as future income. For most people, consumption and income (i.e., saving) are mediated by institutions, not individual decisions. Examples include home mortgage repayment schedules, 401(k) plans, and individual retirement accounts (IRAs); often, these instruments represent an individual's only real savings, with no additional funds being set aside.

Self-control has a cost, and people are willing to pay a price to avoid reigning in their natural impulses. Consumers act as if they are maintaining separate funds within their individual accounting systems, separating income into current income and wealth. The marginal propensity to consume varies according to the source of income (e.g., salary versus bonus), even if the measure taken to activate or to sustain the source of income (e.g., work) is the same. People are more likely to build assets or savings with money they view, or "frame," as wealth, whereas they are less likely to build savings using what they consider to be current income. Many researchers have continued to elaborate on the behavioral life-cycle model, particularly as it relates to retirement savings.

PRACTICAL APPLICATION

Encouraging people to save more is a task that constantly challenges financial advisors. The "Save More Tomorrow Program,"[2] developed by Professors Richard H. Thaler of the University of Chicago and Shlomo Benartzi of the Anderson School of Business at UCLA, aims to help corporate employees who would like to save more but lack the willpower to act on this desire. The program offers many useful insights into saving behavior, and examining it will serve as our practical application discussion in this chapter.

The "Save More Tomorrow Program" has four primary aspects:

1. Employees are approached about increasing their contribution rates a considerable time before their scheduled pay increases occur.
2. The contributions of employees who join the plan are automatically increased, beginning with the first paycheck following a raise.
3. Participating employees' contribution rates continue to increase automatically with each scheduled raise, until rates reach a preset maximum.
4. Employees can opt out of the plan at any time.

Let's examine the results of a trial of the Save More Tomorrow Program (SMTP) by a midsize manufacturing company in 1988. Prior to the adoption of the SMTP, the company suffered from a low participation rate as well as low saving rates. In an effort to increase the saving rates of the employees, the company hired an investment consultant and offered this service to every employee eligible for its retirement savings plan. Of the 315 eligible participants, all but 29 agreed to meet with the consultant and get his advice. Based on information that the employee provided, the consultant used commercial software to compute a desired saving rate. The consultant also discussed with each employee how much of an increase in saving would be considered economically feasible. If the employee seemed very reluctant to increase his or her saving rate substantially, the consultant would constrain the program to increase the saving contribution by no more than 5 percent.

Of the 286 employees who talked to the investment consultant, only 79 (28 percent) were willing to accept the consultant's advice, even with the adjustment to constrain some of the saving rate increases to 5 percent. For the rest of the participants, the planner offered a version of the SMTP, proposing that they increase their saving rates by 3 percentage points a year, starting with the next pay increase. Even with the aggressive strategy of increasing saving rates, the SMTP proved to be extremely popular with the participants. Of the 207 participants who were unwilling to accept the saving rate proposed by the investment consultant, 162 (78 percent) agreed to join the SMTP.

The majority of these participants did not change their minds once the saving increases took place. Only four participants (2 percent) dropped out of the plan prior to the second pay raise, with 29 more (18 percent) dropping out between the second and third pay raises. Hence, the vast majority of the participants (80 percent) remained in the plan through three pay raises. Furthermore, even those who withdrew from the plan did not reduce their contribution rates to the original levels; they merely stopped the future increases from taking place. So, even these workers are saving significantly more than they were before joining the plan.

The key lesson here is that people are generally poor at planning and saving for retirement. They need to have self-discipline imposed on them consistently in order to achieve savings.

Implications for Investors

As previously noted, the primary issue with regard to self-control is the lack of ability to save for retirement. In addition, there are several other self-control behaviors that can cause investment mistakes. We summarize some of these in the feature box.

SELF-CONTROL BIAS: BEHAVIORS THAT CAN CAUSE INVESTMENT MISTAKES

1. Self-control bias can cause investors to spend more today at the expense of saving for tomorrow. This behavior can be hazardous to one's wealth, because retirement can arrive too quickly for investors to have saved enough. Frequently, then, people incur inappropriate degrees of risk in their portfolios in effort to make up for lost time. This can, of course, aggravate the problem.

2. Self-control bias may cause investors to fail to plan for retirement. Studies have shown that people who do not plan for retirement are far less likely to retire securely than those who do plan. Studies have shown that people who do not plan for retirement are also less likely to invest in equity securities.

(Continued)

3. Self-control bias can cause asset-allocation imbalance problems. For example, some investors may prefer income-producing assets, due to a "spend today" mentality. This behavior can be hazardous to long-term wealth because too many income-producing assets can inhibit a portfolio to keep up with inflation. Other investors might favor different asset classes, such as equities over bonds, simply because they like to take risks and can't control their behavior.

4. Self-control bias can cause investors to lose sight of basic financial principles, such as compounding of interest, dollar cost averaging, and similar discipline behaviors that, if adhered to, can help create significant long-term wealth.

RESEARCH REVIEW

This research review examines two academic studies done by Professor Annamaria Lusardi, of Dartmouth College. In 2000, Lusardi wrote "Explaining Why So Many Households Do Not Save."[3] In 1999, she wrote "Information, Expectations, and Savings for Retirement."[4] Lusardi's work examined household savings and asset-ownership behavior in an attempt to assess how differences in planning and saving across households are explained by various factors. In essence, the studies address whether *lack of planning* (which may be interpreted as lack of self-control) plays a key role in explaining differences in savings behavior. The analysis relies on data obtained from the Health and Retirement Study (HRS), a survey based on a sample of U.S. householders born between 1931 and 1941; and the triennial, Federal Reserve–sponsored Survey of Consumer Finances (SCF). Lusardi took two measures to gauge the extent of retirement planning.

1. Planning is measured by responses to the question "How much have you thought about retirement?" Responses, grouped at various income levels, are summarized in Table 19.1. Lusardi classified respondents as "planners" or "nonplanners" on the basis of their responses; those who have "hardly" thought about retirement are nonplanners, whereas those who have thought at least "a little" about retirement are planners.

2. Planning is measured via a "planning index." The index is constructed by assigning "points" to respondents based on survey results. Points are awarded to reflect the extent to which a respondent claims to have

TABLE 19.1 Thinking about Retirement and Savings

	How Much Have You Thought about Retirement?			
Percentile	A Lot	Some	A Little	Hardly at All
5	0	2,010	−120	−500
25	41,300	50,500	28,500	8,800
50	116,200	128,000	92,000	60,000
75	241,000	266,800	208,000	147,000
90	437,000	474,500	485,700	346,500
95	636,500	752,000	1,009,000	613,350
Mean	224,252	239,298	245,304	165,367
(Std. Dev.)	(504,987)	(422,639)	(638,957)	(448,924)
Number of observations	1,331	1,039	681	1,438

Note: This table reports the distribution of total net worth across different responses to the question "How much have you thought about retirement?" All figures are weighted using survey weights.
Source: Annamaria Lusardi, "Explaining Why So Many Households Do Not Save" (working paper, Irving Harris Graduate School for Public Policy Studies, University of Chicago, 2000). Reprinted with permission.

thought about retirement ("hardly at all" merits one point, while "a lot" earns four), and points are added if respondents report engaging in additional planning activities. For example, respondents who have asked the Social Security Administration to calculate their expected retirement benefits receive one extra point. Respondents also receive points for having attended retirement seminars.

Lusardi's empirical analysis showed that householders not planning for retirement tend to have much lower savings than householders who have given thought to retirement. The study controlled for numerous additional variables that might arguably impact savings and also tried substituting various measures of asset accumulation (e.g., financial or total net worth) as proxy variables to provide alternative planning measures. Still, the result remains conclusive: savings levels depend significantly on whether a householder has planned for retirement.

Additionally, planning may have an effect not only on wealth but also on portfolio choice. If obtaining information about complex investment assets, such as stocks, required too much effort, families facing retirement will be less likely to invest in those assets. Thus, the question of whether planning affects stock ownership is also important and can be examined using regression analysis. Again, Lusardi incorporated a wide array of proxy variables to control for resource and preference attributes of households that, though not explicitly measurable, could be expected to bias results. Rather than considering total pension wealth, for example, the analysis distinguished between households whose heads maintain defined contribution, defined benefit, or other types of pensions. The underlying logic here is that plan structure might impact the degree of discretion employees exercise over the allocation of pension assets and that this, in turn, might impact allocation of nonpension assets. The results of this analysis showed that lack of planning is also a strong determinant of portfolio choice. Households that do not plan are less likely to invest in stocks; this result is consistent even after a variety of factors have been accounted for.

In the HRS, respondents were asked to rate their retirement experiences, and to state how they felt retirement compared to their working years (see Table 19.2). More than 54 percent of those respondents who had not thought about retirement rated their retirement experiences poor with

TABLE 19.2 How Has Your Retirement Turned Out?
Retirement and Planning
How Much Have You Thought about Retirement?

How Has Your Retirement Turned Out to Be?	A Lot	Some	A Little	Hardly at All
Very satisfying	0.68	0.50	0.35	0.22
Moderately satisfying	0.28	0.41	0.46	0.35
Not at all satisfying	0.04	0.09	0.19	0.43
Number of observations	343	217	92	520

How Is Your Retirement Compared to the Years Just Before You Retired?	A Lot	Some	A Little	Hardly at All
Better	0.57	0.44	0.35	0.18
About the same	0.22	0.31	0.36	0.24
Not as good	0.11	0.15	0.22	0.54
Retired less than one year ago	0.10	0.10	0.07	0.04
Number of observations	343	217	92	520

Note: This table reports the fraction of respondents according to how they have rated retirement and how much they have thought about retirement.
Source: Annamaria Lusardi, "Explaining Why So Many Households Do Not Save" (working paper, Irving Harris Graduate School for Public Policy Studies, University of Chicago, 2000). Reprinted with permission.

respect to their preretirement years. A large proportion of respondents (79 percent) who thought "a lot" about retirement described their quality of life during retirement as equaling or exceeding that of their preretirement years. This evidence suggestively coincides with the low amount of asset accumulation estimated for nonplanners in Lusardi's previous regressions. Rationally, households that accumulate less savings are probably more likely to experience an unpleasant "surprise" after retirement.

It can be concluded that a large percentage of U.S. households nearing retirement age inadequately plan for retirement. Although many explanations can be generated for these statistics, the reality is that people often simply do not think about retirement or do not want to sacrifice today to have future benefits. Lack of self-control (planning), Lusardi demonstrated, correlates with low aggregate wealth and results in portfolios that are less likely to contain high-return assets, such as stocks. Much research is needed to determine why households fail to plan for retirement and whether the provision of information (e.g., Social Security and pension benefits) might perhaps improve the financial security of many U.S. households.

DIAGNOSTIC TESTING

This section contains a brief diagnostic quiz that deals with issues of self-control.

> **Question 1:** Suppose that you are in need of a new automobile. You have been driving your current car for seven years, and it's time for a change. Assume that you do face some constraints in your purchase as "money doesn't grow on trees." Which of the following approaches are you most likely to take?
>
> **a.** I would typically underspend on a car because I view a car as transportation, and I don't need anything fancy. Besides, I can save the extra money I might have spent on a fancy car and put it away in my savings accounts.
>
> **b.** I would typically purchase a medium-priced model, with some fancy options, simply because I enjoy a nice car. I may forgo other purchases in order to afford a nice car. I don't imagine that I'd go crazy and purchase anything extravagant, but a nice car is something that I value to an extent and am willing to spend money to obtain this.
>
> **c.** When it comes to cars, I like to indulge myself. I'd probably splurge on a top-of-the-line model and select most or all available luxury options. Even if I must purchase this car at the expense of

saving money for the long term, I believe that it's vital to live in the moment. This car is simply my way of living in the moment.

Question 2: How would you characterize your retirement savings patterns?

    a. I consult my advisors and make sure that every tax-favored investment vehicle is maxed out (401(k), IRA, etc.), and I will often save additional funds in taxable accounts.

    b. I will usually take advantage of most tax-favored investment vehicles, though in some cases I'm sure that details may have escaped my attention. I may or may not save something in taxable investment accounts.

    c. I hardly ever save for retirement. I spend most of my disposable income, so very little remains available for savings.

Question 3: How well would you rate your own self-discipline?

    a. I always achieve a goal if it is important to me. If I want to lose 10 pounds, for example, I will diet and exercise relentlessly until I am satisfied.

    b. I can often attain my goals, but sometimes I have trouble sticking to certain difficult things that I have resolved to accomplish.

    c. I have a tremendous amount of difficulty keeping promises to myself. I have little or no self-discipline, and I often find myself reaching out to others for help in attaining key goals.

Test Results Analysis

Questions 1, 2, and 3: People answering "b" or "c" to any of these questions may be susceptible to self-control bias. Please note that self-control is a very common bias!

ADVICE

When a practitioner encounters self-control bias, there are four primary topics on which advice can generally be given: (1) spending control, (2) lack of planning, (3) portfolio allocation, and (4) the benefits of discipline.

    Spending control. Self-control bias can cause investors to spend more today rather than saving for tomorrow. People have a strong desire to consume freely in the present. This behavior can be counterproductive to attaining long-term financial goals because retirement often arrives before investors have managed to save enough money.

This may spur people into accepting, at the last minute, inordinate amounts of risk in their portfolios to make up for lost time—a tendency that actually places one's retirement security at increased risk. Advisors should counsel their clients to pay themselves first, setting aside consistent quantities of money to ensure their comfort later in life, especially if retirement is still a long way off. If an advisor encounters investors who are past age 60 and have not saved enough for retirement, then a more difficult situation emerges. A careful balance must be struck between saving, investing, and risk taking in order to increase the pot of money for retirement. Often, these clients might benefit from examining additional options, such as part-time work (cycling in and out of retirement) or cutting back on consumption. In either case, emphasizing paying oneself first—assigning a sufficient level of priority to future rather than present-day consumption—is critical.

Lack of planning. Self-control bias may cause investors to not plan adequately for retirement. Studies have shown that people who do not plan for retirement are much less likely not to retire securely than those who do plan. People who do not plan for retirement are also less likely to invest in equity securities. Advisors must emphasize that investing without planning is like building without a blueprint. Planning is the absolute key to attaining long-term financial goals. Furthermore, plans need to be written down so that they can be reviewed on a regular basis. Without planning, investors may not be apt to invest in equities, potentially causing a problem with keeping up with inflation. In sum, people don't plan to fail—they simply fail to plan.

Portfolio allocation. Self-control bias can cause asset allocation imbalance problems. Investors subject to this bias may prefer income-producing assets, due to a "spend today" mentality. This behavior can be counterproductive to attaining long-term financial goals because an excess of income-producing assets can prevent a portfolio from keeping up with inflation. Self-control bias can also cause people to unduly favor certain asset classes, such as equities over bonds, due to an inability to reign in impulses toward risk. Advisors must emphasize the importance of adhering to a planned asset allocation. There is a litany of information on the benefits of asset allocation, which can be persuasively cited for a client's benefit. Whether they prefer bonds or equities, clients exhibiting a lack of self-control need to be counseled on maintaining properly balanced portfolios so that they can attain their long-term financial goals.

Benefits of discipline. Self-control bias can cause investors to lose sight of very basic financial principles, such as compounding of interest or dollar cost averaging. By failing to reap these discipline profits over time, clients can miss opportunities for accruing significant long-term wealth. Perhaps the most critical issue is to counsel your clients on the benefits of compounding. There are a number of very effective software programs that can demonstrate that even a minimal, 1 to 2 percent disparity in returns, if compounded over decades, can mean the difference between a comfortable and a subpar retirement. To return to an example that arises frequently in discussions of willpower—the matter of exercising—the benefits of self-discipline in investing, as in physical fitness, are difficult to obtain. The results, however, are well worth it.

NOTES

1. Richard H. Thaler and Hersh M. Shefrin, "The Behavioral Life-Cycle Hypothesis," *Economic Inquiry* 26(4) (1988): 609–643.
2. Richard H. Thaler and Shlomo Benartzi, "Save More Tomorrow: Using Behavioral Economics to Increase Employee Saving," *Journal of Political Economy* 112(1): 5164–5187.
3. Annamaria Lusardi, "Explaining Why So Many Households Do Not Save" (working paper, Irving Harris Graduate School for Public Policy Studies, University of Chicago, 2000).
4. Annamaria Lusardi, "Information, Expectations, and Savings for Retirement," in Henry J. Aaron, ed., *Behavioral Dimensions of Retirement Economics* (Washington, DC: Brookings Institution and Russell Sage Foundation, 1999), 81–155.

CHAPTER 20

Status Quo Bias

Whosoever desires constant success must change his conduct with the times.

—Niccolo Machiavelli (1532)

BIAS DESCRIPTION

Bias Name: Status quo bias
Bias Type: Emotional

General Description

Status quo bias, a term coined by William Samuelson and Richard Zeckhauser in 1988,[1] is an emotional bias that predisposes people facing an array of choice options to elect whatever option ratifies or extends the existing condition (i.e., the "status quo") in lieu of alternative options that might bring about change. In other words, status quo bias operates in people who prefer for things to stay relatively the same. The scientific principle of inertia bears a lot of intuitive similarity to status quo bias; it states that a body at rest shall remain at rest unless acted on by an outside force. A simple real-world example illustrates. In the early 1990s, the states of New Jersey and Pennsylvania reformed their insurance laws and offered new programs. Residents had the opportunity to select one of two automotive insurance packages: (1) a slightly more expensive option that granted policyholders extensive rights to sue one another following an accident, and (2) a less expensive option with more restricted litigation rights. Each insurance plan had a roughly equivalent expected monetary value. In New Jersey, however,

223

the more expensive plan was instituted as the default, and 70 percent of citizens "selected" it. In Pennsylvania, the opposite was true—residents would have to opt out of the default, less-expensive option in order to opt into the more expensive option. In the end, 80 percent of the residents "chose" to pay less.

Technical Description

Status quo bias refers to the finding that an option is more desirable if it is designated as the "status quo" than when it is not.[2] Status quo bias can contribute to the aforementioned inertia principle, but inertia is not as strong as status quo bias. Inertia means that an individual is relatively more reluctant to move away from some state identified as the status quo than from any alternative state not identified as the status quo. People less readily abandon a condition when they're told, "Things have always been this way." Status quo bias implies a more intense "anchoring effect."

Status quo bias is often discussed in tandem with other biases, namely endowment bias (see Chapter 21) and loss aversion bias (see Chapter 17). Status quo bias differs from these two in that it does not depend on framing changes in terms of losses and potential gains.[3] When loss aversion bias and status quo bias cross paths, it is probable that an investor, choosing between two investment alternatives, will stick to the status quo if it seems less likely to trigger a loss—even if the status quo also guarantees a lower return in the long run. Endowment bias implies that ownership of a piece of property imbues that property with some perceived, intangible added value—even if the property doesn't really increase the utility or wealth of the owner. By definition, endowment bias favors the status quo—people don't want to give up their endowments. Loss aversion bias, endowment bias, and status quo bias often combine; and the result is an overall tendency to prefer things to stay as they are, even if the calm comes at a cost.

PRACTICAL APPLICATION

Investors with inherited, concentrated stock positions often exhibit classic status quo bias. Take the case of a hypothetical grandson who hesitates to sell the bank stock he's inherited from his grandfather. Even though his portfolio is underdiversified and could benefit from such an adjustment, the grandson favors the status quo. A number of motives could be at work here. First, the investor may be unaware of the risk associated with holding an excessively concentrated equity position. He may not foresee that if the stock tumbles, he will suffer a significant decrease in wealth. Second, the grandson may experience a personal attachment to the stock, which carries an emotional connection to a previous generation. Third, he may hesitate to sell because of his aversion to the tax consequences, fees/commissions, or other transaction costs associated with unloading the stock.

The advice section of this chapter reviews some strategies for dealing with each of these potential objections—all of which could contribute to status quo–biased behavior.

Implications for Investors

In the following, we review four investment mistakes that can stem from status quo bias.

RESEARCH REVIEW

Samuelson and Zeckhauser's "Status Quo Bias in Decision Making"[4] provides an excellent research paper on status quo bias. It examined a study in which subjects were told that they had each just inherited a large sum of money from an uncle and could choose to invest the money in any one of four possible portfolios. Each portfolio offered a different level of risk and a different rate of return. The scenario was repeated twice; in the first trial, subjects were given only the aforementioned information, with no indication of how the conferring uncle might have invested the money himself. In the second trial, the subjects were informed that the uncle, prior to his death, had invested the sum in a moderate-risk portfolio—one of the four options available to the subjects at present.

As you might expect, the moderate-risk portfolio proved far more popular in the second trial, when it was designated as the status quo, than in the first trial, when all options were equally "new."

This study reinforced the idea that investors tend to prefer upholding the present status. Advisors need to recognize this phenomenon and target their advice accordingly. Status quo bias is strong and, since it is an emotional bias, a lot of skill must be exercised in order to guide clients away from it.

STATUS QUO BIAS: BEHAVIORS THAT CAN CAUSE INVESTMENT MISTAKES

1. Status quo bias can cause investors, by taking no action, to hold investments inappropriate to their own risk/return profiles. This can mean that investors take excessive risks or invest too conservatively.

2. Status quo bias can combine with loss aversion bias. In this scenario, an investor facing an opportunity to reallocate or alter an investment position may choose, instead, to maintain the status quo because the status quo offers the investor a lower probability of realizing a loss. This will be true even if, in the long run, the investor could achieve a higher return by electing an alternative path.

3. Status quo bias causes investors to hold securities with which they feel familiar or of which they are emotionally fond. This behavior can compromise financial goals, however, because a subjective comfort level with a security may not justify holding onto it despite poor performance.

4. Status quo bias can cause investors to hold securities, either inherited or purchased, because of an aversion to transaction costs associated with selling. This behavior can be hazardous to one's wealth because a commission or a tax is frequently a small price to pay for exiting a poorly performing investment or for properly allocating a portfolio.

DIAGNOSTIC TESTING

These questions are designed to detect signs of cognitive errors stemming from status quo bias. To complete the test, select the answer choice that best characterizes your response to each item.

Status Quo Bias Test

Question 1: Your financial advisor presents you with a plan to rebalance your portfolio. This rebalancing would require you to make a number of substantial changes in your portfolio, which may even involve triggering taxable events that are not pleasant but are quite necessary to get your portfolio where it needs to be. Which of the following is most likely?

a. You take action on the recommendation immediately.
b. You say you'll "think about it" to do an honest review and get back to your advisor in a week—and you actually will get back to your advisor in that time.
c. You say you'll "think about it" and get back to your advisor in a week—and you probably won't get back to your advisor and may not for three to six months because you tend to agonize over making substantial changes like this.

Question 2: Your investment portfolio contains a certain high-quality corporate bond. The bond has been providing income for you, and you are happy with it. Your financial advisor analyzes your bond holdings and recommends that you replace the corporate bond with a municipal bond of comparable quality, estimating that you will obtain a better return after capital gains taxes and fees. You aren't familiar with this municipal bond. What is your most likely response?

a. I will sell the corporate and purchase the municipal bond.
b. I will keep things as they are.

Question 3: Suppose that you have inherited a fully liquid investment in a South African gold mine from your eccentric Uncle Jim. You discuss the asset with your financial advisor, and she concludes that your portfolio already contains enough gold and commodities. More important, Uncle Jim's bequest isn't a diversified asset. Your advisor recommends selling it. What is your most likely course of action?

a. I will sell, as recommended by my financial advisor.
b. I will hold on to the gold mine interest, because I don't like to sell or modify things that people pass away and leave to me.

Test Results Analysis

Question 1: Answering "c" demonstrates a classic example of status quo bias.

Question 2: People who select "b" are likelier to suffer from status quo bias than people who select "a." Option "a" probably offers higher returns, but option "b" is, alas, the status quo.

Question 3: In this situation, most people would behave as depicted in "b," even when lacking any cogent rationale for holding the asset. Option "b" suggests status quo bias; "a" does not.

ADVICE

This section offers advice on each of the specific investor errors outlined in the feature box.

> *Holding inappropriate assets.* Education is essential to overcoming this aspect of status quo bias. As previously noted, status quo bias is exceptionally strong and difficult to overcome. Demonstrating the downside risks associated with holding inappropriate assets is often an effective tactic and may motivate people to change their behavior. Another persuasive approach is to demonstrate, based on a single stock position, what could happen to overall wealth levels if the market goes south and then to explicitly link wealth changes with probable lifestyle changes.

> *Status quo bias and loss aversion bias.* Doing nothing is much easier than making a decision. This is especially true when a decision might bring about emotional pain; for example, the decision to sell a losing investment may register the impact of a loss. Sometimes, however, inaction can compromise long-run returns. When clients hesitate to implement changes, advisors should carefully analyze whether adhering to the status quo will affect attainment of financial goals. If you discover that your client's biased behavior will indeed impact his or her wealth down the road, then education is critical. Explain to clients the common cognitive and emotional oversights they may be committing and demonstrate the benefits of decisive action.

> *Status quo bias and emotional attachment.* Emotions are perhaps the least legitimate concerns in asset management. When financial goals are in jeopardy, it can be too risky to sit back and adhere to an affective whim. Advisors need to demonstrate how emotions need to be managed. "Emotional intelligence," a well-publicized topic in popular psychology, offers many insights to this end. Do a little reading, and you may find yourself better equipped to help your clients work through their emotional attachments.

> *Status quo bias and fear of transaction costs.* Taxes and fees are legitimate concerns when it comes to altering an allocation status quo. However, more often than not, these concerns pale in comparison to the other potential implications of holding, or exiting, a poorly performing security. If you are an advisor, run through some financial calculations with your client. Then, be ready to be persuasive in communicating the advantages of diversification and proper asset allocation.

NOTES

1. William Samuelson and Richard J. Zeckhauser, "Status Quo Bias in Decision Making," *Journal of Risk and Uncertainty* 1(1) (1988): 7–59.
2. Daniel Kahneman, J. L. Knetch, and Richard H. Thaler, "The Endowment Effect, Loss Aversion, and Status Quo Bias: Anomalies," *Journal of Economic Perspectives* 5(1) (1991): 193–206.
3. See note 1.
4. Ibid.

CHAPTER 21

Endowment Bias

A wise man should have money in his head, but not in his heart.
—Jonathan Swift

BIAS DESCRIPTION

Bias Name: Endowment bias
Bias Type: Emotional

General Description

People who exhibit *endowment bias* value an asset more when they hold property rights to it than when they don't. Endowment bias is inconsistent with standard economic theory, which asserts that a person's *willingness to pay* for a good or an object should always equal the person's *willingness to accept dispossession* of the good or the object, when the dispossession is quantified in the form of compensation. Psychologists have found, however, that the minimum selling prices that people state tend to exceed the maximum purchase prices that they are willing to pay for the same good. Effectively, then, ownership of an asset instantaneously "endows" the asset with some added value. Endowment bias can affect attitudes toward items owned over long periods of time or can crop up immediately as the item is acquired.

Technical Description

Endowment bias is described as a mental process in which a differential weight is placed on the value of an object. That value depends on whether one possesses the object and is faced with its loss or whether one does not possess the object and has the potential to gain it. If one loses an object that is part of one's endowment, then the magnitude of this loss is perceived to be greater than the magnitude of the corresponding gain if the object is newly added to one's endowment. Professor Richard Thaler of the University of Chicago defines the endowment bias:

> *If out-of-pocket costs are viewed as losses and opportunity costs are viewed as foregone gains, the former will be more heavily weighted. Furthermore, a certain degree of inertia is introduced into the consumer choice process since goods that are included in the individual's endowment will be more highly valued than those not held in the endowment,* ceteris paribus. *This follows because removing a good from the endowment creates a loss while adding the same good (to an endowment without it) generates a gain. Henceforth, I will refer to the underweighting of opportunity costs as the* endowment effect.[1]

In 1989, a researcher named J. L. Knetsch reported results from experiments designed to examine the endowment bias.[2] Knetsch's results provided an excellent practical application of endowment bias and concerned an experiment involving two groups of subjects. The 76 subjects in the first group were each given a coffee mug. They were then asked to complete a questionnaire, after which they were shown some candy bars. It had been determined earlier that the 76 subjects were about evenly divided over whether they generally preferred candy bars or coffee mugs if given a choice. But when told that they could substitute a candy bar for the coffee mug they had been given, 89 percent chose to keep the coffee mug. The second group consisted of 87 subjects. Again, about 50 percent preferred candy bars, and 50 percent preferred coffee mugs. The second group participated in the same exercise as the first group, except this time the candy bars were the endowment good and the coffee mugs were offered subsequently as substitutes. In the second group, 90 percent declined to trade their endowed candy bars. Knetsch concluded that this dramatic asymmetry resulted because "subjects weigh the loss of giving up their initial reference entitlement far more heavily than the foregone gains of not obtaining the alternative entitlement."[3] Neither coffee mugs nor candy bars seemed, in this experiment, innately more desirable by any significant margin; rather, subjects' preferences depended on their respective endowments.

PRACTICAL APPLICATION

Investors prove resistant to change once they become endowed with (take ownership of) securities. We will examine endowment bias as it relates to both inherited securities and purchased securities. Then, we'll look at two common causes of endowment bias.

Inherited Securities

William Samuelson and Richard Zeckhauser[4] performed an enlightening study on endowment bias that aptly illustrates investor susceptibility to this bias. Samuelson and Zeckhauser conducted an experiment in which investors were told to imagine that they had to newly acquire one of four investment options:

1. A moderately risky stock
2. A riskier stock
3. A Treasury security
4. A municipal security

Another group of investors was given the same list of options. However, they were instructed to imagine that they had already inherited one specified item on the list. If desired, the investors were told, they could cede their hypothetical inheritance in favor of a different option and could do so without penalty. In every case, however, the investors in the second group showed a tendency to retain whatever was "inherited." This is a classic case of endowment bias. Most wealth management practitioners have encountered clients who are reluctant to sell securities bequeathed by previous generations. Often, in these situations, investors cite feelings of disloyalty associated with the prospect of selling inherited securities, general uncertainty in determining "the right thing to do," and tax issues.

Purchased Securities

Endowment bias also often influences the value that an investor assigns to a recently purchased security. Here is an example to illustrate this point: Assume that you have a great need for income. How much would you pay for a municipal bond that pays you triple your pretax income? Further assume that you have purchased this bond and that it is performing as expected. Interest rates have not changed, the market for securities is highly liquid, and you have the type of account that offers unlimited transactions for one fee. How much would you demand in exchange for the bond if someone wanted to buy it from you?

Rational economic theories predict that your willingness to pay (WTP) for the bond would equal your willingness to accept (WTA) compensation for it. However, this is unlikely to be the case. Once you are endowed with the bond, you are probably inclined to demand a selling price that exceeds your original purchase price. Many wealth managers have observed that investor decision making regarding both inherited and purchased securities can exhibit endowment bias and that "decision paralysis" often results: Many clients have trouble making decisions regarding the sale of securities that they either inherited or purchased themselves, and their predicament is attributable to endowment bias.

Implications for Investors

There are some practical explanations as to why investors are susceptible to endowment bias. Understanding the origins of endowment bias can help to provide intuition that guards against the mistakes that the bias can cause. First, investors may hold onto securities that they already own in order to *avoid the transaction costs* associated with unloading those securities. This is particularly true regarding bonds. Such a rationale can be hazardous to one's wealth, because failure to take action and sell off certain assets can sometimes invite otherwise avoidable losses, while forcing investors to forgo the purchase of potentially more profitable, alternative assets. Second, investors hold onto securities because of familiarity. If investors know from experience the characteristics of the instruments that they already own (the behavior of particular government bonds, for example), then they may feel reluctant to transition into instruments that seem relatively unknown. Familiarity, effectively, has value. This value adds to the actual market value of a security that an investor possesses, causing WTA to exceed WTP.

The list below contains a summary of investment mistakes that arise from endowment bias.

ENDOWMENT BIAS: BEHAVIORS THAT CAN CAUSE INVESTMENT MISTAKES

1. Endowment bias influences investors to hold onto securities that they have inherited, regardless of whether retaining those securities is financially wise. This behavior is often the result of the heirs' fear that selling will demonstrate disloyalty to prior generations or will trigger tax consequences.
2. Endowment bias causes investors to hold securities they have purchased (already own). This behavior is often the result of decision paralysis, which places an irrational premium on the

compensation price demanded in exchange for the disposal of an endowed asset.

3. Endowment bias causes investors to hold securities that they have either inherited or purchased because they do not want to incur the transaction costs associated with selling the securities. These costs, however, can be a very small price to pay when evacuating an unwise investment.

4. Endowment bias causes investors to hold securities that they have either inherited or purchased because they are familiar with the behavioral characteristics of these endowed investments. Familiarity, though, does not rationally justify retaining a poorly performing stock or bond.

RESEARCH REVIEW

Professor John A. List of the University of Maryland authored a unique and highly relevant paper entitled "Does Market Experience Eliminate Market Anomalies?"[5] that reviewed some key aspects of endowment bias, the lessons of which can be relevant to investors. In the paper, Professor List tried to ascertain the effect of trading expertise on an individual's susceptibility to endowment bias. List's sample population traded sports cards and other sports memorabilia, and the key result of List's empirical analysis was that traders with more real-world experience were less susceptible to endowment bias. Most professional sports memorabilia dealers, for example, showed little biased behavior. List also demonstrated that people who are net sellers learn how to trade better and more quickly, with less biased behavior, than people who are net buyers. These lessons have direct implications for securities markets, and readers should take note:

> Neoclassical models include several fundamental assumptions. While most of the main tenets appear to be reasonably met, the basic independence assumption, which is used in most theoretical and applied economic models to assess the operation of markets, has been directly refuted in several experimental settings. . . . These experimental findings have been robust across unfamiliar goods, such as irradiated sandwiches, and common goods, such as chocolate bars, with most authors noting behavior consistent with an endowment effect. Such findings have induced even the most ardent supporters of neoclassical theory to doubt the validity of certain

neoclassical modeling assumptions. Given the notable significance of the anomaly, it is important to understand whether the value disparity represents a stable preference structure or if consumers' behavior approaches neoclassical predictions as market experience intensifies.

In this study, I gather primary field data from two distinct markets to test whether individual behavior converges to the neoclassical prediction as market experience intensifies. My data gathering approach is unique in that I examine i) trading patterns of sports memorabilia at a sports card show in Orlando, FL, and ii) trading patterns of collector pins in a market constructed by Walt Disney World at the Epcot Center in Orlando, FL. In addition, as an institutional robustness check, I examine explicit statements of value in actual auctions on the floor of a sports card show in Tucson, AZ. All of these markets are natural settings for an experiment on the relationship between market experience and the endowment effect, as they provide natural variation across individual levels of expertise. In the sports card show field experiments, I conduct some of the treatments with professional dealers and others with ordinary consumers. The design was used to capture the distinction between consumers who have intense trading experience (dealers) and those who have less trading experience (non-dealers). A major advantage of this particular field experimental design is that my laboratory is the marketplace: subjects would be engaging in similar activities whether I attended the event or went to the opera. In this sense, I am gathering data in the least obtrusive way possible, while still maintaining the necessary control to execute a clean comparison between treatments. This highlights the naturalness of this particular setting and the added realism associated with my field experiments.

The main results of the study fall into three categories. First, consistent with previous studies, I observe a significant endowment effect in the pooled data. Second, I find sharp evidence that suggests market experience matters: across all consumer types, market-like experience and the magnitude of the endowment effect are inversely related. In addition, within the group of subjects who have intense trading experience (dealers and experienced non-dealers), I find that the endowment effect becomes negligible. Both of these observations extend quite well to statements of value in auctions, where offers and bids are significantly different for naive consumers, but statistically indistinguishable for experienced consumers.

While these empirical results certainly suggest that individual behavior converges to the neoclassical prediction as market *experience intensifies, it remains an open question as to whether the endowment effect is absent for practiced consumers because of experience (treatment effect), or because a prior disposition toward having no such gap leads them to trade more often (selection effect). To provide evidence into this query, I returned to the sports card market approximately one year after the initial sports card trading experiment and examined trading rates for the same group of subjects who participated in the first experiment. Via both unconditional and conditional statistical analyses, which use panel data regression techniques to control for individual static preferences, I find that market experience significantly attenuates the endowment effect.*

Whether preferences are defined over consumption levels or changes in consumption merits serious consideration. If preferences are defined over changes in consumption, then a reevaluation of a good deal of economic analysis is necessary since the basic independence assumption is directly refuted. Several experimental studies have recently provided strong evidence that the basic independence assumption is rarely appropriate. These results, which clearly contradict closely held economic doctrines, have led some influential commentators to call for an entirely new economic paradigm to displace conventional neoclassical theory.

In this study, I depart from a traditional experimental investigation by observing actual market behavior. Examining behavior in four field experiments across disparate markets yields several unique insights. First, the field data suggest that there is an overall endowment effect. Second, within both institutions—observed trading rates and explicit value revelation—I find strong evidence that individual behavior converges to the neoclassical prediction as trading experience intensifies.[6]

Overall, List's data and analysis support the idea that trading expertise negatively correlates with endowment bias. Moreover, by examining trading patterns within two separate market institutions, List provided controls for any unobserved effects that may be specific to one trading forum and thereby bias his result. List's findings do not simply pertain to the sports card show or to Epcot, but to both—and can be applied to the investing behavior of private clients.

DIAGNOSTIC TESTING

The following is a brief diagnostic test that can help to detect endowment bias.

Endowment Bias Test

Question 1: Assume that your dearly departed Aunt Sally has bequeathed to you 100 shares of IBM. Your financial advisor tells you that you are too "tech heavy" and recommends that you sell Aunt Sally's shares. What is your most likely course of action?

a. I will likely hold the IBM shares because Aunt Sally bequeathed them to me.

b. I will likely listen to my financial advisor and sell the shares.

Question 2: Assume that you have purchased a high-quality municipal bond for your portfolio. It has been providing income for you, and you are happy with it. Your financial advisor analyzes your bond holdings and recommends switching to a corporate bond, of comparable quality, with which you are unfamiliar. Your advisor explains that, after taxes and fees, the corporate bond can be expected to provide a slightly better return than your current municipal bond. What is your most likely response?

a. I will stick with the municipal bond because I am familiar with it.

b. I will sell the municipal bond and purchase the corporate bond, even though I am unfamiliar with the corporate bond.

Question 3: Assume that you purchased 100 shares of GE in a self-directed account and paid a commission on the transaction. Shortly following the purchase, you realize that you momentarily overlooked another 100 shares of GE that you already owned in another account. Now, the redundant holdings are causing an imbalance in your overall portfolio. What is your reaction to this situation?

a. Since I paid a commission and I like GE's stock, I will keep the GE even though it may cause an imbalance in my overall portfolio.

b. I am not comfortable with imbalance in my portfolio. I will sell the GE, even though this means that I will have paid two unnecessary commissions.

Test Results Analysis

Question 1: A reluctance to unload Aunt Sally's IBM shares can signal susceptibility to endowment bias.

Question 2: People who decide that they might likely hold on to the municipal bond, due to familiarity with it, are likelier to exhibit endowment bias than people who would be willing to reallocate, even into unfamiliar territory, at a financial advisor's request.

Question 3: Respondents who estimate that they'd be willing to tolerate the imbalance caused by the redundant GE holdings are probably susceptible to endowment bias.

ADVICE

Generally, endowment bias tends to impact investors in four main contexts: (1) inherited securities, (2) purchased securities, (3) commission aversion, and (4) desire for familiarity. Advice can be tailored, specifically, to address each case.

Inherited securities. If you are a professional wealth advisor and you realize that a client's decisions regarding inherited securities, or any other pertinent asset, are being compromised by endowment bias, then asking the client carefully targeted questions is often a useful first step. This way, you can lead clients to discover the "correct" conclusion themselves. In the case of an inherited security, for example, you might ask: "If you had received, as cash, the current value of this security, what portion of that inheritance would you allocate into this specific security?" Often, the answer is none or very little. It can also be useful to explore the deceased's intent in owning the security. "Do you think that Uncle John's primary intent was to leave you this specific number of shares of this specific security? Is it possible that he was concerned about your general financial security?" Again, clients usually affirm the latter conclusion, paving the way to a more sensible allocation. If the client does believe that his or her deceased relative valued, specifically, the opportunity to bequeath holdings in this exact security, then you might need to try a different line of questioning: "Okay, Uncle John wanted you to have these shares. But, if he really didn't want you to sell them, then ... what did he want you to do with them?" Stressing the achievement of financial goals usually persuades the client to listen to facts about how selling enhances the chances of achieving a favorable outcome.

Purchased securities. A similar line of questioning can also help determine if clients are biased in the area of purchased securities, for example, "If you had to convert your current holdings in Security XYZ into cash and then allocate that cash as you see fit, would you end using it to purchase more of Security XYZ? Do you think you'd purchase the same amount of Security XYZ that you currently own?" Often, clients will realize that they might hypothetically behave differently if handling a liquid sum. It is also useful to question the client about his or her intent in owning the security: "What do you hope to accomplish by holding this security, and how is this security helping you to achieve your financial goals?" Often, as in the case of inherited securities, the client will see the light. Stressing a long-term view in financial goals can often persuade clients to be more receptive to facts.

Commision aversion. Commission aversion is a very common phenomenon and can be very detrimental to a portfolio. The "penny wise, pound foolish" proverb is often one of the most salient arguments that you can present to a client in this case, and the best way to do this is to lay out, numerically, potential gains that can be achieved or losses that can be averted by selling versus retaining the security. Then, contrast these sums with the relatively trivial expected sum of any commission fees. More often than not, if you present this logic persuasively, a client will understand the lesson and agree to reallocate.

Desire for familiarity. Familiarity can be a difficult craving to overcome. Comfort is crucial to an investor, and it may not be wise to take a portfolio in any direction with which the client seems significantly uncomfortable. This ends up being especially important in cases where your recommendation ultimately goes sour. The best way to address a client's desire for familiarity, when that desire contradicts your financial advice, is to review the historical performance of the unfamiliar securities that you are suggesting the client acquire. Demonstrate the logic underlying your recommendation. Rather than entirely replacing familiar holdings with new, scary ones, perhaps recommend that the client try out a small purchase of the unfamiliar investment you're recommending. This way, your client can develop familiarity with the new investment instrument and achieve a corresponding comfort level.

NOTES

1. Daniel Kahneman, J. L. Knetsch, and Richard H. Thaler, "The Endowment Effect, Loss Aversion, and Status Quo Bias: Anomalies," *Journal of Economic Perspectives* 5(1) (1991): 193–206.

2. J. L. Knetsch, "The Endowment Effect and Evidence of Nonreversible Indifference Curves," *American Economic Review* 79(5): 1277–1284.
3. Ibid.
4. William Samuelson and Richard Zeckhauser, "Status Quo Bias in Decisions Making," *Journal of Risk and Uncertainty* 1(1): 7–59. With kind permission of Springer Science and Business Media.
5. John A. List, "Does Market Experience Eliminate Market Anomalies?" *Quarterly Journal of Economics* 118 (February 2003): 41–71.
6. Ibid. © 2003 by the President and Fellows of Harvard College and the Massachusetts Institute of Technology. Reprinted with permission of MIT Press Journals.

CHAPTER 22

Regret Aversion Bias

I visualized my grief if the stock market went way up and I wasn't in it—or if it went way down and I was completely in it. My intention was to minimize my future regret, so I split my retirement plan contributions 50/50 between bonds and equities.
—Harry Markowitz, father of Modern Portfolio Theory

BIAS DESCRIPTION

Bias Name: Regret aversion bias
Bias Type: Emotional

General Description

People exhibiting *regret aversion* avoid taking decisive actions because they fear that, in hindsight, whatever course they select will prove less than optimal. Basically, this bias seeks to avoid the emotional pain of regret associated with poor decision making. Regret aversion makes investors, for example, unduly apprehensive about breaking into financial markets that have recently generated losses. When they experience negative investment outcomes, they feel instinctually driven to conserve, to retreat, and to lick their wounds—not to press on and snap up potentially undervalued stocks. However, periods of depressed prices often present the greatest buying opportunities. People suffering from regret aversion bias hesitate most at moments that actually merit aggressive behavior.

Regret aversion does not only come into play only following a loss; it can also affect a person's response to investment gains. People exhibiting regret aversion can be reluctant, for example, to sell a stock whose value has climbed recently—even if objective indicators attest that it's time to pull out. Instead, regret-averse investors may cling to positions that they ought to sell, pained by the prospect that a stock, once unloaded, might soar even higher.

Technical Description

An extensive body of literature in experimental psychology suggests that regret does influence decision making under conditions of uncertainty. Regret causes people to challenge past decisions and to question their beliefs. People who are regret averse try to avoid distress arising from two types of mistakes: (1) errors of commission and (2) errors of omission. Errors of *commission* occur when we take misguided *actions*. Errors of *omission* arise from misguided *inaction*, that is, opportunities overlooked or foregone.

Regret is different from disappointment, because the former implies that the sufferer had some sense of agency in achieving the negative outcome. Also, feelings of regret are more intense when unfavorable outcomes emerge from errors of commission rather than errors of omission. The Implications for Investors section uses an example to examine more concretely the distinction between errors of commission and errors of omission in the context of regret aversion bias.

Regret is most palpable and takes the greatest toll on decision making when the outcomes of forgone alternatives are highly "visible" or "accessible." By the same token, regret becomes a less influential factor when consequences of mistakes are less discernible. Some researchers have proposed theories of choice under uncertainty that incorporate regret bias as a partial explanation for observed violations of traditional expected utility theory. Regret theory assumes that agents are rational but base their decisions not only on expected payoffs but also on expected regret. The Allais paradox (Chapter 2), along with other human tendencies that seem to interfere with utility optimization, make sense from the perspective of regret theory. Regret theory bears some similarities to prospect theory (discussed earlier), and many of its predictions are consistent with the empirical observations of human behavior that constitute the building blocks of prospect theory.

PRACTICAL APPLICATION

The following case study illustrates both aspects of regret bias: *error of commission* and *error of omission*. The case shows a regret-averse investor under two sets of circumstances: (1) an investor experienced a loss and regrets his decision to invest; and (2) an investor missed an opportunity to invest in something that later appreciated in value and regrets his failure to reap profits.

Suppose that Jim has a chance to invest in Schmoogle, Inc., an initial public offering (IPO) that has generated a great buzz following its recent market debut. Jim thinks that Schmoogle has high potential and contemplates buying in because Schmoogle's price has recently declined by 10 percent due to some recent market weakness. If Jim invests in Schmoogle, one of two things will happen: (1) Schmoogle will drop further (Jim made the wrong decision), or (2) Schmoogle will rebound (Jim made the right decision). If Jim doesn't invest, one of two things will happen: (1) Schmoogle will rebound (Jim made the right decision), or (2) Schmoogle will drop further (Jim made the wrong decision).

Suppose that Jim does invest and Schmoogle goes down. Jim will have committed an error of commission because he actually committed the act of investing and will likely feel regret strongly because he actually lost money.

Now suppose that Jim does not invest and Schmoogle goes up. Jim will have committed an error of omission because he omitted the purchase of Schmoogle and lost out. This regret may not be as strong as the regret associated with the error of commission. Why? First, as we learned in Chapter 17, investors dislike losing money more than they like gaining money. Second, in the first possibility, the investor actually committed the act of investing and lost money; in the second possibility, the investor merely did not act and only lost out on the opportunity to gain.

Implications for Investors

Regret aversion causes investors to anticipate and fear the pain of regret that comes with incurring a loss or forfeiting a profit. The potential for financial injury isn't the only disincentive that these investors face; they also dread feeling responsible for their own misfortunes (because regret implies culpability, whereas simple disappointment does not). The anxiety surrounding the prospect of an error of commission, or a "wrong move," can make investors timid and can cause them to subjectively and perhaps irrationally favor investments that seem trustworthy (e.g., "good companies"). Suppose that regret-averse Jim is now considering two investments, both with equal projected risk and return. One stock belongs to Large Company, Inc., while the other confers a share in Medium-Size Company, Inc. Even though, mathematically, the expected payoffs of investing in these two companies are identical, Jim will probably feel more comfortable with Large Company. If an investment in Large Company, Inc., fails to pay off, Jim can rationalize that his decision making could not have been too egregiously flawed, because Large Company, Inc., must have had lots of savvy investors. Jim doesn't feel uniquely foolish, and so the culpability component of Jim's regret is reduced. Jim can't rely on the same excuse, however, if an investment in Medium-Size Company fails. Instead of exonerating himself ("Lots of high-profile people made the same mistake that I did—perhaps some market anomaly is at fault?"), Jim may condemn himself ("Why did I do that? I shouldn't have invested in Medium-Size. Only small-time players invested in Medium-Size, Inc. I feel stupid!"), adding to his feelings of regret. It's important to recall here that Large Company and Medium-Size Company stocks were, objectively, equally risky. This underscores the fact that aversion to regret is different from aversion to risk. We review in the following six investor mistakes that can stem from regret aversion bias. Remedies for these biases will be reviewed in the Advice section.

RESEARCH REVIEW

Hersh Shefrin and Meir Statman,[1] in their paper entitled "Explaining Investor Preference for Cash Dividends," highlighted *regret* as a reason that investors prefer stocks that pay dividends. They argued that this is true because by paying dividends, investors can avoid, in some measure, the frustration that is felt when taking an action that leads to a less than desirable outcome. As previously noted, regret is stronger for errors of commission (cases where people suffer because of an action they took) than for errors of omission (cases where people suffer because of an action they failed to take). Suppose that an investor buys stock in Company A, which does not pay a dividend. In order to extract cash flow from this investment consumption, an investor would have to sell some stock. If the stock subsequently goes up in value, the investor feels substantial regret because the error is one of commission; he can readily imagine how not selling the stock would have left him better off. Conversely, suppose the investor invests in Company D, which does pay a dividend. With Company D, the investor would be able to extract cash flow from dividends, and, thus, a rise in the stock price would not have caused so much regret. This time, the error would have been one of omission: to be better off, the investor would have had to reinvest the dividend.

REGRET AVERSION BIAS: BEHAVIORS THAT CAN CAUSE INVESTMENT MISTAKES

1. Regret aversion can cause investors to be too conservative in their investment choices. Having suffered losses in the past (i.e., having felt pain of a poor decision regarding a risky investment), many people shy away from making new bold investment decisions and accept only low-risk positions. This behavior can lead to long-term underperformance, and can jeopardize investment goals.

2. Regret aversion can cause investors to shy away, unduly, from markets that have recently gone down. Regret-averse individuals fear that if they invest, such a market might subsequently continue its downward trend, prompting them to regret the decision to buy in. Often, however, depressed markets offer bargains, and people can benefit from seizing, decisively, these undervalued investments.

3. Regret aversion can cause investors to hold on to losing positions too long. People don't like to admit when they're wrong, and they will go to great lengths to avoid selling (i.e., confronting the reality of) a losing investment. This behavior, similar to loss aversion, is hazardous to one's wealth.

4. Regret aversion can cause "herding behavior" because, for some investors, buying into an apparent mass consensus can limit the potential for future regret. The demise of the technology stock bubble of the late 1990s demonstrated that even the most massive herd can stampede in the wrong direction.

5. Regret aversion leads investors to prefer stocks of subjectively designated *good companies,* even when an alternative stock has an equal or a higher expected return. Regret-averse investors may feel that "riskier" companies require bolder decision making; hence, if the investment fails, the consequences reflect more dramatically on an individual's judgment than do the consequences of investing in a "routine," "safe," or "reliable" stock. With increased perception of personal responsibility, of course, comes increased potential for regret. Investing in *good companies* may not permit investors any more return or less return than those companies perceived to be risky.

6. Regret aversion can cause investors to hold on to winning stocks for too long. People fear that by selling a stock that has been doing well, they might miss out on further imminent gains. The danger here is that in finance, as in physics, whatever goes up must come down.

DIAGNOSTIC TESTING

These questions are designed to detect signs of emotional bias stemming from regret aversion. To complete the test, select the answer choice that best characterizes your response to each item.

Regret Aversion Bias Test

Question 1: Suppose that you make an investment in mutual fund ABC and that over the next 12 months ABC appreciates by 10 percent. You contemplate selling ABC for normal portfolio rebalancing purposes, but then come across an item in the *Wall Street Journal* that sparks new optimism: Could ABC climb even higher? Which answer describes your likeliest response, given ABC's recent performance and this new information?

   a. I think I'll hold off and sell later. I'd really kick myself if I sold now and ABC continued to go up.

   b. I'll probably sell. But I'll still kick myself if ABC appreciates later on.

   c. I'll probably sell the stock without any second thoughts because rebalancing is important—regardless of what happens to ABC's price after the transaction.

Question 2: Suppose that you've decided to acquire 200 shares of LMN mutual fund. You purchase 100 shares now at $30 apiece and strategize to wait a few days before picking up the additional 100. Further suppose that soon after your initial buy, the market takes a comprehensive dip. LMN is now trading at $28, with no change in fundamentals. Which answer most closely matches your thought process in this situation?

   a. I will probably wait until the stock begins to go back up before buying the remaining 100 shares. I really don't want to see LMN fall below $28 because I'd regret my initial decision to buy in.

   b. I will probably buy the remaining 100 shares. If LMN ends up going below $28, though, I will probably regret my decision.

   c. I will probably buy the remaining 100 shares. Even if LMN falls below $28, I don't think I'll experience a lot of regret.

Question 3: Suppose you have decided to invest $5,000 in the stock market. You have narrowed your choices down to two mutual funds: one run by Big Company, Inc, and one run by Small Company, Inc. According to your calculations, both funds have equal risk and return characteristics. Big Company is a well-followed, eminently established company, whose investors include many large pension funds. Small company has performed well but has not garnered the same kind of public profile as Big Company. It has few well-known investors. Which answer most closely matches your thought process in this situation?

   a. I will most likely invest in Big Company because I feel safe taking the same course as so many respected institutional investors. If

Big Company does decline in value, I know I won't be the only one caught by surprise—and with so many savvy professionals sharing my predicament, I could hardly blame myself for excessively poor judgment.

b. I will most likely invest in Big Company because if I invested in Small Company and my investment failed, I would feel like a fool. Few well-known investors backed Small Company, and I would really regret going against their informed consensus only to discover that I was dead wrong.

c. I would basically feel indifferent between the two investments, since both generated the same expected parameters for risk and return.

Test Result Analysis

Questions 1, 2, and 3: People answering "a" or "b" to any question may harbor susceptibility to regret aversion bias.

ADVICE

This section is organized to address each of the pitfalls of regret aversion bias that are enumerated in the feature box.

Investing too conservatively. No matter how many times an investor has been "burned" by an ultimately unprofitable investment, risk (in the context of proper diversification) is still a healthy ingredient in any portfolio. Demonstrating to clients the long-term benefits of adding risky assets to a portfolio is essential. Efficient frontier research can be very helpful here. Investing too conservatively doesn't place an investor's assets in any acute danger—by definition, an excess of conservatism denotes a relative absence of risk. However, refusing to assume a risk often means forgoing a potential reward. Investors who swear off risky assets due to regret aversion may see less growth in their portfolios than they could otherwise achieve, and they might not reach their investment goals.

Staying out of the market after a loss. There is no principle more fundamental in securities trading than "buy low, sell high." Nonetheless, many investors' behavior completely ignores this directive. Again, human nature is to chase returns, following "hot" money. Of course, it is possible to profit from following market trends . . . the problem is, you never know when the balloon is going to pop and cause, for example, yesterday's coveted security to plummet 40 percent in an afternoon. Disciplined portfolio management is crucial to long-term success. This means buying at times when the market is low and selling at the times when the market is up.

Holding losing positions too long. An adage on Wall Street is "The first loss is the best loss." While realizing losses is never enjoyable, the wisdom here is that following an unprofitable decision, it is best to cut those losses and move on. Everyone missteps occasionally—even the world's savviest traders. Hedge funds, for example, can place mistaken bets (remember the Asian financial crisis?) and usually admit to these mistakes, even though this means registering losses of hundreds of millions of dollars. Advise your clients that they shouldn't regret realizing their losses. If people can learn to feel less grief when realizing that they have incurred losses, then the pain of owning up to a loss can be reduced and the effects of regret aversion in such instances can be lessened.

Herding behavior. If you're a practitioner and you believe that a decision your client has made reflects a herd mentality, then it can help to stop and question the investor's motivations. For example, you might ask your client to pinpoint whether the trade at hand relates to any particular long-term financial goal. Often, investors subject to pack mentalities have a hard time answering this question well. Disconcerted by their own hesitation, many clients at this point will step back and reconsider the consensus of the herd. Others, though, may rationalize: "This is my time to take a risk." This is not, in and of itself, a dangerous statement. Investors are permitted, on occasion, to gamble. They must, however, understand the stakes and the magnitudes of the gambles they undertake. Advisors can help by reminding their clients of the outcomes of some other "flyers" that have been taken in the past, so that, at the very least, a speculative decision can be grounded in an unbiased, historical perspective.

Preference for good companies. Investors often think they can save face (especially with their spouses) by buying stock in good companies like GE or Coca-Cola. Such household names have seen their ups and downs, however, just like competitor firms. Don't let clients limit themselves to good companies simply because they fear the regret they might experience if an investment in a lesser-known company doesn't work out. Remember that high-profile brands don't necessarily deliver returns either. GE and Coke are certainly recognizable, but that doesn't mean that either company's stock constitutes a sure thing.

Holding winners too long. It's time to entertain one final Wall Street axiom: "You never get hurt taking a profit." This is not to say that you should not let winners run. However, if you find numerous, objective considerations that favor selling a security and if the only reason not to sell is because you fear regretting a missed opportunity should the investment appreciate after you sell it, then it's time to take a step back.

Remember that you may also experience regret when a stock begins to decline after you've held it for too long. Moreover, a helpful approach is to attempt to set aside any emotions that might be impacting the sell decision. Once you feel certain, make a choice—and stick to it. You can always buy in again later on if the stock does indeed represent a good investment opportunity.

NOTES

1. Hersh Shefrin and Meir Statman, "Explaining Investor Preference for Cash Dividends," *Journal of Financial Economics* 13 (June 1984): 253–282. Reprinted in Richard H. Thaler, ed., *Advances in Behavioral Finance* (New York: Russell Sage Foundation, 1993).

CHAPTER 23

Affinity Bias

My yachts were, I suppose, outstanding status symbols.
—Paul Getty

BIAS DESCRIPTION

Bias Name: Affinity bias

Bias Type: Emotional

Subtype: Information processing

General Description

Affinity bias refers to an individual's tendency to make irrationally uneconomical consumer choices or investment decisions based on how they believe a certain product or service will reflect their values. This idea focuses on the *expressive benefits* of a product rather than on what the product or service actually does for someone (the utilitarian benefits). A common example of this behavior in the consumer product realm is when one purchases wine. A consumer may purchase a fine bottle of well-known wine in a restaurant or wine shop for hundreds of dollars to impress their dinner guests, while a bottle that costs much less could be equally delicious but would not convey the same status. Automobiles are another example. A person may purchase a Range Rover or a similar sport utility vehicle because they want to be viewed by others as someone who is "outdoorsy" (sometimes regardless of the extent to which the person actually engages in outdoor activities) when a much more affordable vehicle would easily transport them from point A to point B. Similarly, in the investment realm, individuals may invest in certain companies, such as those that produce Range Rovers, because they feel that this company reflects their values or self-image. This behavior may lead to suboptimal investment results if the company producing the product or service is poorly managed or has financial or business-related problems.

Technical Description

A technical way of describing the phenomenon listed above is to describe the products as having either expressive or image-related value as opposed to utilitarian or functional value. As a practical example, advertisers target their consumers with different types of advertising by using two common approaches to influence consumer behavior: value-expressive (image) and utilitarian (functional) appeal[1] (see Park, Jaworski, and MacInnis 1986[2]; Snyder and DeBono 1985). The value-expressive strategy involves building a "personality" for a product or creating an image of the product user with which the consumer can identify. This value-expressive advertising appeal has the innovative objective of creating an image of the generalized user of the advertised product (or brand). However, the utilitarian strategy involves informing the target consumers about one or more key benefits that they may perceive as highly functional or important. The utilitarian advertising strategy is simply a creative strategy that highlights the functional features of the product (or brand). Those who are subject to affinity bias will focus on value-expressive characteristics rather than utilitarian benefits.

Practical Application: Affinity Bias

A useful application of affinity bias in the investment realm is *patriotism*. Investors who concentrate their holdings in their home country or state gain the expressive benefit of patriotism but may potentially lose the utilitarian benefits of high returns and low risk that come to those who invest elsewhere. Adair Morse and Sophie Shive[3] (2003) of the University of Chicago Booth School of Business and the University of Notre Dame, respectively, found that patriotism continuously affects investment behavior in their study, "Patriotism in Your Portfolio." They explored the role of devotion and loyalty to one's country in explaining an "equity home bias" and found that investors in more patriotic countries and regions within the United States discriminate more in favor of domestic stocks. Much like betting on the home team despite unfavorable odds or allocating retirement savings only to one's own company stock, patriotic investors choose to invest more of their stocks in firms based in their homeland. For example, the study found that U.S. investors hold 92 percent of their equity portfolio in domestic stock, although portfolio theory suggests that the optimally diversified portfolio should consist of only one third invested in domestic stocks.

Using data on 33 countries from the U-M World Values Survey, the researchers found that more patriotic countries and regions within the United States hold smaller foreign equity positions—in other words, investors discriminate in favor of domestic stocks. For example, Americans and South Africans invest less in foreign stocks than do several European investors, while investors in the very patriotic regions of Texas, Oklahoma, Louisiana, and Arkansas invest less in international equities than do investors in the less patriotic New England states.

Morse and Shive found that patriotism accounts for an additional 7 percent of the cross-country variation in foreign equity holdings. Further, a 10 percent decrease in patriotism is associated with a 29 to 48 percent increase in foreign equity in the home country portfolio. The study also presented evidence that U.S. demand for French stocks traded in the United States declined in reaction to French opposition to the recent war in Iraq. The proportion of American Depositary Receipts (ADRs) sold increased by 15 to 18 percent during the prewar period of anti-French sentiment and the average U.S. price of the ADR decreased relative to the French price (ADRs are certificates issued by a U.S. depository bank, representing foreign shares held by the bank).

Overall, Morse and Shive say their research has two implications: patriotic behavior explains a part of the mysterious equity home bias and policies aimed at increasing investors' portfolio diversification may need to account for "irrational" investor behavior. Shive said of her research:

> *Patriotism results in a winner's curse in the sense that the person valuing a stock most highly will ultimately be the highest bidder. . . . The citizens of a country will likely be the highest bidders for their own country's assets, thus possibly driving up prices in their own market.*[4]

Implications for Investors

One of the previously referenced implications for affinity bias is that investors decide to invest in weak or otherwise unsound companies that reflect expressive characteristics rather than utilitarian characteristics in a misguided attempt to achieve investment success. A classic example of this can be found in individuals who invest in retail chain stores that produce popular products such as blue jeans, watches, or other products that reflect expressive benefits, only to discover that the company is a disaster from an investment standpoint. Other investors may also wish to invest in companies that they feel reflect their environmental, social, or governance values (ESG), which may or may not prove to be a successful strategy. Some studies have shown that ESG-type (socially responsible) investing is a successful strategy, while others have shown that ESG is not a winning investment strategy. Regardless, investors and their advisors need to be aware that some clients may wish to invest in companies that reflect their social values and that this behavior has investment implications. Another implication of affinity bias is that some investors may wish to invest in things that convey status but that they know little about or that may involve risks, such as investing in hedge funds or other alternative investments that their social acquaintances are investing in, in order to demonstrate status or be part of an investment club—only to find that they made a bad decision by doing so. Finally, patriotic behavior may cause investors to have home country bias, which can limit the success of any portfolio, especially in the globally diverse world we now live in.

The box below summarizes affinity bias behaviors that can cause poor investment outcomes.

AFFINITY BIAS BEHAVIORS THAT CAN LEAD TO POOR INVESTMENT OUTCOMES

1. Investors subject to affinity bias can make investments in companies that make products or deliver services that they like but don't examine carefully enough the soundness of the investment characteristics of those companies.
2. Investors subject to affinity bias can invest in companies that reflect their ESG values but don't carefully examine the soundness of the investment characteristics of those companies.
3. Investors subject to affinity bias can invest in their home countries at the expense of investing in foreign countries due to home country bias.
4. Investors subject to affinity bias can sometimes invest in "sophisticated" investment products that convey status only to find they have invested in something they don't understand, which can be "hazardous to your wealth."

RESEARCH REVIEW

In an interesting twist on the subject of home equity bias, Evangelos Benos and Marek Jochec[5] of the University of Illinois wrote a compelling paper entitled "Liberalism and Home Equity Bias," which found that countries whose citizens have liberal ideals are less biased toward domestic equity. Their data from 30 countries suggested that economic as well as social liberalism is associated with proportionally higher foreign equity holdings. The results held true even after controlling for standard rational and behavioral explanations of the home equity bias, as well as country and time fixed effects. In today's investing world, investors should hold the world market portfolio in some proportion depending upon their unique circumstance. Regardless, some investors ignore the currency and diversification benefits of international equity investing and hold portfolios that are concentrated disproportionately on domestic equity. This is known as *home equity bias* and has been documented by several studies[6] [see French and Poterba[7] (1990), Cooper and Kaplanis[8] (1994), etc.] Putting aside real potential problems such as taxes and capital restrictions, foreign accounting issues, and differing legal environments that might make foreign investments unattractive, these information costs also appear to be small when compared to the potential benefits of international diversification [See Lewis[9] (1999)].

The home equity bias is one of the big, yet to be fully understood puzzles in financial economics. This is largely because the potential rational explanations that have been proposed so far cannot fully account for its magnitude. In an attempt to explain why investors forgo important diversification benefits associated with international investing, researchers have more recently been adding variables to their empirical specifications that proxy for behavioral factors such as familiarity and patriotism. In this paper, the authors are trying to find reasons why a given set of people might not be susceptible to this bias. They examined whether liberalism (or conservatism) has any incremental explanatory power with respect to the level of the home equity bias. They made a distinction between social and economic liberalism not only because these are different notions per se, but also because they suspected that each one may separately affect people's investment behavior. Using data from 30 countries, we then examine if these metrics help to explain the home equity bias after controlling for the level of a country's degree of liberalization, the potential cost of information acquisition, the country's risk-adjusted average stock market return, and the familiarity of the country's residents with foreign cultures and their level of patriotism. They found that liberal societies, in both the economic and social sense, are conditionally less biased toward domestic stock. The effect is economically significant: a one standard deviation increase in our social (economic) liberalism metric is associated with a 2 percent (5 percent) drop in the level of home equity bias. They interpret these results as evidence that people's investment decisions are influenced by their core beliefs about the economy and the society in which they live. It may come as no surprise that societies that have less trust of the open market and instead favor more government intervention are less likely to invest in foreign equities. It is, however, less apparent why social liberalism/conservatism should have any effect on an individual's investment behavior. They suggest that social liberalism is a proxy for a society's willingness to accept changes in general, and since in historical terms international investing is relatively modern, socially liberal societies are more likely to pioneer the transition to international investing.

DIAGNOSTIC TESTING

This section contains a diagnostic quiz that can help to detect susceptibility to affinity bias. In the Advice section that follows, you will find guidelines for scoring responses to this quiz, along with corresponding suggestions for managing outcome bias.

Question 1:

	Strongly Disagree	Disagree	Neutral	Agree	Strongly Agree
I invest in companies that make products I like, such as cars, watches, or clothing.	☐	☐	☐	☐	☐

Question 2:

	Strongly Disagree	Disagree	Neutral	Agree	Strongly Agree
I invest in companies that reflect my personal values such as environmental, social, or governance values.	☐	☐	☐	☐	☐

Question 3:

	Strongly Disagree	Disagree	Neutral	Agree	Strongly Agree
My investment portfolio does not contain much in the way of international investments.	☐	☐	☐	☐	☐

Question 4:

	Strongly Disagree	Disagree	Neutral	Agree	Strongly Agree
I have made investments in "sophisticated" investment products because it made me feel like a better investor or because my associates were doing it and I wanted to invest like them.	☐	☐	☐	☐	☐

ADVICE

If you agreed or strongly agreed with any of these questions, you may be susceptible to affinity bias.

> **Question 1:** Investors who are susceptible to affinity bias may decide to invest in weak or otherwise unsound companies that reflect expressive characteristics rather than utilitarian characteristics in a misguided attempt to find investment success. As noted earlier, a classic example of this is retail chain stores that have a popular product such as blue jeans, watches, or other products that reflect expressive benefits, only to find that they are not a sound investment. Investors and advisors need to ask themselves first why they are making the investment—not just based on the product that is manufactured or promoted.

> **Question 2:** Some investors may invest in companies that they feel reflect their ESG values, which may or may not prove to be a successful strategy. Some studies have shown that ESG-type (socially responsible) investing is a successful strategy, while others have shown that ESG is not a winning investment strategy. Regardless, investors and their advisors need to be aware that some clients may wish to invest in companies that reflect their social values, and this may have investment implications.

> **Question 3:** Another implication of affinity bias is that some investors may wish to invest in things that convey status, but that they know nothing about or are unaware of the risks of, such as investing in hedge funds or other alternative investments that their social acquaintances are investing in, in order to demonstrate status or be part of an investment club—only to find that they made a bad

decision by doing so. This is something that advisors and their clients need to carefully monitor because capital can be lost if unwise investments are made in the name of status.

Question 4: Finally, patriotic behavior may cause investors to have home country bias, which can limit the success of any portfolio, especially in the globally diverse world we live in now. A simple analysis to identify what percentage of the investor's portfolio involves international investments is a good way to begin a conversation about this bias. I would encourage investors to take advantage of the diversification and currency benefits of international investing.

NOTES

1. M. Joseph Sirgy, "Value-Expressive Versus Utilitarian Advertising Appeals: When and Why to Use Which Appeal," *Journal of Advertising* 20 (3) (1991): 23–33.
2. Park, C. Whan, Bernard J. Jaworski and Deborah J. MacInnis. "Strategic Brand Concept-Image Management," *Journal of Marketing* 50 (1986): 135–145.
3. Synder, Mark and Kenneth G. DeBono. "Appeals to Image and Claims About Quality: Understanding the Psychology of Advertising," *Journal of Personality and Social Psychology*, 49 (3) (1985): 586–597.
4. Adair Morse and Sophie Shive, "Patriotism in Your Portfolio," Journal of Financial Markets 14 (2011): 411–440.
5. Adair Morse and Sophie Shive, "Patriotism in Your Portfolio," Journal of Financial Markets 14 (2011): 438.
6. Evangelos Benos and Marek Jochec, "Liberalism and Home Equity Bias" (University of Illinois Urbana-Champaign (2009): 1–26.
7. Ibid, pg. 1.
8. Kenneth French and James Poterba. "Investor Diversification and International Equity Markets", *American Economic Review* 81 (1991): 221–226.
9. Ian Cooper and Evi Kaplanis. "Home Bias in Equity Portfolios, Inflation Hedging and International Capital Market Equilibrium", *The Review of Financial Studies* 7 (1) (1994): 45–60.
10. Karen Lewis. "Trying to Explain Home Bias in Equities and Consumption." *Journal of Economic Literature* 37 (1999): 571–608.

Five

Application of Behavioral Finance to Asset Allocation and Case Studies

We have covered the foundations of behavioral finance micro—the biases—so our discussion now turns to the main focus of this book: practical application of behavioral finance for investors and advisors. The next chapter establishes a basic framework for integrating behavioral finance insights into portfolio structure, and presents the concept of best practical allocation. Chapter 25 takes the concepts presented in this chapter and applies them in a case study format to reinforce learning.

CHAPTER 24

Application of Behavioral Finance to Asset Allocation

Successful investing is anticipating the anticipations of others.
—John Maynard Keynes, English economist, 1883 to 1946

What a difference five years makes! In the first edition of the book, I discussed why only a few of the many biases that have been identified in behavioral finance research are used when creating and implementing an asset allocation program with clients and investors. Behavioral finance is coming closer to the mainstream and is being incorporated by financial services firms into the asset allocation process. Take, for example, the following passage from the most recent Merrill Lynch/CapGemini World Wealth Report:

> *Emotional factors are a prominent feature of the HNWI psyche today, and wealth management firms and Advisors must incorporate those emotional factors into stronger portfolio management and risk capabilities so as to properly support client goals and needs. With billions of assets still in motion post-crisis, wealth management firms are embracing change, leveraging key tenets of behavioral finance to rebuild investor trust and confidence and drive further innovation into their offerings and service models.*[1]

The fact that this annual wealth report has recognized behavioral finance so prominently is truly remarkable and evidence that behavioral finance has made tremendous strides (perhaps the first edition helped the cause!). The best part about this development is that it is true! Firms that decide to help their clients by incorporating behavioral finance into the investment process will have a higher likelihood of success going forward. And this activity will be a real help to their clients in terms of making them feel comfortable with their portfolio and confident that they will reach their financial goals. The wealth report will be referenced again in the next section, and there will be more to come on this subject.

PRACTICAL APPLICATION OF BEHAVIORAL FINANCE

This book intends not only to familiarize financial advisors and investors with 20 of the major biases unearthed in behavioral finance research, as was done in the last 20 chapters, but also to demonstrate how to apply behavioral finance in the process of developing and implementing an asset allocation plan. The central question for advisors when applying behavioral finance biases to the asset allocation decision is: When should advisors attempt to *moderate*, or counteract, biased client reasoning to accommodate a predetermined asset allocation? Conversely, when should advisors *adapt* asset allocation recommendations to help biased clients feel more comfortable with their portfolios?[2] Furthermore, how extensively should the moderate-or-adapt objective factor into portfolio design? Later in the chapter we explore the use of quantitative parameters to indicate the magnitude of the adjustment an advisor might implement in light of a particular bias scenario.

The chapter, which reviews the practical consequences of investor bias in asset allocation decisions, might, with any luck, sow the seeds of a preliminary thought process for establishing an industry-standard methodology for detecting and responding to investor biases. This chapter, first, examines the limitations of typical risk tolerance questionnaires in asset allocation; next, it introduces the concept of best practical allocation, which in practice is an allocation that is behaviorally adjusted; then it identifies clients' behavioral biases and discusses how discovering a bias might shape an asset allocation decision; as noted, it also reviews a quantitative guideline methodology that can be utilized when adjusting asset allocations to account for biases.

Limitations of Risk Tolerance Questionnaires

Those who read the last edition of this book will be reminded that this section pointed out the limitations of risk tolerance questionnaires. It noted that in an attempt to standardize asset allocation processes, financial service firms ask and may, for compliance reasons, require their advisors to administer risk tolerance questionnaires to clients and potential clients prior to drafting any asset allocation. In the absence of any other diagnostic analysis, this methodology is certainly useful and generates important information. However, there are a number of factors that restrict the usefulness of risk tolerance questionnaires. Aside from ignoring behavioral issues, an aspect shortly examined, a risk tolerance questionnaire can also generate dramatically different results when administered repeatedly but in slightly varying formats to the same individual. Such imprecision arises primarily from inconsistencies in the wording of questions. Additionally, most risk tolerance questionnaires are administered once and may not be revisited. Risk tolerance can vary directly as a result of changes and events throughout life. Another critical issue with respect to risk tolerance questionnaires is that many advisors interpret their results too literally. For example, some clients might indicate that the maximum loss they would be willing to tolerate in a single year would comprise 20 percent of their total assets. Does that mean that an ideal portfolio would place clients in a position to lose 20 percent? No! Advisors should set portfolio parameters that preclude clients from incurring the maximum specified tolerable loss in any given period. For these reasons, risk tolerance questionnaires provide, at best, broad guidelines for asset allocation and should only be used in concert with other behavioral assessment tools.

Proof that others are now starting to agree with this idea is contained in the World Wealth report referenced earlier:

> *Risk and Scenario Analysis is now being used more extensively to help HNW clients understand the extremes, with risk positioned as a series of ups and downs not an average. Firms are extending the possible extremes (increasing the standard deviations) in their models of "what could happen?," as many pre-crisis models did not account for the extremes that ultimately occurred. But more importantly, risk analysis is being revamped to include a more thorough client goal assessment. Previously, clients may have been simplistically assigned the typical labels (conservative/moderate/aggressive), and consequently provided the appropriate models in which to invest, based on a very basic outline of their objectives. That label served as a proxy for risk tolerance—categorizing the client's willingness to pursue or avoid risk, while often using simple volatility to quantify that risk. The crisis proved the flaws in that approach since strategies to avoid volatility, for example, did not necessarily limit downside risk. The more sophisticated scenario approaches, beginning with client goals rather than just a risk "label," assist in identifying the emotional triggers that could ultimately help to better optimize a client portfolio for risk." From the behavioral finance perspective, in fact, risk tolerance questionnaires may work well for institutional investors but fail regarding psychologically biased individuals. An asset allocation that is generated and executed based on mean-variance optimization can often result in a scenario in which*

a client demands, in response to short-term market fluctuations and the detriment of the investment plan, that his or her asset allocation be changed. Moving repeatedly in and out of an allocation can cause serious, long-term, negative consequences. Behavioral biases need to be identified before the allocation is executed so that such problems can be avoided.[3]

BEST PRACTICAL ALLOCATION

Practitioners are often vexed by their clients' decision-making processes when it comes to structuring investment portfolios. Why? As noted in the previous section, many advisors, when designing a standard asset allocation program with a client, first administer a risk tolerance questionnaire, then discuss the client's financial goals and constraints, and finally recommend the output of a mean-variance optimization. Less-than-optimal outcomes are often a result of this process because the client's interests and objectives may not be fully accounted for. According to Kahneman and Riepe, financial advising is "a prescriptive activity whose main objective should be to guide investors to make decisions that serve their best interest."[4] Clients' interests may indeed derive from their natural psychological preferences—and these preferences may not be served best by the output of a mean-variance model optimization output. Investors may be better served by moving themselves up or down the efficient frontier, adjusting risk and return levels depending on their behavioral tendencies.

More simply, a client's best practical allocation (which may also be referred to as a behaviorally modified allocation) may be a slightly underperforming long-term investment program to which the client can comfortably adhere, warding off an impulse to "change horses" in the middle of the race. In other cases, the best practical allocation might contradict clients' natural psychological tendencies, and these clients may be well served to accept risks in excess of their individual comfort levels in order to maximize expected returns. The remainder of this book develops an understanding of how, exactly, a real client situation might be construed in order to determine a particular allocative approach. In sum, the right allocation is the one that helps the client to attain financial goals while simultaneously providing enough psychological security for the client to sleep at night. The ability to create such optimal portfolios is what advisors and investors should try to gain from this book.

In creating a behaviorally modified portfolio, it is critically important to distinguish between emotional and cognitive biases and to consider the level of wealth of the investor in question. Individual biases should be assessed primarily for the purpose of identifying which type of biases dominate (cognitive or emotional) and what action should be taken in response to observed behaviors and with regard to the investor's overall wealth level. The two basic forms of action are either to adapt to the bias or to moderate the impact of the bias. When investors adapt to a bias, they accept it and make decisions that recognize and adjust for the bias rather attempting to reduce the impact of the bias. The resulting portfolio represents an alteration of the rational portfolio; the alteration responds to the investor's biases while considering financial goals and level of wealth. When investors and advisors moderate the impact of a bias, they recognize the bias and attempt to reduce or even eliminate the bias within the individual investor rather than accepting the bias. The resulting portfolio is similar to the rational portfolio, and a program is adopted to reduce or eliminate the investor's biases.

The next section examines guidelines for determining a modified portfolio including an explanation of how to assess one's wealth level. It adopts the perspective of a private wealth manager working with an individual client. The approach can be used with modifications in other situations.

GUIDELINES FOR DETERMINING BEST PRACTICAL ASSET ALLOCATION

This section has been adapted from an article entitled "Incorporating Behavioral Finance into Your Practice," which I, with my colleague John Longo, originally published in the March 2005 *Journal of Financial Planning*. It sets forth two guidelines for constructing a best practical allocation (also referred to as a behaviorally modified asset allocation) in light of client behavioral biases. These guidelines are not intended as prescriptive absolutes, but rather should be consulted along with other data on risk tolerance, financial goals, asset class preferences, and so on. The guidelines are general enough to fit almost any client situation; however, exceptions can occur. Later on, some case studies provide a better sense of how these guidelines are applied in practice.

To review, recall that when considering behavioral biases in asset allocation, financial advisors must first determine whether to moderate or to adapt to "irrational" client preferences. This basically involves weighing the rewards of sustaining a calculated, profit-maximizing allocation against the outcome of potentially affronting the client, whose biases might position them to favor a different portfolio structure entirely. The guidelines laid out in this section offer guidelines for resolving the puzzle "When to moderate, when to adapt?"

Guideline I: Moderate Biases in Less Wealthy Clients; Adapt to Biases in Wealthier Clients

Guideline I. The decision to moderate or adapt to a client's behavioral biases during the asset allocation process depends fundamentally on the client's level of wealth. Specifically, the wealthier the client, the more the practitioner should adapt to the client's behavioral biases. The less wealthy, the more the practitioner should moderate a client's biases.

Rationale. Clients who outlive their assets constitute a far graver investment failure than do clients who are unable to accumulate wealth. The likelihood of a client's outliving his or her assets is a function of the level of wealth. If a bias is likely to endanger a client's standard of living, moderating is an appropriate course of action. If a bias will only jeopardize the client's standard of living if a highly unlikely event occurs, adapting may be more appropriate. However, the potential impact of low-probability, high-impact events should be discussed with the client.

Guideline II: Moderate Cognitive Biases; Adapt to Emotional Biases

Guideline II. The decision to moderate or adapt to a client's behavioral biases during the asset allocation process depends fundamentally on the type of behavioral bias the client exhibits. Specifically, clients exhibiting cognitive errors should be moderated, while those exhibiting emotional biases should be adapted to.

Rationale. Because cognitive errors stem from faulty reasoning, better information and advice can often correct these biases. Conversely, emotional biases originate from feelings or intuition rather than from conscious reasoning, and so are more difficult to correct.

Regarding the determination of "high" and "low" wealth levels: naturally, the determination of high wealth level and low wealth level is a subjective one that must be determined by the advisor in concert with the client. In this context, wealth is determined in relation to lifestyle, and not just based on level of assets. Some people have high levels of assets but also have an extravagant financial lifestyle to match, implying a "low" level of wealth; in other words, some people have a lot of assets but also spend accordingly. This is related to standard of living risk. Standard of living risk (SLR) is the risk that the current or a specified acceptable lifestyle may not be sustainable. For example, an individual with modest assets and a modest

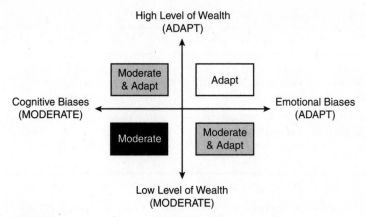

FIGURE 24.1 Visual Depiction of Guidelines I and II
Source: M. Pompian and J. Longo, "Incorporating Behavioral Finance into Your Practice," *Journal of Financial Planning* (March 2005). Reprinted with permission of the Financial Planning Association. For more information on the Financial Planning Association, please visit www.fpanet.org or call 1-800-322-4237.

lifestyle that he or she does not wish to alter may not have an SLR, and as such might be viewed as having a moderate to high level of wealth. However, an individual with a high level of assets and an extravagant lifestyle that he or she wishes to maintain may have an SLR; this individual, regardless of level of assets, might be viewed as having a low to moderate level of wealth.

In some cases, heeding Guidelines I and II simultaneously yields a blended recommendation. For instance, a less wealthy client with strong emotional biases should be both adapted to and moderated. Figure 24.1 illustrates this situation. Additionally, these guidelines reveal that two clients exhibiting the same biases should sometimes be advised differently. In Chapter 25, the case studies will add clarity to this complex framework, while also illustrating how practitioners can apply Guidelines I and II to determine the best practical allocation.

QUANTITATIVE GUIDELINES FOR INCORPORATING BEHAVIORAL FINANCE IN ASSET ALLOCATION

To override the mean-variance optimizer is to depart from the strictly rational portfolio. The following is a recommended method for calculating the magnitude of an acceptable discretionary deviation from default of the mean-variance output allocation.

TABLE 24.1 Deviations from "Rational" Portfolio

	Bias Type—Cognitive	Bias Type—Emotional
High wealth level/Low SLR	Modest asset allocation change Suggestion: +/– 5–10% max per asset class	Stronger asset allocation change Suggestion: +/– 10–15% max per asset class
Low wealth level/High SLR	Close to the rational asset allocation Suggestion: +/– 0–3% max per asset class	Modest asset allocation change Suggestion: +/– 5–10% max per asset class

A key concept in creating a behaviorally modified allocation is to decide how much it should deviate from the "rational" allocation of traditional finance. Table 24.1 is a useful guideline for determining how much to adjust an allocation for behavioral bias.

Note that the percentages listed in the chart are suggested percentage adjustments from the "rational" allocation to asset classes based on behavioral bias. In terms of the magnitude of the suggested changes, to some these ranges may appear too narrow or too small in absolute terms, while others may view them as reasonable. The amount of change that is appropriate to modify an allocation will in large part depend on how many asset classes are used in the allocation. A 5 percent change in 10 asset classes, for example, could yield a substantial tilt to or away from risky assets, while for an asset allocation with four asset classes, 5 percent would not be enough. It is important to recognize the relative differences between these cases. The case requiring the least adjustment to the rational portfolio is a low-wealth-level client with cognitive bias. Here, low-wealth investors need to modify their behavior to reach their financial goals and, with cognitive bias, should be able to adjust behavior to match the rational allocation with appropriate education and information. If an adjustment is needed, a +/– 0–2 percent maximum asset class adjustment is suggested. We will see an example of this case in the case studies later. The case that will likely require the most adjustment per asset class is emotional bias at high wealth level. Here, a +/–10 percent maximum adjustment per asset class is suggested. The rationale for such a potentially high adjustment is that a wealthy investor with emotional bias may need substantial flexibility due to the fact that emotional biases are difficult to correct; a high wealth level permits flexibility. The "middle of the road" cases are the high wealth level with cognitive biases and the low wealth level with emotional bias. With these two cases, a suggested maximum asset class adjustment is +/–5 percent. The rationale for this level of adjustment is that there is a need to both adapt and moderate to behavioral biases, and the offsetting that takes place likely requires a modest adjustment. Naturally, these are only conceptual guidelines, and actual client situations will likely require additional customization.

Later in the book we will review an alternative way of classifying assets to incorporate behavioral finance principles into the asset allocation process.

INVESTMENT POLICY AND ASSET ALLOCATION

Behavioral biases can and should be accounted for in the investment policy development and asset allocation selection process by both investors and their advisors. Behavioral finance considerations may have their own place in the constraints section of the investment policy statement, along with liquidity, time horizon, taxes, legal and regulatory environment, and unique circumstances. Responses to questions such as the following may help develop the behavioral finance considerations that impact on investment decisions and the resulting portfolio:

1. Which biases does the client show evidence of?
2. Which bias type dominates (cognitive or emotional)?
3. What effect do the client's biases have on the asset allocation decision?
4. What adjustment should be made to a "rational" (risk tolerance–based) asset allocation that accounts for the client's behavioral makeup?
   a. When should behavior be *moderated* to counteract the potentially negative effects of these biases on the investment decision-making process?
   b. When should asset allocations be created that *adapt* to the investor's behavioral biases so that they can comfortably abide by their asset allocation decisions?
   c. What is an appropriate *behaviorally modified asset allocation* (referred to as a behaviorally modified portfolio) for an investor?
   d. Once the decision is made to recommend a modified portfolio, what quantitative parameters should be used when putting the recommendation into action?

In the next chapter, we will review two case studies to help demonstrate these concepts.

NOTES

1. "World Wealth Report Spotlight," Capgemini, Inc., accessed March 17, 2011, at www.capgemini.com/services-and-solutions/by-industry/financial-services/solutions/wealth/new-service-model-for-hnw-clients/.

2. M. Pompian and J. Longo, "A New Paradigm for Practical Application of Behavioral Finance: Creating Investment Programs Based on Personality Type and Gender to Produce Better Investment Outcomes," *Journal of Wealth Management* (Fall 2004).
3. Capgemini and Merrill Lynch Global Wealth Management, "2010 World Weath Report," *World Wealth Report* (2010): 28.
4. D. Kahneman and M. Riepe, "Aspects of Investor Psychology," *Journal of Portfolio Management* (Summer 1998): 52–64.

CHAPTER 25

Case Studies

Things do not change; we change.
—Henry David Thoreau

Congratulations! If you've gotten this far in the book, you should have developed your practical understanding of behavioral finance micro along the way. In this chapter, we'll draw on all our discussions so far regarding specific behavioral biases and examine two fictional advisor-client case studies.

Obviously, every advisory relationship is unique, and there is no absolute, definitive way to diagnose and counteract client biases. As an advisor, you should read this chapter while keeping in mind how you might handle similar situations in your own practice. You should focus most on applying the methodological process—diagnosis, effects assessment, response determination, best practical allocation—outlined.

The following case studies involve two hypothetical investors, Mr. Nicholas and Mrs. Alexander, and their advisor, Mr. Gerard Spencer. Considering two dimensions, level of wealth and type of dominant biases, these case studies will consider two extreme examples: an investor with high wealth and emotional biases (Mr. Nicholas), and an investor with lower wealth and cognitive biases (Mrs. Alexander). To keep the book to a reasonable length, we will not review the two other extreme examples: an investor with high wealth and cognitive biases and an investor with lower wealth and emotional biases. Still, readers should understand that most cases will likely fall in between the two cases presented here in terms of behavioral adjustments to "rational" portfolio allocations.

These case studies were designed to answer the following four key questions in determining an investor's modified portfolio:

1. Which biases does the client show evidence of?
2. What effect do the client's biases have on the asset allocation decision?
3. What action should Mr. Spencer take: moderate or adapt to these biases?
4. What is the appropriate behaviorally modified asset allocation for each client?

In the real world of investing, each client and each advisor is different; therefore, these case studies illustrate an approach to diagnosing and devising strategies for behaviorally biased clients rather than specific strategies. In each case, put yourself in the role of the advisor, Mr. Spencer, and consider how you (Spencer) would deal with the client given the situation and how you would approach the issues presented. The case studies will contain the following format, which is a simulation of the approach that advisors might encounter with a client:

- Introductory description of the case.
- Identification of behavioral finance biases.
- Effect of biases on asset allocation decision.
- Action to be taken in response to identified biases (moderate or adapt).
- Recommendation for the behaviorally modified asset allocation.

These cases involve hypothetical investors and are not intended to represent all investor types. Each client is unique and will differ from the clients described in these case studies. What is important is to follow the process that is being described on how to identify biases, how to determine what the appropriate course of action is for dealing with the biases, and how to adjust or not adjust the rational mean-variance portfolio recommendation for biased behavior.

Capital Markets Assumptions: For each of the case studies, assume that for the past three years, the stock market has experienced moderate and steady increases and interest rates have been stable. For simplicity, we will assume that the investors in the case studies will be limited to investing in three asset classes: stocks, bonds, and cash. Diagnosis for biases is done in two steps in the following way. First, a basic questionnaire (Table 25.1) is given that assesses the 20 biases presented in the previous chapters. *Note that the choice of responses would normally be in a multiple-choice format, but in the interest of length, only the questions are shown here.* The questions do not follow the order of presentation of biases in the book but instead intersperse emotional, belief perseverance, and information processing biases because it is advisable to not cluster questions about similar types of

TABLE 25.1 Basic Diagnostic Questions for Behavioral Bias

Behavioral Bias	Diagnostic Question
Loss aversion	Imagine you make an investment that drops 25% in the first six months. You are unsure if it will come back. What would you normally do (NOT what you *think* you should do; what you *would* do)?
Endowment	How would you describe your emotional attachment to possessions or investment holdings?
Status quo	How would you describe the frequency of your trading?
Anchoring	You purchase a stock at $50 per share. It goes up to $60 in a few months, and then it drops to $40 a few months later. You are uncertain what will happen next. How would you respond to this scenario?
Mental accounting	Generally, do you categorize your money by different financial goals, or do you look at the bigger financial picture?
Regret aversion	Have you ever made an investment that you have regretted making? How did that affect your future investing decisions?
Hindsight	Do you believe investment outcomes are generally predictable or unpredictable?
Outcome	What's most important is that my investments make money—I'm not that concerned with following a structured plan.
Affinity	Do you invest in companies that make products you like or companies that reflect your personal values?
Cognitive dissonance	You purchase a stock and it goes down because the company's important new product launch is delayed indefinitely. The validity of your investment thesis is challenged. What is your immediate reaction to this news? Would you buy more or sell if those were the only two choices?
Self-attribution	Do you tend to attribute a winning investment to uncontrollable things such as good economic conditions or a good industry or your own investment prowess?
Recency	Have you made an investment based on a recent, successful track record only to find that you purchased at the top of the market?
Framing	Assume you have agreed to a financial plan created by your adviser that has a projected return of 9% and an annual standard deviation of +/–15% (a typical plan). Would it surprise you to know that statistically in the worst case, the plan's return could be negative 36% or more in 1 year out of 100? Would this information cause you to rethink your risk tolerance?

(continued)

TABLE 25.1 (*Continued*)

Behavioral Bias	Diagnostic Question
Conservatism	Assume you make an investment based on your own research. An advisor presents you with information that contradicts your belief about this investment. How would you respond?
Availability	Do you ever make investment decisions (such as selecting a mutual fund or online broker) based on word-of-mouth or name recognition?
Representativeness	Have you ever made a new investment because of its apparent similarity to a past successful investment (e.g., a tech stock or value stock) without doing research to validate the new investment's merits?
Overconfidence	Suppose you make a winning investment. How do you generally attribute the success of your decision?
Confirmation	Suppose you make an investment based on your own research. The investment doesn't move up as much as you thought it might. How are you likely to respond?
Illusion of control	You are offered two free lottery tickets. You may either select your own numbers or have a machine do it. What would you do?
Self-control	Do you tend to save or spend disposable income?

biases. Second, after reviewing the responses, the advisor focuses on biases identified by the questionnaire and delves further into them with the client to help create a modified portfolio.

CASE STUDY A: MR. NICHOLAS

Mr. Michael Nicholas ("Mr. N") is a single, 59-year-old, hardworking, international pharmaceutical marketing executive (an employee of a large multinational company). He earns a salary of $600,000 annually. He has residences in both Geneva and New Jersey and generally lives within his annual income net of taxes. He occasionally spends more than his net income, but in other years he saves and invests. His current portfolio is worth approximately $4 million. It reached this value primarily because of some successful high-risk biotechnology investments as well as stock options granted by his employer. Mr. N is a widower and has no children. His primary financial goal is to retire comfortably at age 68 with a reduced spending level of $150,000 and to bequeath any assets remaining at his death to his alma mater, Tulane University. Mr. N's financial advisor, Mr. Clayton Spencer, has been working with Mr. N for less than a year. During that time, Spencer has proposed a comprehensive financial plan. Despite Spencer's recommendations, however, Mr. N's asset allocation has remained the same, at nearly 80 percent equities, with 35 percent in his employing company's publicly traded stock. Still, Spencer has developed a good working relationship with Mr. N.

Spencer believes that Mr. N. is a well-grounded, fairly rational person, but he also believes that Mr. N has some behavioral issues to address. In Spencer's view, the most important issue is that Mr. N has not taken action yet on the new, more conservative allocation that Spencer proposed months ago of 50 percent stocks, 40 percent bonds, and 10 percent cash. Spencer worries about the lack of diversification in Mr. N's portfolio. Spencer's concern is that a severe downward market fluctuation or drop in Mr. N's employing company's stock may cause him to sell assets irrationally, affecting his long-term financial plan. Spencer's financial plan demonstrates that even with a somewhat less aggressive portfolio, Mr. N could still meet his primary financial objectives if he could save just $25,000 annually. Spencer believes that one of the issues is that Mr. N thinks of himself as a good investor because of the biotechnology bets that worked out well for him in the past. Spencer suspects that Mr. N hasn't changed his allocation because he thinks Spencer's allocation recommendation is too conservative. Spencer also notices that Mr. N constantly worries about missing out on hot stocks that go up, which his friends are investing in. Spencer decides to ask Mr. N to take a behavioral bias diagnostic questionnaire. When Spencer gets the answers to the questionnaire, he decides to focus on three biases: *regret aversion, overconfidence*, and *self-control*. Spencer asks Mr. N further questions on these three biases. Table 25.2 shows Mr. N's answers to these questions in **bold**.

Through this process, Spencer finds that Mr. N is indeed susceptible to the following emotional biases:

- *Regret-aversion bias* (the tendency to avoid making a decision for fear the decision may cause regret later).
- *Overconfidence bias* (the tendency to overestimate one's investment savvy).
- *Self-control bias* (the tendency to spend today rather than save for tomorrow).

As part of the original financial planning process, Spencer administered a risk tolerance questionnaire to Mr. N for the purpose of generating a mean-variance optimization portfolio recommendation. When Spencer generated

APPLICATION OF BEHAVIORAL FINANCE TO ASSET ALLOCATION

APPLICATION OF BEHAVIORAL FINANCE TO ASSET ALLOCATION

TABLE 25.2   Mr. Nicholas's Bias Diagnostic Tests

Regret Aversion Diagnostic Test

Question 1: Suppose you make an investment in mutual fund BBB, and over the next six months, BBB appreciates by your target of 20 percent. You contemplate selling but then come across an item in the financial press that rehashes the company's recent successes and also sparks new optimism. You wonder whether BBB could rise further. Which response describes your likeliest reaction given ABC's recent performance and the press article?

 a. I think I'll hold off and wait to see what happens. I'd really "kick" myself if I sold now and BBB continued to go up.
 b. I'll probably sell because ABC has hit the target I set, and I try to stick to the targets I set.

Question 2: Suppose you have decided to invest $25,000 in one individual company stock, and you have narrowed your choice down to two companies: Big, Inc., and Medium, Inc. Big is a well-followed, eminently established company whose shareholders include many large pension funds. Medium is newer but has performed well; it has not garnered the same kind of public profile as Big, and it has few well-known investors. According to your calculations, both stocks are expected to have very similar risk and return payoffs. Which answer most closely matches your thought process in this situation?

 a. I would probably feel indifferent between the two investments because both generated the same expected parameters with respect to risk and return.
 b. I will most likely invest in Big because if I invested in Medium and my investment failed, I would feel foolish. Few well-known investors backed Medium, and I would really regret going against their informed consensus only to discover that I was wrong.
 c. I will most likely invest in Big because I feel safe taking the same course as so many respected institutional investors. If Big does decline in value, I know I won't be the only one caught by surprise. With so many savvy professionals sharing my predicament, I could hardly blame myself for poor judgment.

Scoring Guidelines: People answering "a" in Question 1 and/or "b" or "c" in Question 2 may harbor susceptibility to regret aversion bias.

Overconfidence Bias Diagnostic Test

Question 1: How difficult do you think it was to predict the collapse of the credit bubble in the United States from 2008 to 2009?
 a. Easy
 b. Somewhat easy
 c. Somewhat difficult
 d. Difficult

TABLE 25.2 *(Continued)*

Question 2: Assume that from 1926 through 2009, the compound annual return for equities was approximately 9 percent. In any given year, what returns do you expect your equity investments to produce?

a. Below 9 percent
b. About 9 percent
c. Above 9 percent
d. **Well above 9 percent**

Question 3: How much ability do you believe you have in picking investments that will outperform the market?

a. Absolutely no ability
b. Little if any ability
c. Some ability
d. **A fair amount of ability**

Scoring Guidelines: Answering "a" or "b" in Question 1, answering "c" or "d" in Question 2, or answering "c" or "d" in Question 3 indicates susceptibility to overconfidence bias.

Self-Control Bias Diagnostic Test

Question 1: Suppose that you are in need of a new automobile. You have been driving your current car for seven years, and it's time for a change. Which of the following approaches are you most likely to take?

a. I would typically "underspend" on a car because I view a car as transportation and I don't need anything fancy. Besides, I can save the extra money I might have spent on a fancy car and put it away in my savings accounts.
b. I would typically purchase a medium-priced model, with some fancy options, simply because I enjoy a nice car. I may forgo other purchases in order to afford a nice car. I would not purchase anything extravagant, but a nice car is something that I value to an extent and am willing to spend money to obtain.
c. **When it comes to cars, I like to indulge myself. I'd probably splurge on a top-of-the-line model and select most or all available luxury options. Even if I must purchase this car at the expense of saving money, for the long term, I believe that it's vital to "live in the moment." This car is simply my way of living in the moment.**

Question 2: How would you characterize your retirement savings patterns?

a. I consult my advisors and make sure that every tax-favored investment vehicle is "maxed out" (e.g., 401(k), IRA), and I will often save additional funds in taxable accounts.
b. I will usually take advantage of most tax-favored investment vehicles, though in some cases I'm sure that details may have escaped my attention. I may or may not save something in taxable investment accounts.
c. **I hardly ever save for retirement. I spend most of my disposable income, so very little remains available for savings.**

Scoring Guidelines: People answering "b" or "c" to Questions 1 and 2 may be susceptible to self-control bias. Lack of self-control is very common.

the optimization recommendation, Mr. N's proposed asset allocation was 50 percent stocks, 40 percent bonds, and 10 percent cash. Spencer's job is now to answer the following three questions:

1. What effect do Mr. N's biases have on the asset allocation decision?
2. Should Spencer moderate or adapt to Mr. N's biases?
3. What is an appropriate behaviorally modified asset allocation for Mr. N?

Solutions to Mr. Nicholas Case Study

Effect of Biases Mr. Nicholas has emotional biases that provide a clear indication of what allocation he would naturally prefer, which is one dominated by equities. Mr. Nicholas's overconfidence leads him to be more comfortable with equities than may be appropriate. This overconfidence, as well as a potential endowment bias, may explain why he has chosen to hold a substantial part of his portfolio in his employing company's stock. Additionally, Mr. N is likely to experience regret if he misses a major market move. However, he has a high need for current income that supplements his "spend today" mentality (self-control bias), and he may need the "ballast" of fixed-income investments in the event of a market downturn. Because his level of wealth is high, however, he does have some flexibility with his allocation to favor equity over fixed income.

Moderate or Adapt? When considering level of wealth, Mr. Nicholas clearly does not run a standard of living risk, which argues for adapting to his biases. Additionally, his behavioral biases are principally emotional (overconfidence, regret aversion, self-control). Given these facts, and that he naturally prefers an allocation favoring equity, Spencer now has the information with which to make the graph shown in Figure 25.1 and the "moderate, adapt, or both moderate *and* adapt" recommendation.

Spencer decides that the appropriate recommendation is to *adapt* to Mr. N's biases and create a more aggressive portfolio that Mr. N can adhere to and be comfortable with. Spencer also recommends that Mr. N reduce his company stock position by 50 percent and reduce spending, if possible. At the same time, Spencer will run a cash flow analysis to ensure that in the event of a market downturn, Mr. N's living expenses will not be at risk. Spencer also advises a comfortable cash reserve.

Behaviorally Modified Portfolio Decision The mean–variance optimizer's recommended allocation was 50 percent stocks, 40 percent bonds, and 10 percent cash. Using guidelines presented earlier in the reading for

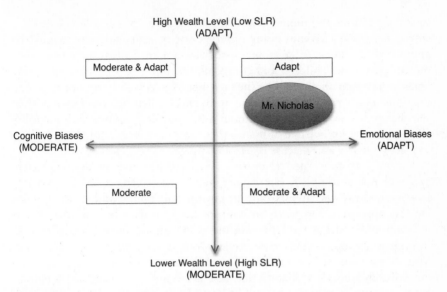

FIGURE 25.1 Illustration of Mr. Nicholas's Case Study Information

emotional biases at a high wealth level, in Spencer's judgment, an appropriate behaviorally modified asset allocation is an allocation of **60 percent stocks, 30 percent bonds, and 10 percent cash.** When Spencer checks his financial planning software to make sure that this allocation will statistically ensure that Mr. N will have adequate living expenses in the event of a market downturn, it shows that the behaviorally modified asset allocation indeed works. Thus, Spencer recommends this allocation to Mr. N, explaining how he arrived at that particular allocation recommendation.

CASE STUDY B: MRS. ALEXANDER

Mrs. Angela Alexander ("Mrs. A") is an 85-year-old widow from Australia with a modest lifestyle and no income beyond what her investment portfolio of $1.5 million generates (about $90,000 per year) and a small government pension of $10,000 annually. Her advisor, Mr. Gerard Spencer, has known Mrs. A for about 10 years. Although Mrs. A did not clearly articulate her investment goals when Spencer first started working with her, over time Spencer has learned that Mrs. A's primary investment goals are (1) to not lose money and (2) to maintain the purchasing power of her assets after fees and taxes. Her desire to not lose money stems from the fact that she recalls that her parents grew up in a lower-middle-class family and she was one of seven children and money was always tight. One of her tendencies is to spread her money around many different banks, and she speaks regularly about various "buckets" of money—such as one for generating her income, one for gifts to her children and grandchildren, and one for paying her bills. Spencer has been challenged by the fact that Mrs. A is quite stubborn in her opinions and rarely, if ever, listens to Spencer when he recommends that she change her way of thinking about her investment money and portfolio allocation. Her knowledge of financial concepts is limited, but she is willing to meet regularly and discuss issues with Spencer over tea.

Spencer is concerned that she is too conservative in her approach and will not accomplish one of her key goals—keeping her purchasing power—because she invests only in government bonds and cash. By taking this approach, her portfolio will not keep up with her spending after inflation and taxes in the long run; therefore, she is putting herself at risk to outlive her assets. As Spencer reflects one day on his relationship with Mrs. A, he realizes that the only recommendation she has accepted is to buy sovereign bonds to slightly increase her returns. Spencer suspects that behavioral biases are influencing Mrs. A and not permitting her to feel comfortable with changing her portfolio. Spencer asks her if she will take a 20-question assessment to examine her investor behavior. She agrees. Based on the answers to the assessment, Spencer decides to delve further into three biases: *anchoring, mental accounting,* and *loss aversion.* Spencer provides Mrs. A with additional questions on these three biases. Table 25.3 shows Mrs. A's answers in **bold**.

Spencer's suspicions are confirmed. Mrs. A is subject to the following biases:

- *Loss aversion bias* (the tendency to feel the pain of losses more acutely than the pleasure of gains).
- *Anchoring and adjustment bias* (the tendency to believe that current market levels are "right"; up or down directional estimates are made from the current level).
- *Mental accounting bias* (the tendency to segregate money into different "accounts.")

As part of the original asset allocation process, Spencer also administered a risk tolerance questionnaire to Mrs. A for the purpose of generating a mean-variance optimization portfolio recommendation. When Spencer generated the optimization recommendation, Mrs. Alexander's "rational" asset allocation was 75 percent bonds, 15 percent stocks, and 10 percent cash; her actual allocation is 100 percent bonds. Spencer is convinced that Mrs. A needs to have a riskier portfolio than the one she currently has and that the

TABLE 25.3 Mrs. Alexander's Bias Diagnostic Tests

Anchoring Bias Diagnostic Test

Question 1: Suppose you own a four-bedroom house and have decided it is time to "downsize" to a smaller house. You are not in a rush to sell your house, but taxes and general expenses on your home are significant and you want to sell it as soon as possible. Your real estate agent, whom you have known for many years and trust, lists your home for sale at $800,000. You paid only $300,000 for the house 10 years ago, so you are thrilled. The house has been on the market for several months, and you have not had any serious offers. One day, you get a phone call from your agent saying he needs to come over right away. When he arrives, he tells you that World-Books, a major employer in town, just declared bankruptcy and 1,000 people are out of work. He has been in meetings all week with his colleagues, and they estimate that real estate prices are down about 10 percent across all types of homes in your area. He says that you must decide at what price you now want to list your home based on this new information. You tell him that you will think it over and get back to him shortly. Please select one of the following that would be your answer:

a. You decide to keep your home on the market for $800,000.
b. **You decide to lower your price by 5 percent to $760,000.**
c. You decide to lower your price by 10 percent to $720,000.
d. You decide to lower your price to $700,000 because you want to be sure you get a bid on the house.

Scoring Guidelines: Mrs. A chose "b," and thus she may be susceptible to anchoring bias. It is clear that if she wants to sell her home, she should lower her price by 10 percent. Mrs. A demonstrates that she is "anchored" to $800,000 and will not fully adjust to the updated information.

Mental Accounting Bias Diagnostic Test

Question 1: How do you tend to think about your money?
a. I tend to think about my money as one "pot," and money is spent out of that one pot.
b. **I tend to segregate my money into various accounts, such as money for paying bills, money for traveling, and money for education.**
c. I tend to segregate my money based on its source, such as pension, interest income, or capital gains.

Scoring Guidelines: Mrs. A selected "b." People who select "b" or "c" may be susceptible to mental accounting bias.

Loss Aversion Diagnostic Test

Question 1: Suppose you are presented with the following investment choices. Please choose between the following two outcomes:

a. **An assured gain of $400**
b. A 25 percent chance of gaining $2,000 and a 75 percent chance of gaining nothing.

(continued)

TABLE 25.3 *(Continued)*

Question 2: You are then asked to choose between the following two outcomes:
  a. An assured loss of $400
  b. A 50 percent chance of losing $1,000, and a 50 percent chance of losing
     nothing

Scoring Guidelines

Question 1: Loss-averse investors are likely to opt for the assurance of a profit in
  "a," even though the expected value of "b" is $500.

Question 2: Loss-averse investors are more likely to select "b" even though the
  expected value in B is –$500 and the loss in A is only $400.

By making both these choices, Mrs. A appears to exhibit loss aversion.

---

reason she is invested so conservatively is primarily because of behavioral
biases. Spencer's job is now to answer the following three questions:

1. What effect do Mrs. A's biases have on the asset allocation decision?
2. Should Spencer moderate or adapt to Mrs. A's biases?
3. What is an appropriate behaviorally modified asset allocation for
   Mrs. A?

Solutions to Mrs. Alexander Case Study

Effect of Biases   Mrs. Alexander's biases are consistent and demonstrate to
Spencer a clear allocation preference for bonds. Because Mrs. Alexander does
not want to put her principal at risk (which is manifested by loss aversion
bias) and separates her money into mental accounts (mental accounting), she
would naturally prefer the safe and secure asset allocation of 100 percent
bonds that she now has. Additionally, because the stock market rises and
falls regularly, she will likely make irrational conclusions about what the
"right" level of the overall stock market should be (anchoring bias); as a
result, she will be wary of any exposure to equities. Thus, if Spencer as her
advisor presented her with an allocation of 100 percent bonds, she would be
likely to immediately agree with that recommendation. However, Spencer
understands that she has a bias toward such an allocation.

Moderate or Adapt?   Mrs. Alexander's level of wealth—which, while not
low, is not high—puts her at a relatively high standard of living risk (SLR).
If Spencer *adapts* to her biases and recommends an allocation of 100 percent
bonds, Spencer's financial planning software tells him that Mrs. Alexander
runs the risk of outliving her assets, a clearly unacceptable outcome. Spencer

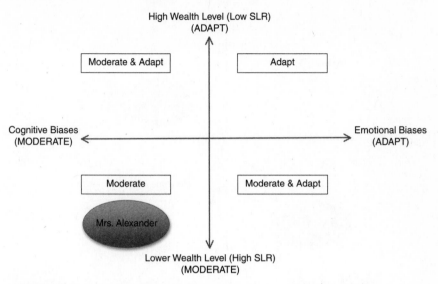

FIGURE 25.2 Illustration of Mrs. Alexander's Case Study Information

needs to help her understand that she would be at risk if she accepted a 100 percent bond portfolio. Because her biases are principally cognitive (mental accounting, anchoring), and these types of biases can be corrected with education and advice, Spencer is confident he can help her make changes. Spencer now has the information needed to make a moderate versus adapt decision as illustrated in the table seen in Figure 25.2.

Behaviorally Modified Portfolio Decision Spencer decides that an appropriate course of action is to *moderate* Mrs. A's bias preferences, so he recommends that she accept some risk in her portfolio. Spencer reasons that an appropriate moderation of Mrs. A's biases will result in the "rational" allocation of **75 percent bonds, 15 percent equity, and 10 percent cash** (the mean-variance recommendation). Spencer checks his financial planning software to make sure that this allocation will statistically ensure that Mrs. A will not outlive her money. The software shows that this allocation is acceptable. Spencer explains to Mrs. A how an allocation based on her biases may have led to an allocation such that her resources would have likely been depleted before her death. Thus, Spencer recommends the **75 percent bonds, 15 percent equity, and 10 percent cash** allocation to Mrs. A. Also, Spencer will continue a program of investor education on the risk of outliving one's assets.

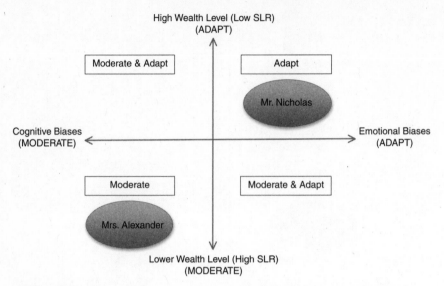

FIGURE 25.3 Illustration of Outcomes of Individual Investor Case Studies
Source: M. Pompian and J. Longo, "Incorporating Behavioral Finance into Your Practice." *Journal of Financial Planning* (March 2005). Reprinted with permission of the Financial Planning Association. For more information on the Financial Planning Association, please visit www.fpanet.org or call 1-800-322-4237.

SUMMARY OF CASE STUDIES

Figure 25.3 illustrates the outcomes of the two case studies, plotted on a common set of axes for easy reference.

As an advisor, you may encounter cases resembling either or both of the scenarios entertained here. Or you may happen on less common cocktails of cognitive and emotional biases. Whatever scenario you encounter, it is hoped that this chapter laid out a useful template methodology that you can expand and tailor in response to your individual client situations. In general, bias type determines the feasibility of and wealth levels determine the advisability of moderating versus adapting to a client. Sometimes, the mean-variance output will be correct; other times the use of the quantitative guidelines presented in Chapter 24 should help to determine the most appropriate course of action.

Six

Behavioral Investor Types

The last section of the book, Chapters 26 and 27, bring us to the section that ties together many of the concepts learned in the book. In these two chapters, I introduce a new concept I developed to make behavioral finance easier to apply in practice. The main idea is that people fall into four basic types of investors, and the distinguishing characteristics of the four types are the biases they have when making investment decisions. More specifically, we are trying to identify the biases that *dominate* one's investor personality. As you will see, there are biases that are associated with each type; however, it is important to realize that just because investors are specific types, they aren't necessarily exempt from the biases of other types. Behavioral Investor Types (BITs) or BITS as I call them, are meant to help both investors and advisors quickly identify who they are dealing with and how best to avoid common mistakes associated with that specific type. Chapter 26 goes over the process of identifying each type and Chapter 27 goes into more detail about each type.

Behavioral Investor Type Diagnostic Process

An individual's self-concept is the core of his personality. It affects every aspect of human behavior: the ability to learn, the capacity to grow and change. A strong, positive self-image is the best possible preparation for success in life.
—Dr. Joyce Brothers, American Psychologist, Columnist and Author

Since the popping of both the technology stock bubble in March of 2000 and subsequent popping of the credit bubble in 2008, behavioral finance has taken center stage with the financial advisory world. But for many financial advisors and individual investors—from now on I will call them, collectively, Financial Market Participants or FMPs—behavioral finance is still an unfamiliar and unused subject. There are many FMPs, however, who have taken the time to read and learn about behavioral finance and use it in practice with good results. Why have they done so? These FMPs realize that being successful is just as much about understanding behavior as it is about understanding financial analysis. And they have observed that behavioral finance can provide tools that can help them "get inside" the head of themselves and their clients. In this chapter, we will be exploring a way to easily apply behavioral finance in practice by segmenting investors by their behavioral traits. By doing so, we can learn how best to help FMPs reach their financial goals. Before we get into the details of how to classify clients into "Behavioral Investor Types" or BITs using a process I call "Behavioral Alpha," let's examine the background of how BITs were developed.

BACKGROUND OF THE DEVELOPMENT OF BEHAVIORAL INVESTOR TYPES

When I first began researching behavioral finance in the early to mid-1990's, my intention was to simply do a better job for my clients by creating port-folios that compensated for the irrational investor behaviors I witnessed. Later, I began writing on the subject in 1998, after seeing the benefits of applying behavioral finance research to my advisory practice. At that time, my intent was to (hopefully) make a contribution to my industry and the clients we serve by demonstrating the benefits that behavioral finance can deliver. My thought process then was relatively simple: doesn't it make sense that people who behave differently (i.e., have different personality types) might want to invest differently? After doing some original research on this topic, and publishing a paper on it entitled "A New Paradigm for Practical Application of Behavioral Finance: Creating Investment Programs Based on Personality Type and Gender to Produce Better Investment Out-comes" in the *Journal of Wealth Management*, I was quite satisfied; but that satisfaction was short-lived. Through the process of educating myself and others on behavioral finance, I was indeed able to help my clients understand and improve their investor behavior. However, I quickly re-alized that if behavioral finance were to be used by a large number of FMPs to create better investment portfolios, three key challenges needed to be tackled.

First, financial advisors needed a guidebook to teach them the basics of what behavioral biases were and how to diagnose their client's irrational behaviors. Without an understanding of the basics, behavioral finance would not be used. Second, even if advisors could diagnose a client's biases, they needed to know what to do with that information. For example, given a certain set of behaviors, should they attempt to change the behavior of the client to match an allocation they think is right for the client, or should they change the allocation to match the client's behavior? Third, the industry needed a common behavioral finance language. Behavioral biases, as then articulated, were not user-friendly because there was not a widely accepted "industry standard" language for describing and communicating these biases to other advisors or to clients.

So, in 2002, I set out to meet these challenges. The first step was the pub-lication of an article in the *Journal of Financial Planning* (JFP) entitled "The Future of Wealth Management: Incorporating Behavioral Finance into Your Practice." In this article, readers were given some practical steps to take to adjust a client's asset allocation for irrational biases they encountered, as-suming they could recognize irrationally biased behaviors in their clients. The ability to recognize biases, of course, was a big assumption; I noted in that article that no "handbook" existed that financial advisors could turn to for the basics of diagnosing and treating behavioral biases. As it turned out, I wrote that book; in April of 2006, Wiley published the first edition of *Behavioral Finance and Wealth Management*, which, among other topics, defined twenty of the most common behavioral biases advisors encounter in their daily client work and described how to diagnose and treat these biases. In addition to delivering basic information on behavioral finance, it also established the framework for an industry standard language of communicating and diagnosing biases. After the JPF article and the book were completed, I felt satisfied that I had met these three challenges; once again, however, that satisfaction was ephemeral.

There was still a missing piece to the puzzle. Even if advisors had been trained in irrational biases, could understand how to apply this knowledge to their clients, and could communicate in industry standard parlance, they still needed a way to make the process efficient, almost second nature, in terms of incorporating behavioral finance into the everyday practice of providing financial advice. In other words, advisors needed to be able to adroitly recognize investor behavior at a high level, so they could quickly and effectively diagnose and treat that client's irrational behavior.

The method for doing this, as we will see in this chapter, is called Behavioral Alpha. The word "alpha" is used for two reasons. First, the dictionary definition of alpha is "first" or "the beginning." It is my belief that before an asset allocation is created, financial advisors first need to take inventory of a client's behavior—hence behavioral alpha. Secondly, in the context of the financial world, the word *alpha* has become synonymous with describing performance above expectations. In the context of behavioral alpha, my belief is that by taking inventory of an investor's behavior prior to creating an investment plan, the advisor will have performance results that exceed expectations because the client will be able to more comfortably adhere to an allocation that has been custom-designed for them.

The development of behavioral investor types or BITs is essentially a continuation and refinement of my previous work in the aforementioned JFP article published in March 2003 and was intended to get behavioral finance over the proverbial "goal line;" to a place where FMPs feel more confident that they can use behavioral finance easily and effectively in practice.

PSYCHOGRAPHIC MODELS OF INVESTOR BEHAVIOR

Much of current economic and financial theory is based on the assumptions that individuals act rationally and consider all available information in the decision-making process. Behavioral finance challenges these assumptions.

Psychographic models classify individuals according to certain characteristics, tendencies, or behaviors. By segmenting individuals by personality type and gender and correlating these variables with specific investor biases, we can lay the groundwork for applying many of the biases that behavioral finance literature explores (e.g., Khaneman and Tversky).[1]

If certain groups of investors prove susceptible to certain biases, then practitioners can recognize behavioral tendencies before investment decisions are made and, likely, produce better investment outcomes. Psychographic classifications are particularly relevant with regard to individual investment strategy and risk tolerance. An investor's background, past experiences, and attitudes can play a significant role in decisions made during the asset allocation process. It is important to note that because psychology is involved, no exact diagnosis can be made of any individual or situation. Although there are limitations to this type of analysis, if financial market participants can gain an understanding of their behavioral tendencies, the result is likely to be better investment outcomes.

Two studies—Barnewall,[2] and Bailard, Biehl, and Kaiser (BB&K)[3]— apply useful models of investor psychographics and will be reviewed in the next section. However, both studies predate significant findings in the behavioral finance literature, including important biases discovered in recent years. Further, the models Barnewall and BB&K applied leave out references to specific behavioral biases. The Barnewall model—one of the first and most used—distinguished investors by their passivity or activity in creating wealth. Although it usefully described certain individual investors, and can be used in the behavioral investor type diagnostic process, it has limitations. For example, investors aren't just differentiable according to how they've arrived at their wealth. They are, after all, human beings and possess unique, complicated, intellectual and emotional attribute arrays. Moreover, investors are gendered. It might seem regressive to suggest that gender identity preordains financial decision making, and we certainly don't go that far. However, our data does strongly insinuate that when it comes to investing, men and women reason differently. Barnewall didn't take any of these factors into account. The modern investment era demands a better model. The BB&K model featured some of the principles of the Barnewall model; but, by classifying investor personalities according to level of confidence and method of action, it introduced additional segmentation. Like the Barnewall model, the BB&K model is useful in working with certain clients and may explain in general terms why a person is predisposed to certain investor behaviors. However, the BB&K model neither scientifically described personality type nor links investor behaviors with recently identified investor biases, limiting its utility. As noted, neither study had the benefit of the behavioral finance literature that informs this book.

EARLY PSYCHOGRAPHIC MODELS

We will now review these two models of investor psychographics from the 1980s. We will then move to more recent models of investor behavior.

Barnewall Two-Way Model

One of the oldest and most prevalent psychographic investor models, based on the work of Marilyn MacGruder Barnewall and intended to help investment advisers interface with clients, distinguishes two relatively simple investor types: passive and active. Barnewall notes that "passive investors" are defined as those investors who have become wealthy passively—for example, by inheritance or by risking the capital of others rather than risking their own capital (managers who benefit when their companies do well are examples of the latter category). Passive investors have a greater need for security than they have tolerance for risk. Occupational groups that tend to have passive investors include corporate executives, lawyers with large regional firms, certified public accountants (CPA) with large CPA companies, medical and dental non-surgeons, small business owners who inherited the business, politicians, bankers, and journalists. Further, the smaller the economic resources an investor has, the more likely the person is to be a passive investor. The lack of resources gives individuals a higher security need and a lower tolerance for risk.

"Active investors" are individuals who have been actively involved in wealth creation through investment, and they have risked their own capital in achieving their wealth objectives. Active investors have a higher tolerance for risk than they have need for security. Related to their high risk tolerance is the fact that active investors prefer to maintain control of their own investments. Their tolerance for risk is high because they believe in themselves. When active investors sense a loss of control, their risk tolerance drops quickly. They are involved in their own investments to the point that they gather tremendous amounts of information about the investments. By their involvement and control, they feel that they reduce risk to an acceptable level, which is often fallacious (Barnewall 1987).

Barnewall's work suggests that a simple, non-invasive overview of an investor's personal history and career record could signal potential pitfalls to guard against in establishing an advisory relationship. Her analysis also indicates that a quick, biographic glance at a client could provide important context for portfolio design.

Bailard, Biehl, and Kaiser Five-Way Model

The Bailard, Biehl, and Kaiser (BB&K) model features some of the principles of the Barnewall model, but by classifying investor personalities along two axes—level of confidence and method of action—it introduces an additional dimension of analysis. Bailard, Biehl, and Kaiser (1986) provide a graphic representation of their model (Figure 26.1). Kaiser (1990) explains:

> *The first (aspect of personality) deals with how confidently the investor approaches life, regardless of whether it is his approach to his career, his health, or his money. These are important emotional choices, and they are dictated by how confident the investor is about some things or how much he tends to worry about them. The second element deals with whether the investor is methodical, careful, and analytical in his approach to life or whether he is emotional, intuitive, and impetuous. These two elements can be thought of as two "axes" of individual psychology; one axis is called the "confident–anxious" axis and the other is called the "careful–impetuous" axis* [see Figure 26.1].

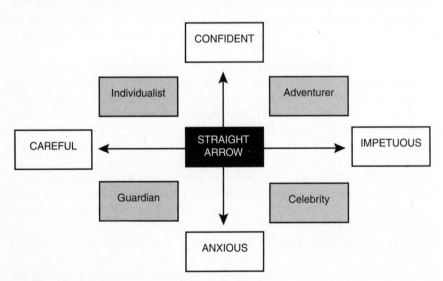

FIGURE 26.1   Bailard, Biehl, and Kaiser Model

- The **Adventurer:** Adventurers may hold highly undiversified portfolios because they are confident and willing to take chances. Their confidence leads them to make their own decisions and makes them reluctant to take advice. This presents a challenge for an investment adviser.

- The **Celebrity:** Celebrities like to be the center of attention. They may hold opinions about some things, but to a certain extent recognize their limitations and may be willing to seek and take advice about investing.

- The **Individualist:** Individualists are independent and confident, which may be reflected in their choice of employment. They like to make their own decisions but only after careful analysis. They are pleasant to advise because they will listen and process informational rationally.

- The **Guardian:** Guardians are cautious and concerned about the future. As people age and approach retirement, they may become guardians. They are concerned about protecting their assets and may seek advice from those they perceive as being more knowledgeable than themselves.

- The **Straight Arrow:** Straight arrows are sensible and secure. They fall near the center of the graph. They are willing to take on some risk in the expectation of earning a commensurate return.

FIGURE 26.2 BB&K Classifications

Figure 26.1 includes a synopsis of BB&K's descriptions of each of the five investor personality types that the model generates (Kaiser 1990).

Although this model may be useful, it is possible that investors do not approach all parts of their life with equal confidence or care. It is important to focus on the approach to investing rather than placing undue focus on evidence from other aspects of their life. In addition, a limitation of all categorization schemes is that an individual's behavior patterns may change or lack consistency.

THE BEHAVIORAL ALPHA PROCESS: A TOP-DOWN APPROACH

The Behavioral Alpha approach is a multi-step diagnostic process that results in clients being classified into one of four behavioral investor types

(BITs). Bias identification, which is done near the end of the process, is narrowed down for the advisor by giving the advisor clues as to which biases a client is likely to have, based on the client's BIT. BITs were designed to help advisors make rapid yet insightful assessments of what type of investor they are dealing with before recommending an investment plan. The benefit of defining what type of investor an advisor is dealing with up-front is that client behavioral surprises that result in a client wishing to change his or her portfolio as a result of market turmoil can be mitigated. If an advisor can limit the number of traumatic episodes that inevitably occur throughout the advisory process by delivering smoother (read here: expected) investment results, because the advisor had created an investment plan that is customized to the client's behavioral make-up, a stronger client relationship is the result. BITs, however, are not intended to be "absolutes" but rather "guide posts" to use when making the journey with a client; dealing with irrational investor behavior is not an exact science. For example, an advisor may find that he or she has correctly classified a client as a certain BIT, but finds that the client has traits (biases) of another.

There are four behavioral investor types: Preservers, Followers, Independents, and Accumulators. Each BIT is characterized by the type of bias that dominates an investor's personality. One of the most important concepts advisors should keep in mind as they go through these articles is that the least risk tolerant BIT and the most risk tolerant BIT are driven by emotional biases, while the two BITS in between these two extremes are mainly affected by cognitive biases. Emotional clients tend to be more difficult clients to work with and advisors who can recognize the type of client they are dealing with prior to making investment recommendations will be much better prepared to deal with irrational behavior when it arises.

THE BIT IDENTIFICATION PROCESS

Step 1: Interview client and identify active or passive traits. Most advisors begin with a client interview, which consists mainly of a question-and-answer session intended to gain an understanding about a client's objectives, constraints, and past investing practices. This interview should tell the advisor whether a client is an active or passive investor. In other words, has the client in the past (or does the client now) put capital at risk to build wealth? It is important to make a distinction between investing in a diversified portfolio and risking capital. Risking capital involves doing things such as building companies (big or small), investing in speculative real estate using leverage, or working for oneself rather than for a large company.

TABLE 26.1 Test for Active or Passive Traits

Question	Response A	Response B
Have you earned the majority of your wealth in your lifetime?	Yes	No
Have you risked your own capital in the creation of your wealth?	Yes	No
Which is stronger: your tolerance for risk to build wealth or the desire to preserve wealth?	Tolerance for risk	Preserve wealth
Would you prefer to maintain a degree of control over your investments or prefer to delegate that responsibility to someone else?	Maintain control	Delegate
Do you have faith in your abilities as an investor?	Yes	No
If you had to pick one of two portfolios, which would it be?	80-percent stocks/20-percent bonds	40-percent stocks/60-percent bonds
Is your wealth goal intended to continue your current lifestyle or are you motivated to build wealth at the expense of current lifestyle?	Build wealth	Continue Current lifestyle
In your work or personal life, are you generally a "self-starter" in that you seek out what needs to be done and then do it, or do you normally take direction?	Self-starter	Take direction
Are you "income motivated," or are you willing to put your capital at risk to build wealth?	Capital at risk	Income motivated
Do you believe in the concept of borrowing money to make money/operate a business, or do you prefer to limit the amount of debt you owe?	Borrow money	Limit debt

Understanding active and passive traits is important because passive investors tend toward certain biases and active investors tend toward different biases, which we will see later in the chapter. Table 26.1 shows questions that probe the active/passive nature of clients. A preponderance of "A" answers indicates an active investor; "B" answers indicate a passive investor.

Step 2: Administer risk-tolerance questionnaire. Once the advisor has classified the investor as active or passive, the advisor administers a traditional risk-tolerance questionnaire (not included here). The expectation

General Type	PASSIVE		ACTIVE	
Risk Tolerance	Conservative	Moderate	Growth	Aggressive
Dominant Biases	Emotional	Cognitive	Cognitive	Emotional
BIT	Preserver	Follower	Independent	Accumulator
Biases	Status Quo	Regret	Conservatism	Affinity
	Endowment	Outcome	Availability	Overconfidence
	Loss Aversion	Cognitive Dissonance	Confirmation	Self-Control
	Mental Accounting	Hindsight	Representativeness	Illusion of Control
	Anchoring	Framing	Self-Attribution	
		Recency		

FIGURE 26.3 Biases Associated with each Behavioral Investor Type

is that active investors will rank medium-to-high for risk tolerance and that passive investors will rank moderate-to-low for risk tolerance (Figure 26.3). Naturally, this will not always be the case. With an unexpected outcome, the advisor should defer to risk tolerance in determining which biases to test for.

Step 3: Test for Behavioral Biases and Confirm Behavioral Investment Type (BIT). The third step is to test for and confirm that the client has certain behavioral biases. For instance, if an investor is passive, and the risk-tolerance questionnaire reveals a very low risk tolerance, the investor likely has the biases associated with a *preserver*. If the investor is passive and the questionnaire reveals a low-to-medium risk tolerance, the investor likely has the biases associated with a *follower*. If an investor is active and has a medium-to-high risk tolerance, the investor likely has the biases associated with an *individualist*. Finally, if an investor is active and has a high risk tolerance, the investor likely has the biases associated with an *accumulator*. When the client is tested for behavioral biases of a passive preserver, for example, and the test confirms that the client has these biases, then the BIT diagnosis is confirmed. Figure 26.3 provides an overview of the characteristics of each BIT and Figure 26.4 illustrates the entire diagnostic process.

Note that in the figure above clients at either end of the scale are emotionally biased in their behavior while clients in the middle are cognitively biased, which makes sense. Clients with a high need for security are

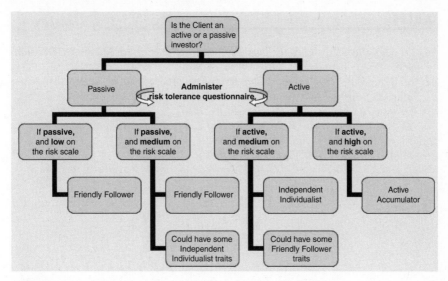

FIGURE 26.4 The Behavioral Investor Type Diagnostic Process

emotionally driven; they get very emotional about losing money and very uneasy during times of stress or change. Similarly, very aggressive investors also are emotional. They typically suffer from overconfidence and mistakenly believe they can control their investment outcomes. In between are the investors who mainly suffer cognitive biases and need education and information to make better investment decisions. But of primary importance is this: *Clients who are emotional investors need to be advised differently than those who make mainly cognitive errors.* When advising emotional investors, advisors must focus on how the investment program impacts important emotional issues such as financial security, retirement, or future generations, not quantitative details such as standard deviations and Sharpe ratios. The quantitative approach is more effective with clients who are less emotional and tend to make cognitive errors (see Figure 26.4).

SUMMARY

Now that we have an understanding of the basics of how to identify behavioral investor types, we will now move to Chapter 27 that will review the specific details of each type and advice for overcoming the biases associated with each type.

NOTES

1. Daniel Kahneman and Amos Tversky, "Prospect Theory: An Analysis of Decision under Risk," Econometrica 47 (1979): 263–91.
2. M. Barnewall, "Psychological Characteristics of the Individual Investor," in Asset Allocation for the Individual Investor, ed. William Droms (Charlottesville, VA: Institute of Chartered Financial Analysts, 1987).
3. Thomas Bailard, David Biehl, and Ronald Kaiser, *Personal Money Management*, 5th ed. (Chicago: Science Research Associates, 1986).
4. M. Barnewall, "Psychological Characteristics," see note 2.
5. T. Bailard, D. Biehl, and R. Kaiser, *Personal Money Management*, see note 3.

CHAPTER 27

Behavioral Investor Types

No theory of the universe can be satisfactory which does not adequately account for the phenomena of life, especially in that richest form which finds expression in human personality.
                                                        —B. H. Streeter

INTRODUCTION

Behavioral investor types (BITs) were designed to help financial market participants (FMPs) make a speedy yet insightful assessment of what type of biases dominate investment decision making. Based on my experience as a financial advisor, combined with the research I have done in behavioral finance, I have identified four BITs: the Preserver, the Follower, the Independent, and the Accumulator. Each BIT has biases that are associated with it, which will be discussed extensively in the next section. BITs are not intended to be "absolutes" but rather "guideposts." For example, you may find that you have classified yourself or a client as a Preserver, but find that they have traits (biases) of a Follower or even an Individualist. The grouping or clustering of biases to define a BIT is done to show that certain investors have a strong *tendency* to certain biases that can dominate investment decision-making behavior. The goal of the use of BITs is to discover irrational behaviors and then, ultimately, to create a behaviorally modified (best practical) asset allocation (that we learned about in earlier chapters) that FMPs can comfortably adhere to, to meet long-term financial goals.

One of the most important concepts readers should keep in mind as they go through the next four sections in this chapter is that the least risk-tolerant BIT and the most risk-tolerant BIT clients are emotionally biased in their behavior. In the middle of the risk scale are BITs that are affected mainly by cognitive biases. This should make intuitive sense. Investors who have a high need for security (i.e., a low risk tolerance) do so because emotion is driving this behavior; they get emotional about losing money and get uneasy during times of stress or change. Similarly, highly aggressive investors are also emotionally charged people who adamantly want to accumulate assets. They typically suffer from a high level of overconfidence and mistakenly believe they can control the outcomes of their investments. In between these two extremes are the investors who suffer mainly from cognitive biases and can benefit from education and information about their biases so they can make better investment decisions.

A brief diagnostic is provided for each of the biases associated with each BIT. Advice, which is geared toward the advisor, is also provided. An overarching point that readers should keep in mind as they proceed is that investors who are emotional about their investing need to be advised differently than those who make mainly cognitive errors. When advising emotionally charged investors, advisors need to focus on how the investment program being created impacts important emotional issues like financial security, retirement, or the goals for future generations rather than focusing on portfolio details like standard deviation and Sharpe ratios. A quantitative approach is more effective with clients who are less emotional and tend to make cognitive errors. Emotional clients tend to be more difficult clients to work with, and advisors who can recognize the type of client they are dealing with prior to making investment recommendations will be much better prepared to deal with irrational behavior when it arises. At the end of the day, the goal is to build better long-term relationships with clients; BITs are designed to help in this effort. In the next section, we begin with a passive, conservative investor, the Preserver.

PRESERVER

> **Basic type:** Passive
> **Risk tolerance level:** Low
> **Primary bias:** Emotional

Preservers are, as the name implies, passive investors who place a great deal of emphasis on financial security and preserving wealth rather than taking risk to grow wealth. Because they have gained wealth by not risking their own capital, Preservers may not be highly financially sophisticated. A common situation is a Preserver who has gained wealth through inheritance or conservatively by working in a large company. Some Preservers are "worriers" in that they obsess over short-term performance (losses) and are slow to make investment decisions because they aren't entirely comfortable with change—which is consistent with the way they have approached their professional lives—being careful not to take excessive risks.

Many Preservers are focused on taking care of their family members and future generations, especially funding life-enhancing experiences such as education and home buying. Because the focus is on family and security, Preserver biases tend to be emotional rather than cognitive. As age and wealth level increase, this BIT becomes more common. Although not always the case, many Preservers enjoy the wealth management process—they like the idea of being catered to because of their financial status—and thus are generally good clients. Behavioral biases of Preservers tend to be emotional, security-oriented biases such as endowment bias, loss aversion, and status quo. Preservers also exhibit cognitive biases such as anchoring and mental accounting. The following is a description of the biases just discussed (this should be a review for you) and a simple diagnostic for each bias.

Loss Aversion Bias

Bias type: Emotional

Preservers tend to feel the pain of losses more than the pleasure of gains as compared to other client types. As such, these Preservers may hold on to losing investments too long—even when they see no prospect of a turnaround. Loss aversion is a very common bias and is seen by large numbers of financial advisors with this type of client.

Simple diagnostic for loss aversion bias: On a scale of 1 to 5, with 5 being full agreement, how much do you agree with the following:

The pain of financial loss is at least two times stronger than the pleasure of financial gain.

Answering 3 to 5 shows a tendency toward loss aversion bias.

Status Quo Bias

Bias type: Emotional

Preservers often prefer to keep their investments (and other parts of their life for that matter) the same or keep the "status quo." These investors tell themselves "things have always been this way" and thus feel safe keeping things the same.

Simple diagnostic for status quo bias: On a scale of 1 to 5, with 5 being full agreement, how much do you agree with the following:

When considering changing my portfolio, I spend time thinking about options but often end up changing little or sometimes nothing.

Answering 3 to 5 shows a tendency toward status quo bias.

Endowment Bias

Bias type: Emotional

Preservers, especially those who inherit wealth, tend to assign a greater value to an investment they already own (such as a piece of real estate or an inherited stock position) than they would if they didn't possess that investment and had the potential to acquire it.

Simple diagnostic for endowment bias: On a scale of 1 to 5, with 5 being full agreement, how much do you agree with the following:

I sometimes get attached to certain of my investments, which may cause me not to take action on them.

Answering 3 to 5 shows a tendency toward endowment bias.

Anchoring Bias

Bias type: Cognitive

Investors in general, and Preservers in particular, are often influenced by purchase points or arbitrary price levels, and tend to cling to these numbers when facing questions like "should I buy or sell this investment?" Suppose that the stock is down 25 percent from the high that it reached five months ago ($75/share vs. $100/share). Frequently, a Preserver client will resist selling until its price rebounds to the $100/share it achieved five months ago.

Simple diagnostic for anchoring bias: On a scale of 1 to 5, with 5 being full agreement, how much do you agree with the following:

When thinking about selling an investment, the price I paid is a big factor I consider before taking any action.

Answering 3 to 5 shows a tendency toward anchoring bias.

Mental Accounting Bias

Bias type: Cognitive

Many Preservers treat various sums of money differently based on where these sums are mentally categorized. For example, Preservers often segregate their assets into safe "buckets." If all of these assets are viewed as safe money, suboptimal overall portfolio returns are usually the result.

Simple diagnostic for mental accounting bias: On a scale of 1 to 5, with 5 being full agreement, how much do you agree with the following:

I tend to categorize my investments in various accounts, for example, leisure, bill pay, college funding, etc.

Answering 3 to 5 shows a tendency toward mental accounting bias.

Advice for Preservers

After reviewing this section, readers might correctly conclude that Preservers are difficult to advise because they are driven mainly by emotion. This is true; however, they are also greatly in need of good financial advice. Advisors should take the time to interpret behavioral signs provided to them by Preserver clients. Preservers need "big picture" advice, and advisors shouldn't dwell on details like standard deviations and Sharpe ratios or else they will lose the client's attention. Preservers need to understand how the portfolio they choose to create will deliver desired results to emotional issues such as family members or future generations. Once they feel comfortable discussing these important emotional issues with their advisor, and a bond of trust is established, they will take action. After a period of time, Preservers are likely to become an advisor's best clients because they value greatly the advisor's professionalism, expertise, and objectivity in helping make the right investment decisions.

FOLLOWER

Basic type: Passive

Risk tolerance level: Low to medium

Primary bias: Cognitive

Followers are typically passive investors who do not have their own ideas about investing. They often follow the lead of their friends and colleagues in investment decisions, and want to be in the latest, most popular investments without regard to a long-term plan. One of the key challenges of working with Followers is that they often overestimate their risk tolerance. Advisors need to be careful not to suggest too many "hot" investment ideas—Followers will likely want to do all of them. Some don't like, or even fear, the task of investing, and many put off making investment decisions without professional advice; the result is that they maintain, often by default, high cash balances. Followers generally comply with professional advice when they get it, and they educate themselves financially, but can at times be difficult because they don't enjoy or have an aptitude for the investment process. Biases of Followers are cognitive: recency, hindsight, framing, regret, cognitive dissonance, and outcome.

Recency Bias

Bias type: Cognitive

Recency bias is a predisposition for investors to recall and emphasize recent events and/or observations. Followers may extrapolate patterns where none really exist. Recency bias ran rampant during the bull market period between 2003 and 2007 when many investors wrongly presumed that the stock market, particularly energy, housing, and international stocks, would continue gains. Moderate investors are known to enter or hold on to investments when prices are peaking, which can end badly, with sharp price declines.

Simple diagnostic for recency bias: On a scale of 1 to 5, with 5 being full agreement, how much do you agree with the following:

When considering the track record of an investment, I put more weight on how it has performed recently versus how it has performed historically.

Answering 3 to 5 shows a tendency toward recency bias.

Hindsight Bias

Bias type: Cognitive

Followers often lack independent thoughts about their investments and are susceptible to hindsight bias, which occurs when an investor perceives investment outcomes as if they were predictable. The result of hindsight bias is that it gives investors a false sense of security when making investment decisions, emboldening them to take excessive risk without recognizing it.

Simple diagnostic for hindsight bias: On a scale of 1 to 5, with 5 being full agreement, how much do you agree with the following:

When reflecting on past investment mistakes, I see that many could have been easily avoided.

Answering 3 to 5 shows a tendency toward hindsight bias.

Framing Bias

Bias type: Cognitive

Framing bias is the tendency of Followers to respond to situations differently based on the context in which a choice is presented (framed). Often,

Followers focus too restrictively on one or two aspects of a situation, excluding other considerations. The use of risk tolerance questionnaires provides a good example. Depending on how questions are asked, framing bias can cause investors to respond to risk tolerance questions in an either unduly risk-averse or risk-taking manner. For example, when questions are worded in the gain frame (e.g., an investment goes up), then a risk-taking response is more likely. When questions are worded in the "loss" frame (e.g., an investment goes down), then risk-averse behavior is the likely response.

Simple diagnostic for framing bias: On a scale of 1 to 5, with 5 being full agreement, how much do you agree with the following:

I trust more the advice of national investment firms than smaller, local firms.

Answering 3 to 5 shows a tendency toward framing bias.

Cognitive Dissonance Bias

Bias type: Cognitive

In psychology, cognitions represent attitudes, emotions, beliefs, or values. When multiple cognitions intersect–for example when a person believes in something only to find out it is not true—Followers try to alleviate their discomfort by ignoring the truth and/or rationalizing their decisions. Investors who suffer from this bias may continue to invest in a security or fund they already own after it has gone down (average down) even when they know they should be judging the new investment with objectivity. A common phrase for this concept is "throwing good money after bad."

Simple diagnostic for cognitive dissonance bias: On a scale of 1 to 5, with 5 being full agreement, how much do you agree with the following:

When making investment decisions, I tend to focus on the positive aspect of an investment rather than on what might go wrong with the investment.

Answering 3 to 5 shows a tendency toward cognitive dissonance bias.

Regret Aversion Bias

Bias type: Emotional

Followers often avoid taking decisive actions because they fear that, in hindsight, whatever course they select will prove less than optimal. Regret aversion can cause some investors to be too timid in their investment choices because of losses they have suffered in the past.

Simple diagnostic for regret aversion bias: On a scale of 1 to 5, with 5 being full agreement, how much do you agree with the following:

Poor past financial decisions have caused me to change my current investing behavior.

Answering 3 to 5 shows a tendency toward regret aversion bias.

Advice for Followers

Advisors to Followers first and foremost need to recognize that Followers often overestimate their risk tolerance. Risky trend-following behavior occurs in part because Followers don't like situations of ambiguity that may accompany the decision to enter an asset class when it is out of favor. They also may convince themselves that they "knew it all along" when an investment idea goes their way, which also increases future risk-taking behavior. Advisors need to handle Followers with care because they are likely to "say yes" to investment ideas that make sense to them, regardless of whether the advice is in their best long-term interest. Advisors need to encourage Followers to take a hard look at behavioral tendencies that may cause them to overestimate their risk tolerance. Because Follower biases are mainly cognitive, education on the benefits of portfolio diversification and sticking to a long-term plan is usually the best course of action. Advisors should challenge Follower clients to be introspective and provide data-backed substantiation for recommendations. Offering education in clear, unambiguous ways so they have the chance to "get it" is a good idea. If advisors take the time, this steady, educational approach will generate client loyalty and adherence to long-term investment plans.

INDEPENDENT

Basic type: Active

Risk tolerance: Medium to high

Primary bias: Cognitive

With Independents, we are entering the realm of the active investor. As we reviewed in earlier articles, these investors have been actively involved in their wealth creation, typically risking their own capital in achieving their wealth objectives. Active investors have a higher tolerance for risk than they have need for security. Their tolerance for risk is high because they believe in themselves. Related to their high risk tolerance is the fact that active investors prefer to maintain at least some amount of control of their own investments. They want to get very involved in investment decision making and aren't afraid to roll up their sleeves and do due diligence on contemplated investments. Let's turn our attention to the first of two active behavioral investor types, the Independent Individualist (II).

An Independent is an active investor with medium-to-high risk tolerance who is strong-willed and an independently minded thinker. Independents are self-assured and "trust their instincts" when making investment decisions; however, when they do research on their own, they may be susceptible to acting on information that is available to them rather than getting corroboration from other sources. Sometimes advisors find that an Independent client made an investment without consulting anyone. This approach can be problematic because, due to their independent mind-set, these clients often irrationally cling to the views they had when they made an investment, even when market conditions change, making advising Independents challenging. They often enjoy investing, however, and are comfortable taking risks, but often resist following a rigid financial plan.

Some Independents are obsessed with trying to beat the market and may hold concentrated portfolios. Of all behavioral investor types, Independents are the most likely to be contrarian, which can benefit them—and lead them to continue their contrarian practices. Independent Individualist biases are cognitive: conservatism, availability, confirmation, representativeness, and self-attribution.

Conservatism Bias

Bias type: Cognitive

Conservatism bias occurs when people cling to a prior view or forecast at the expense of acknowledging new information. Independents often cling to a view or forecast, behaving too inflexibly when presented with new information. For example, assume an investor purchases a security based on the knowledge about a forthcoming new product announcement. The company then announces that it is experiencing problems bringing the product to market. Independents may cling to the initial, optimistic impression of the new product announcement and may fail to take action on the negative announcement.

Simple diagnostic for conservatism bias: On a scale of 1 to 5, with 5 being full agreement, how much do you agree with the following:

I don't easily change my views about investments once they are made.

Answering 3 to 5 shows a tendency toward conservatism bias.

Availability Bias

Bias type: Cognitive

Availability bias occurs when people estimate the probability of an outcome based on how prevalent that outcome appears in their lives. People exhibiting this bias perceive easily recalled possibilities as being more likely than those prospects that are harder to imagine or difficult to comprehend. As an example, suppose an Independent is asked to identify the "best" mutual funds. Many of these investors would perform a Google search and, most likely, find funds from firms that engage in heavy advertising—such as Fidelity or Schwab. Investors subject to availability bias are influenced to pick funds from such companies, despite the fact that some of the best-performing funds advertise very little if at all.

Simple diagnostic for availability bias: On a scale of 1 to 5, with 5 being full agreement, how much do you agree with the following:

I often take action on a new investment right away, if it makes sense to me.

Answering 3 to 5 shows a tendency toward availability bias.

Representativeness Bias

Bias type: Cognitive

Representativeness bias occurs as a result of a flawed a perceptual framework when processing new information. To make new information easier to process, some investors project outcomes that resonate with their own preexisting ideas. An Independent might view a particular stock, for example, as a value stock because it resembles an earlier value stock that was a successful investment—but the new investment is actually not a value stock. For instance, a high-flying biotech stock with scant earnings or assets drops 25 percent after a negative product announcement. Some Independents may take this situation to be representative of a "value" stock because it is cheap; but biotech stocks don't typically have earnings, while traditional value stocks have had earnings in the past but are temporarily underperforming.

Simple diagnostic for representativeness bias: On a scale of 1 to 5, with 5 being full agreement, how much do you agree with the following:

Many investment choices I make are based upon my knowledge of how similar past investments have performed.

Answering 3 to 5 shows a tendency toward representativeness bias.

Self-Attribution (Self-Enhancing) Bias

Bias type: Cognitive

Self-attribution bias refers to the tendency of Independents to ascribe their successes to innate talents while blaming failures on outside influences. For example, suppose an Independent makes an investment in a particular stock that goes up in value. The reason it went up is not due to random factors such as economic conditions or competitor failures (the most likely reason for the investment success), but rather to the investor's investment savvy (likely not the reason for the investment success.) This is classic self-enhancing bias.

Simple diagnostic for self-attribution bias: On a scale of 1 to 5, with 5 being full agreement, how much do you agree with the following:

I often find that many of my successful investments can be attributed to my decisions, while those that did not work out were based on the guidance of others.

Answering 3 to 5 shows a tendency toward self-attribution bias.

Confirmation Bias

Bias type: Cognitive

Confirmation bias occurs when people observe, overvalue, or actively seek out information that confirms their claims, while ignoring or devaluing evidence that might discount their claims. Confirmation bias can cause investors to seek out only information that confirms their beliefs about an investment, and not seek out information that may contradict their beliefs. This behavior can leave investors in the dark regarding, for example, the imminent decline of a stock. Independents often find themselves subject to this bias.

Simple diagnostic for confirmation bias: On a scale of 1 to 5, with 5 being full agreement, how much do you agree with the following:

When an investment is not going well, I usually seek information that confirms I made the right decision about it.

Answering 3 to 5 shows a tendency toward confirmation bias.

Advice for Independents

Independents can be difficult clients to advise due to their independent mindset, but they are usually grounded enough to listen to sound advice when it is presented in a way that respects their independent views. As we have learned, Independent Individualists are firm in their belief in themselves and their decisions, but can be blinded to contrary thinking. As with Followers, education is essential to changing behavior of Independents; their biases are predominantly cognitive. A good approach is to have regular educational discussions during client meetings. This way, the advisor doesn't point out unique or recent failures, but rather educates regularly and can incorporate concepts that he or she feels are appropriate for the client. Because Independents' biases are mainly cognitive, education on the benefits of portfolio diversification and sticking to a long-term plan is usually the best course of action. Advisors should challenge Independents to reflect on how they make investment decisions and provide data-backed substantiation for recommendations. Offering education in clear, unambiguous ways is an effective approach. If advisors take the time, this steady, educational approach should yield positive results.

ACCUMULATOR

> **Basic type:** Active
> **Risk tolerance:** High
> **Primary bias:** Emotional

With Accumulators, we continue within the realm of the active investor. As we reviewed in earlier articles, active investors have been actively involved in their wealth creation, typically risking their own capital in achieving their wealth objectives. Active investors have a higher tolerance for risk than they have need for security. Their tolerance for risk is high because they believe in themselves. Related to their high risk tolerance is the fact that active investors prefer to get very involved in investment decision making and aren't afraid to roll up their sleeves and do due diligence on contemplated investments. Let's turn our attention now to the last of the two active behavioral investor types, the Accumulator.

The Accumulator is the most aggressive behavioral investor type. These clients are entrepreneurial and often the first generation to create wealth, and they are even more strong-willed and confident than Independents. At high wealth levels, they often have controlled the outcomes of noninvestment activities and believe they can do the same with investing. This behavior can lead to overconfidence in investing activities. Left unadvised, they often trade too much, which can be a drag on investment performance. Accumulators are quick decision makers but may chase higher-risk investments than their friends. If successful, they enjoy the thrill of making a good investment.

Some Accumulators can be difficult to advise because they don't believe in basic investment principles such as diversification and asset allocation. They are often "hands-on," wanting to be heavily involved in the investment decision-making process. Biases of Accumulators are overconfidence, self-control, affinity, and illusion of control.

Overconfidence Bias

Bias type: Emotional

Overconfidence is best described as unwarranted faith in one's own thoughts and abilities, which contains both cognitive and emotional elements. Overconfidence manifests itself in investors' overestimation of the quality of their judgment. Many Accumulators claim an above-average aptitude for selecting stocks; however numerous studies have shown this to be a fallacy. For example, a study done by researchers Odean and Barber showed that after trading costs (but before taxes), the average investor underperformed the market by approximately 2 percent per year due to unwarranted belief in their ability to assess the correct value of investment securities.

Simple diagnostic for overconfidence bias: On a scale of 1 to 5, with 5 being full agreement, how much do you agree with the following:

I am confident that my investment knowledge is above average and I can accurately predict how my investments will do.

Answering 3 to 5 shows a tendency toward overconfidence bias.

Self-Control Bias

Bias type: Emotional

Self-control bias is the tendency to consume today at the expense of saving for tomorrow. The primary concern for advisors with this bias is a client with high risk tolerance coupled with high spending. For example, suppose you have an Accumulator client who prefers high volatility investments and has high current spending needs and suddenly the financial markets hit some severe turbulence. This client may be forced to sell solid long-term investments that have had been priced down due to current market conditions just to meet current expenses.

Simple diagnostic for self-control bias: On a scale of 1 to 5, with 5 being full agreement, how much do you agree with the following:

I will buy things I want even if they are not the best financial choices.

Answering 3 to 5 shows a tendency toward self-control bias.

Affinity Bias

Bias type: Emotional

Affinity bias refers to an individual's tendency to make irrationally un-economical consumer choices or investment decisions based on how they believe a certain product or service will reflect their values. Accumulators sometimes succumb to this bias.

Simple diagnostic for affinity bias: On a scale of 1 to 5, with 5 being full agreement, how much do you agree with the following:

I invest in companies that make products I like or companies that reflect my personal values.

Answering 3 to 5 shows a tendency towards affinity bias.

Illusion of Control Bias

Bias type: Cognitive

The illusion of control bias occurs when investors believe that they can control or, at least, influence investment outcomes when, in fact, they cannot. Accumulators who are subject to illusion of control bias believe that the best way to manage an investment portfolio is to constantly adjust it. For example, trading-oriented Accumulators who accept high levels of risk, believe themselves to possess more "control" over the outcome of their investments than they actually do because they are "pulling the trigger" on each decision.

Simple diagnostic for outcome bias: On a scale of 1 to 5, with 5 being full agreement, how much do you agree with the following:

I am more likely to have a better outcome if I make my own investment choices rather than relying on others.

Answering 3 to 5 shows a tendency toward outcome bias.

Outcome Bias

Bias type: Cognitive

Outcome bias refers to the tendency of individuals to decide to do something—such as make an investment in a mutual fund—based on the outcome of past events (such as returns of the past five years) rather than by observing the process by which the outcome came about (the investment process used by the mutual fund manager over the past five years). Accumulators often are prone to outcome bias.

Simple diagnostic for outcome bias: On a scale of 1 to 5, with 5 being full agreement, how much do you agree with the following:

What's most important is that my investments make money—I'm not that concerned with following a structured plan.

Answering 3 to 5 shows a tendency toward outcome bias.

Advice for Accumulators

Aggressive clients are generally the most difficult clients to advise, particularly those who have experienced losses. Because they like to control or at least get deeply involved in the details of investment decision making, they tend to eschew advice that might keep their risk tolerance in check. And they are emotionally charged and optimistic that their investments will do well, even if that optimism is irrational. Some Accumulators need to be monitored for excess spending, which, when out of control, can inhibit performance of a long-term portfolio. The best approach to dealing with these clients is to take control of the situation. If the advisor lets the Accumulator client dictate the terms of the advisory engagement, they will always be at the mercy of the client's emotionally driven decision making and the result will likely be an unhappy client and an unhappy advisor. Advisors to Accumulators need to demonstrate the impact financial decisions have on family members, lifestyle, or the family legacy. If these advisors can prove to the client that they have the ability help the client to make sound long-term decisions, they will likely see their Accumulator clients fall into step and be better clients that are easier to advise.

SUMMARY

We have just reviewed the basics of the four behavioral investor types. I hope this gives you an overview of what the key aspects of each BIT is and how best to adjust behavior to account for these biases. For a more detailed review of BITs, I plan to publish another book in the near future that reviews in much more detail each BIT and how to work with each one. For a more complete discussion of behavioral investor types, please see *Behavioral Finance and Investor Types: Managing Behavior for Better Investment Decision Making*, to be published later in 2012 by John Wiley.

Index